# Chuck Hagel

---

# Chuck
# Hagel

## Moving Forward

CHARLYNE BERENS

*University of Nebraska Press*
*Lincoln & London*

© 2006 by the Board of Regents of the University of Nebraska
All rights reserved
Manufactured in the United States of America

Library of Congress Cataloging-in-Publication Data
Berens, Charlyne.
Chuck Hagel: moving forward / Charlyne Berens.
p.  cm.
ISBN-13: 978-0-8032-1075-2 (cloth: alk. paper)
ISBN-10: 0-8032-1075-2 (cloth: alk. paper)
1. Hagel, Charles Timothy, 1946–
2. Legislators—United States—Biography.
3. United States. Congress. Senate—Biography.
I. Title.
E840.8.H23B47  2006
973.931092—dc22
2006004323

# Contents

# Illustrations

# Acknowledgments

I can't think of a new way to phrase it, so I'll just say that this book would not have been written without the help and support of a passel of fine people.

I appreciate the support and encouragement of Dean Will Norton and the College of Journalism and Mass Communications at the University of Nebraska–Lincoln and of Jim and Rhonda Seacrest, who have helped foster research by the college faculty.

I am grateful to all who served as sources for the book, offering their insights and expertise about Senator Hagel in particular and politics and government in general. Those who offered especially helpful perspectives and gave generously of their time included Rutgers political scientist Ross Baker; Delaware senator Joe Biden; Senator Hagel's wife, Lilibet; former Nebraska congressman John Y. McCollister; CNN's Judy Woodruff; and the *Washington Post*'s Helen Dewar.

Mike Buttry, Senator Hagel's communications director, was endlessly patient and cheerful in responding to my myriad requests for access and references—as well as points of information.

And Senator Hagel himself, of course, made it possible for this book to be more than just a digest of previously published and broadcast stories. I am enormously grateful that he was willing to answer scores of questions, thoughtfully and with good humor.

He gave me hours of time and took considerable risk in giving me access to so many of his ideas, thoughts, and reflections with no right of pre-publication review. I appreciate it.

Quotes and paraphrases not footnoted in the text should be assumed to come from personal interviews with the people cited.

Finally I am grateful to my husband, Denny, for listening to me complain when things weren't working and rejoicing with me when they were. He's the best.

# Chuck Hagel

# 1

## Who Is This Guy?

IT'S LATE AUGUST 2004, and the Republicans are celebrating in New York City. It's a foregone conclusion that they will nominate incumbent George W. Bush for a second term as president. Not much to watch there.

But some other scenarios are playing themselves out among the delegates and party enthusiasts. After all, it's only four years until the Oval Office will be wide open, and it's not too early for potential Republican candidates to start positioning themselves to be anointed in 2008. The routine involves going to the right parties, meeting the right people, getting interviews with the top media—not just the hometown folks but those who can make a person's name a household word around the nation's collective dinner table.

Chuck Hagel, Nebraska's senior senator, is playing the game. Only a few weeks before the start of the festivities, he finally confirmed that he was considering taking a shot at the 2008 presidential nomination, something many observers had long expected he'd do. Now he's laying some groundwork.

He's been invited to speak at a morning gathering of the Iowa delegation and will drop in at an afternoon reception hosted by the New Hampshire delegation and make a few remarks there too. The potential candidate and the party leaders from the two states with the earliest caucus and primary election will size up each other's moves.

Hagel takes the opportunity to compliment his hosts. "You started the process, and you're going to have an awful lot to do with how it ends," he tells the Iowa delegates in the morning. "You shape and mold the outcomes from start to finish," he says to the New Hampshire delegates in the afternoon.[1]

The senator may be making the required moves, but he's not always saying the expected things. Instead of gliding along, telling his audiences what he thinks they want to hear, he tends to talk about the things he thinks are important. Sometimes they do not reflect Republican orthodoxy.

Several days before Bush will make his speech to accept the nomination, for instance, Hagel is interviewed on the PBS *NewsHour with Jim Lehrer*. The topic is the role the war in Iraq is playing in the presidential campaign. Reporter Margaret Warner asks whether Iraq is a "real negative" for the president.

Hagel does a delicate turn. "It's a major issue." There are other issues, too, of course, but, "Yes, it's an issue."

Warner reminds Hagel that, back in June, he said the occupation of Iraq had been poorly planned and had actually spread terror cells throughout the world. Does he still think that's true?

Well, yes. "We didn't think about consequences. We didn't think about the long term," he says.

And when the president addresses the convention and America's voters, what should Mr. Bush say about the nation's involvement in Iraq?

Some careful footwork: "It is very complicated. And we are going to need relationships. We are going to need associations, seamless networks of cooperation with our allies. . . . And if he can clearly define that, then I think the American public will continue to give him the latitude that presidents must have in the imple-

WHO IS THIS GUY?

mentation of foreign policy." Some internationalist advice for a president who seems determined to be a nationalist.[2]

Earlier in the week Hagel surprised some observers by co-hosting a reception at Bob Kerrey's home in Greenwich Village. The two men became friends when they represented Nebraska together in the Senate, and in 2004 Kerrey, the Democrat, is president of the New School University in New York. The reception is billed as a kickoff for a New School forum, a series of roundtable discussions on urban issues that, Kerrey says, both parties' policy makers need to confront. Crossing party lines in the midst of a convention is not exactly commonplace, but Hagel takes advantage of the opportunity to promote some of his own policy views.

And he takes advantage of the convention's media spotlight as well. He doesn't get to make a speech to the convention this time, as he had done in 2000 when he nominated his friend John McCain. But he gets plenty of attention off the floor itself.

Hagel is interviewed live on CNN's *American Morning*. The possibility that he will be the party's chosen one in 2008 is discussed in stories in major papers like the *New York Times*, the *Los Angeles Times*, and the *Boston Globe*, as well as in wire-service stories that run in papers around the nation.

Then, as the convention ends, Hagel becomes really blunt. "The Republican Party has come loose of its moorings," he tells reporters. He doesn't blame Bush for the mess, but he laments what his party has done during the previous four years. For one thing, the Congress, with Republican majorities in both houses, has run up the largest deficits in the nation's history. For another, Republicans have embraced a foreign policy that has put the United States at odds with many of its longtime allies and fed Americans' suspicion that multilateral institutions like the United Nations and NATO are a nuisance at best and a threat at worst.

Once upon a time, he says, the Republicans made a name for themselves as an internationalist party, reaching out to build consensus all over the world. Now they're turning their back on their reputation and their friends. It's a position he thinks is dead wrong.[3]

Well. In the wake of his party's party, Hagel is not in the mood to celebrate the GOP's condition or direction. Instead of joining the post-celebration euphoria, he contributes to the morning-after headaches. Is this any way to navigate the treacherous road to the White House?

Maybe, but it's risky. Most people who want to win delegates' support try to keep in step with those delegates, not challenge them to change their ways. But Chuck Hagel is not afraid of challenge—or risk. He may be jumping through mandatory hoops on the way to a possible presidential nomination, but he's leaping through some of them a bit sideways or even backward, pausing occasionally to stick his finger in his party's eye.

For all the frustration Hagel expresses about the Republican Party—and sometimes about politics in general—he is philosophically in tune with many of the party's traditional positions. The man who grew up in independent-minded Nebraska and made a fortune in the cell-phone industry believes ardently in free trade, in as little government intervention as possible, in fostering a climate that lets people do for themselves, and in a government that interferes in people's lives only when it has to. It is primarily on matters of foreign relations that he parts company with his party.

But he loves his job in the Senate—just as he has loved all the other jobs he's had: aide to a Nebraska congressman, lobbyist for Firestone Tire, deputy director of the Veterans Administration, cell-phone entrepreneur, head of the USO, investment banker. Quite a list for a man born in 1946. Hagel has not done much sitting around.

As one of his former employees said, "He's always pleased but never satisfied." Cheerful and optimistic but driven and impatient. Eager to learn and create but also eager for the next thing. Loyal to friends and long-held values but ready to change things he believes have gone wrong. Defender of Republican principles and politicians but quick to speak out when he thinks they've gone awry. A true conservative in philosophy but a moderate in attitude and approach. As one observer put it, Hagel is that highly evolved political animal: principled but open for business.[4]

WHO IS THIS GUY?

It's a philosophy grounded in both nature and nurture. Hagel grew up in small towns in Nebraska, the son of a committed independent Republican who communicated to his sons his interest in the nation's business and the way he thought it should be run. Hagel was sixteen when his father died of a brain aneurysm. The oldest of four boys, he became the one on whom his mother leaned and to whom his brothers looked for guidance.

Things were going well until he graduated from high school and headed to college. After several tries in four-year institutions, he finished a one-year degree from a broadcasting institution in Minneapolis and got a radio job in Lincoln.

By that time the United States was up to its armpits in Vietnam, and young men like Hagel who weren't in college were prime targets for the draft. His draft board gave him fair warning, telling him to get himself enrolled somewhere if he wanted to avoid Uncle Sam's beckoning finger. But Hagel took another route: he enlisted in the army before it could draft him.

Basic training went well, and Hagel was offered a special assignment in a top-secret missile program. Rather than becoming fodder for the Vietnam War machine, he was to be sent to Germany for an elite assignment. Instead he volunteered to go to Vietnam.

It nearly killed him, several times. But, in other ways, it gave him back his life. After a year of Vietnam's miserable heat, nearly constant danger, and violent campaigns like the Tet Offensive, Chuck Hagel came back to the United States ready to get on with things—and with both a loyalty to the U.S. military and a belief he should do all he could to prevent his nation's being involved in another war.

The young man who had floundered his way through several semesters at several colleges now earned a bachelor's degree in history then made his way to Washington where he talked his way into an almost-volunteer job with one of Nebraska's congressmen. From there on, his intellectual and political smarts, his Nebraska work ethic, and his charm took him steadily upward—with a few blips on the trajectory.

President Reagan appointed Hagel deputy director of the Veterans Administration, but he quit in less than a year, frustrated by differences with a director he thought was indifferent or even hostile to Vietnam vets. It looked like political suicide, but in retrospect it seems perfectly in character.

Hagel was out of work and pretty much out of financial resources. But he sold his car, cashed in his insurance policies, and put everything he could scrape together into a "Dick Tracy" venture: cellular phones. It sounded like science fiction in the early 1980s, but Hagel convinced investors to commit to his firm, Vanguard, and the effort paid off enormously for the investors and for the firm itself.

The Wild West atmosphere of cell-phone franchise awards would later lead to questions about just how legal all Vanguard's activities were, but no one was found guilty of breaking the law. And the boy who grew up poor in Nebraska ended up a millionaire after his company turned cellular science fiction into reality.

So then what? Hagel could have spent his career maintaining and building the company and quietly enlarging his personal fortune, but when the next opportunity knocked, the restless Hagel welcomed it with enthusiasm. He spent three years salvaging the United Service Organization (USO) which had been facing bankruptcy. It was risky. If he had failed, his reputation would have slipped in Washington's power circles. But he took the chance and he succeeded.

After a few more years in Washington government-service jobs, Hagel moved back to Omaha and took a position with an investment bank. The job included revitalizing a small, struggling company that made vote-counting machines. That connection came back to haunt him.

Then he ran for the U.S. Senate, another risk. Outside Republican circles in Douglas County, not many residents of the Cornhusker State had heard of Hagel before he started campaigning for the 1996 election. Had he lost, no one would have been surprised. But by November enough Nebraskans were impressed with Hagel that they passed over a popular sitting governor and sent the

WHO IS THIS GUY?

political unknown to Washington to take his place in the nation's legislature.

So there he was, a freshman senator in a body where seniority makes all the difference. We shouldn't have heard much from him besides the usual press releases issued by his office for the state's media. But the stars converged for Hagel, ensuring that his affinity for and skill in international affairs coincided with a series of circumstances that moved him rapidly into leadership on the Senate's Foreign Relations Committee.

Then, in 2001, the nation was attacked and went to war in Afghanistan and, later, Iraq. Foreign affairs were suddenly relevant again, and people like Hagel, who had both a background in and policy influence on America's relations with the rest of the world, were the darlings of the media.

Sure, a senator always runs at least a little risk in talking to a reporter or getting in front of a TV camera to talk about his work and his beliefs, but he can always give the pat answer, parrot the party line, mouth the official doctrine. Unless he's Chuck Hagel.

Hagel, the loyal Republican, has time and again taken shots at his party's and his president's engagement—or lack of it—with the rest of the world. Hagel the internationalist has been unafraid to scold his colleagues for their unilateralist tendencies. The media love this stuff, but a lot of Republicans don't.

So now he's considering a run for the presidency. Just how will his outspokenness affect that aspiration?

On the one hand Hagel's independence may draw support from people who have had enough of knee-jerk partisanship from both sides of the aisle. His belief that the nations of the world are interconnected and that the United States must not try to go it alone may draw support from those of both parties who agree with that internationalist position.

On the other hand loyal Republicans—both those in power and those who will vote in the primaries—don't always appreciate Hagel's very public poking and prodding of their heroes and their positions. Sure, he votes with them nearly all the time, but when he disagrees he does it loudly and publicly and on some of the highest-profile policies.

Hagel says he knows it's a risk, but he says he's just being who he is. If he were to shut up and be a good soldier, he wouldn't be doing the job he was elected to do. And he says he learned a long time ago that people can accomplish a lot if they're not afraid to try—and to risk failure.

Despite the irritation he causes some of his supporters at home, he could probably get reelected to the Senate indefinitely. Nebraskans may be conservative, but they're also stubbornly independent, and many of them like the way Hagel often bluntly speaks his mind. They say his willingness to level with them makes them feel that he respects them.

But much as he loves his work as a senator, Hagel says he's not planning to make it his last career. He wants to see what else he can accomplish before the years catch up with him and dampen some of his stamina and energy.

Hagel's brother and some of his friends say the man does what he makes up his mind to do. If he decides to give his heart to a run for the nation's top spot, he'll win the job—just as he won election to the Senate in 1996, coming from out of nowhere.

It was that election that first drew my interest. How could someone who had been away from the state for most of his adult life move back home, enter the campaign as a long shot, and actually cross the finish line in first place?

It wasn't long after the election that Americans were first exposed to Hagel's criticism of his party's positions. Many Nebraskans, including some Democrats, seemed to like what they were hearing from this Republican who sees the world as a web of interconnections and isn't afraid to say it. Even those who disagreed with many of his policy positions often respected Hagel's willingness to take a stand on his principles and his willingness to consider changing his mind when the evidence suggested he should.

He is, of course, a skillful politician. But Hagel also seems genuinely interested in people and what they have to say. His friends and colleagues say he treats everyone with respect, including the waitresses and security guards and mailroom clerks, who would be easy to ignore.

The senator seems genuinely concerned about his work and the nation and people he serves. And he seems genuinely unafraid to say what he thinks, even when that may rock the political boat. He has a commonsense approach to his work in Congress—and toward life in general.

Hagel has been involved in two circumstances that some have labeled scandals: the machinations by which Vanguard got some of its cell-phone franchises, and his work for and continued ownership of a small amount of stock in a company that makes voting machines. If Hagel becomes a serious candidate for the presidency, his opponents will look to use those incidents for political advantage. And journalists will try to unearth even more information than has already been found and published.

But where some see a rash businessman manipulating the cell-phone franchise system, others see an enthusiastic entrepreneur. Where some see a politician owning a conflict-of-interest share in the machines that count votes, others see an investor holding onto stock in a company he once helped run. But there's more to the story than that.

Chuck Hagel is a Nebraskan who has built on his midwestern ethic, taken advantage of opportunities as they arose—including those that posed risks to his personal and political reputation—and developed his political acumen along the way.

He is a complex person who has achieved some major successes in life and is poised to take a shot at another. He's moving forward. He's worth knowing.

# 2

## The Early Years

IT WAS A BEAVER CLEAVER KIND OF WORLD.

In many ways Chuck Hagel seems to have lived the stereotypical 1950s childhood: traditional family, nice towns, lots of kids to play with, good schools to attend. But instead of putting down deep roots in one community, as the stereotype might demand, the Hagel family was on the move. Led by their father, the family was always looking for the next—and better—place. They lived in five Nebraska towns between 1946 and 1961, when they settled in Columbus.

The children in those Nebraska communities played baseball and football, went to school, and pretty much stayed out of trouble, at least in part because everybody knew everybody else. As John Gottschalk, one of Hagel's schoolmates in Rushville, recalled, "In those kinds of towns, a village really did raise the children."

At least one child raised in those Nebraska villages learned well that moving on could mean moving forward, that energy and restlessness constructively applied could mean leadership, that the risk of new challenges could open new worlds. Those lessons of child-hood took Chuck Hagel all the way to the United States Senate. They may take him to even higher office.

## Getting to Know Western Nebraska

Charles Timothy Hagel was born in North Platte on October 4, 1946. His father, Charles Dean Hagel, an Ainsworth native, had served in the South Pacific during World War II and had taken a job managing the Cook Paint and Varnish store in North Platte when the war ended. In 1947 the family moved to Ainsworth so Charles Hagel could work at the family lumberyard there. Three more Ha-gel boys—Tom, Mike, and Jim—were born in that town, and people who knew the Hagels in Ainsworth remember a good-looking fam-ily that lived in a modest home and struggled to make ends meet.

They were pillars of their Catholic church, where Charles, the oldest son, and Tom, the next in line, were altar boys. A long-time Ainsworth resident, Sid Salzman, remembers how Charles, the father, served on the building committee for the first Catho-lic church in Ainsworth—and actually helped with the construc-tion—and how his wife Betty helped with church dinners.

The Hagels were solid citizens, hard workers, said Gerry Os-born, who also still lives in Ainsworth. But they were also fun-loving people, people who liked to go dancing when they could. The four boys were lively and mischievous but never in any real trouble. Salzman said, "They were active, shall we say?" He added, "I was thirty, and they were eight. You just tolerate them when they're that age."

Their search for something to do led the two older boys to Gerry Osborn's Little League baseball program. Chuck, known then by his middle name, Tim, was especially enthusiastic, Osborn said.

"He ended up being a fairly proficient young player," the re-tired postmaster remembers, "but he was competing against kids four years older" in the fledgling program, and the difference be-tween a ten-year-old and a fourteen-year-old is significant.

But Chuck never lacked for energy. In fact Osborn remembers him as having a type A personality before anyone had coined the term. The coach said he kept close watch over Chuck, afraid that the young player's enthusiasm would lead to his getting hit by a batter or a ball.

Osborn's policy was that every boy on the team would play part of a game. Some would start, and others would be sent in as substitutes. Chuck Hagel knew he had to take his turn, but "when he was a sub, he just paced until it was his turn to go into the game," Osborn remembers. Osborn tried to teach his teams sportsmanship along with baseball skills. "I told them, 'We will cheer, but we will not jeer,'" he said. He wanted his players to emphasize the good things their own teams were doing, not get down on their opponents. It was OK to pace and to be impatient; it was not OK to gripe.

But as much as he loved to keep moving, Hagel was forced to settle down for some quiet times during the summer. His mother corralled him and his brother Tom for an hour or so every day and made them practice Latin so they would be good altar boys. Not that they learned the language; they just memorized the Latin prayers so they could recite them at the appropriate place in the Mass and do what their parents expected them to do.

The Hagel family might have stayed in Ainsworth indefinitely had the economic opportunities been better. Instead they moved from Ainsworth to Rushville, in Nebraska's northern panhandle, where Charles had landed a job in another lumberyard.

It was in Rushville that Tim Hagel changed his name. He was eleven years old and in the fifth grade, and his parents enrolled him and his brothers in a Catholic grade school that happened to be too small to offer athletics. "If you wanted to be involved in sports, you went over to the public school," Hagel said.

When he showed up at a Rushville Junior High intramural football practice, the coach asked Hagel who he was. He mumbled a response that must not have been too effective because the coach did not invite him to join the team. But Tim Hagel didn't give up. He asked his mother to dye a white T-shirt black, the team's color, and went back to sit on the bleachers and watch the practices for the next three days, hoping to be noticed. Finally the coach asked the persistent outsider if he wanted to play. Hagel jumped at the chance.

When the coach asked his name, Hagel recited his full name—as it appeared on his report cards: Charles Timothy Hagel. The coach said, "OK, Chuck, get out there." And that was that.

At the supper table that evening, Hagel told his family he was changing his name. His brothers snickered, and his dad asked what the new moniker would be. His grandfather, Charles Leo, had a lumberyard in Ainsworth and was known as Charlie. His father, a lumberyard manager, was Charles Dean and went by Charles. So the family had called the third-generation Charles Hagel by his middle name: Tim. But once the coach had dubbed him Chuck, the eager football player was only too happy to stay with it. "I actually kind of liked my new identity," he said.

His parents didn't object, but it took a while before they adapted completely. Mike Hagel, the third son, remembered that their mother, Betty Dunn Hagel, would step out on the back porch to call the kids home for dinner every evening. "She had that yell: 'Bo-ways! Supper!' And no matter where you were, you'd better get going home." When their mom was in a hurry, she'd reel off all four of their names, Mike said, and, for a couple of years after the Rushville coach renamed the oldest brother Chuck, "Tim" was still among the names his mother called.

By the time the Hagels moved to Rushville, Chuck was old enough that girls were starting to notice him and vice versa. Lynn Gottschalk Roper, now of Lincoln, was a year or so behind Chuck in school and remembers that he was "awfully cute" and that he broke her best friend's heart when he broke up with the girl. "I had to spend days consoling her," she said.

Even if they hadn't broken up, Chuck Hagel and his girlfriend would have been separated when the family moved again. In 1958, when Chuck was twelve, they left Rushville for Scottsbluff and what their dad hoped would be another step up in the lumber business. "He always felt a little bit trapped. He didn't have the education. It was a very difficult deal. . . . Some people took advantage of him," Chuck Hagel said.[1]

Things could get tough at home, too, Hagel admitted. Although it never led him to be abusive, Charles's drinking problem could make life difficult for his family. But as an adult, Hagel said he refused to dwell on it. "I've seen too many politicians, especially, blame their fathers for the difficulties they had growing up," he said. Hagel preferred to accept things as they were and go on.

All that moving wasn't easy for the boys. Hagel said it was hard to leave friends who, the young brothers were sure, were the best friends they'd ever have in their lives. But the upside was meeting new people, making new friends. He recalled, "You're just forced to have to deal with things." The Hagel boys learned how to adapt, to reach out, to develop survival skills they'd use the rest of their lives.

That ability to survive ran in the family, said Mike Hagel, now a commercial artist in Omaha: "Dad could sell ice to Eskimos" and "Mom loved to laugh." He thinks those were genetic traits that helped the boys embrace change and the chance to move on.

Moving so much made the family closer, said Tom Hagel, the second Hagel son, who teaches law at the University of Dayton. "When you're a kid and move to a new town, for a while all you've got are your brothers, until you start making friends again." And Chuck was the leader of the gang of four, partly because he was the oldest and partly because "he is and always was an absolutely natural leader," Tom said.

Mike remembers that when the boys played army "Chuck was always the general. The rest of us were privates." But when neighborhood squabbles arose, Chuck would defend his brothers from the other kids.

That didn't mean there was always peace and unity at home. "I don't want to say we fought, but we were brothers," Mike said. Their household was not exactly tranquil. As the oldest son, Chuck carried the burden of his father's expectations, Tom said.[2]

Mike agreed: "Chuck was a carbon copy of my father. Chuck never rebelled. In my opinion, once you get used to seeking and getting everyone's approval, it's like a drug. You want to keep it. He was the classic All-American perfect son. Still is."

One expectation forced on Hagel early in his life was that he would be responsible for his younger brothers. "I always had to take my brothers along to the movies," he said.[3] "That was not all that attractive, but I didn't fight it. We moved so much that we had to rely on each other. We were very, very close."

### Moving On, Moving Up

Their father convinced himself that moving on, helping rescue yet another lumber company, was a chance to move forward, and his sons bought into that idea. "Each place we moved we thought was a little better than where we'd been," Hagel said. That is, until Charles lost his job in Terrytown, just west of Scottsbluff, in 1960 and the family was forced to move to York, the only place Charles was able to find lumberyard work when he needed it. The family had to sell the western Nebraska house—the first house they'd ever owned—and move into the basement of a hotel in York for six months. "We didn't have anything," Hagel remembers.

That may have been a low point, but, generally, the Hagels were probably typical of what Mike Hagel described as a lower-middle-class family. They hadn't owned a television until 1958. For entertainment they listened to radio shows like *Gunsmoke* and traded comic books with neighborhood kids. They read the community newspaper and listened to their father's stories about his experiences in World War II.

Charles and Betty Hagel were interested in history, politics, and world events. Betty had been a Democrat before she married Charles, but by the time their boys were old enough to remember, both parents were Republicans. The boys were, too—except for Tom. Deadpan, Mike Hagel explains the aberration this way: "Tom was born on November, 2, 1948, the day Truman defeated Dewey. He's been a Democrat ever since."

Politics and world affairs may not have been the centerpiece of every dinner table conversation, but the boys heard enough about them that they got interested. Chuck, especially, was hooked. He was fascinated by history and said it still provides a strong frame of reference for him. "What's fascinated me about it all is how individuals have really changed the world, not just in politics but in everything," he said.

History so intrigued him that he memorized the succession of U.S. presidents' names even though he didn't have to. And he loved flags and tried to memorize which flag belonged to which nation. Not that he was a complete geek. "I had my baseball-card moments and my football-card moments, and I enjoyed that too," he said. "But it was a personal thing," the flags.

He started subscribing to *Time* and *Newsweek* when he was in junior high, although he said it never occurred to him at that point that he would someday be one of the people who appeared in those publications. "My favorite was Hugh Sidey's column on the presidency," he remembers now. And one of his favorite perks in his current life was the opportunity to get to know Sidey.

But he wouldn't have talked about that in the late 1950s. Afraid it would mess up his image as a sports-loving Nebraska kid, Hagel didn't tell his friends he subscribed to the magazines. Of course, everyone found out after his brothers spilled the beans, trying to embarrass their sibling.

Even more than history and current events, church was a mainstay of the Hagels' lives. Betty was a devout Catholic, and Charles, who had been a Congregationalist, joined her church after they were married. They raised their boys to be churchgoers. Attendance was not voluntary. "You went to church on Sunday, and you went to the holy days of obligation," Mike remembers.

At the time, Chuck said, the boys were likely to get restless, to think it was a waste of time to be sitting in church when they could be out doing things. But then, Chuck recalled, "When you look back, you understand why it was important and how much fortification it gave you for the later years." Now an Episcopalian, Hagel said his faith is still important to him. "Anyone who has a strong faith and belief in God is anchored to a world that is well beyond the corporal 'now' universe that we live in." That means, he said, that the responsibilities and passions of today are just a small part of the big picture. He doesn't dwell on it as he makes day-to-day decisions in the Senate but a clear understanding of what he believes and the role it plays in his life underpins everything he does.

In the Hagel household, hard work was next to godliness. All the boys got jobs as soon as they were able. Chuck earned money delivering papers in Ainsworth when he was seven. In Rushville he and his brother Tom stacked ten-pound bags of potatoes and ice at the local grocery store. Later, in the same town, Chuck was a carhop at a local drive-in, using a booster stool to make him tall enough to hang the trays on the car windows. The boys manually set pins in a bowling alley. They shoveled snow and mowed lawns.

That work ethic came from the family's German background, Tom said. "It was almost a message—a subtle message—that your value as a human being and to society depended a lot on work. If you were a good worker, that was one of best things you could say about anybody."

After only a few years in York, Charles left the world of lumberyards to take a job with Gerhold Concrete in Columbus, a town that would become a more permanent home for the family, the town where the older Hagel boys would graduate from high school. Chuck was a sophomore when the family moved to Columbus and enrolled him in St. Bonaventure Catholic High School, now Scotus High. He was an outsider among students who had been going to school together for years, but he fit right in. His classmate Dave Kudron remembers, "He was easy to get along with. He made friends easily."

Hagel played football and basketball and went out for track. He was on the student council and in the honor society as well as in Sodality, a Catholic young people's organization. "He was a kid you never could keep busy because he was so busy," his football coach Dean Soulliere, now retired, said.

Sports were a great way to get to know new people and make new friends, and Hagel embraced them. Anything he lacked in athletic ability he made up for in effort. For instance, Tom Hagel said Chuck really didn't have a lot of talent in basketball, but he wanted to play so badly that he just drove himself until he made the team. "He was kind of the comic relief in some games," Tom recalls, "moderately good, at best, but just entirely focused on it."

Hagel did better in football, Soulliere said, and he was definitely a leader on the field and off. He got along with all sixty-six members of his class, not just the athletes. He had dates for the dances and special occasions, but he hung out most with a group of guys that included Kudron and Larry Dowd. Dowd's family moved to Columbus the same summer the Hagels did, and he and Chuck Hagel quickly became friends. It didn't take long before pretty much all two hundred or so of the students at St. Bonaventure knew Hagel. Dowd recalls, "He was real outgoing." Almost aggressively friendly, Soulliere said.

And it wasn't just the students who knew and liked the new guy. Hagel also got along with everybody's parents, Dowd said. "He seemed to know how to talk to adults real well."

Kudron, now a manufacturing manager in the building division at Behlen Manufacturing in Columbus, remembers how comfortable Hagel was with his friends' families: "Chuck was noted for walking into someone's house and going right to the fridge. He'd take a piece of celery or a cold chicken leg—like he was at home."

Coach Soulliere said, "That's his strong suit: he fits in wherever he goes."

Chuck Hagel, the guy with lots of practice moving to a new community and making friends, had done it again. Things were going great—until Christmas Day 1962.

It was Chuck's junior year in high school. The Hagels were preparing to have relatives at their home for Christmas dinner, so Betty Hagel had gone to an early church service on Christmas morning. Charles and the boys had planned to go later. But when Betty returned home, she found her husband dead of a brain aneurysm. He was thirty-nine.

Chuck walked his mother to the neighbors' house to begin making funeral arrangements. Nothing would ever be the same.

*A Different World*

Up to that point, Mike Hagel said, the boys had been carefree and rambunctious, despite their jobs and their church obligations. When their dad died, things changed. The burden fell especially hard on Chuck. Their father had adored his oldest son and always expected Chuck to be responsible for the younger ones. Now that responsibility came in spades.

"He took over the role not really as the father but as the head male in the pack," Mike said. "He kept us in line pretty good. We raised a little hell, but you knew you didn't want to cross Chuck because it would get to Mom—and you never wanted to cross Mom."

John Y. McCollister, a former Nebraska congressman and a friend of the family, understands what Mike meant. "Betty Hagel was tough," McCollister said. By herself, she had to manage four boys, each with a strong personality. She was definitely in charge, he added. But with the toughness came great affection, and McCollister observed that the boys returned the love: "I can't describe the respect and affection they had for her."

Mike Hagel gets excited talking about it: "You've got to understand about my mother. We are who we are because of that woman. . . . She was a phenomenal woman. She was our best friend along with being our mother—and I don't say that lightly."

When their father died, "we grew up really quick," Mike said. "We were the men here now, particularly Chuck."

Dowd remembers how Chuck's group of high school friends would gather regularly at the Hagel home to play cards. Mike, thirteen at the time of his father's death, was building a model car for a contest sponsored by General Motors. "Every time we were there, Chuck would be sure to show us Mike's car," Dowd said. "We saw every stage of it. He was the proud father—who wasn't the father."

Charles Hagel's death had both an emotional and practical impact on the family. Since the Hagels had left Ainsworth, Betty had always had a job outside the home. But now she became the sole full-time breadwinner—as a secretary at the Rural Electrification Association office in Columbus—and the boys' part-time jobs took on new importance.

"It had the effect of bringing us closer together as well as making us more self-reliant," Tom Hagel said. "Whatever we were going to get out of life, we had to get ourselves."

Chuck held multiple jobs, at various times working at Frank Murphy's Texaco station; at a junkyard outside the nearby town of Richland; at the Jack and Jill store, where he bagged and stocked; and at Tom Riley's Chevron station. One summer he worked part-time at Adams Clothing Store in Columbus. Another summer he worked for Gerhold Concrete, shoveling cement for a highway project, and for Cornhusker Public Power, sawing down tree limbs that threatened power lines.

Despite the jobs and the extra responsibility at home, Chuck Hagel continued to enjoy a typical teenager's life in small-town Nebraska. Dowd and Hagel didn't spend a lot of weekend evenings at home. Their adventures included attending dances at the Oak Ballroom in nearby Schuyler, where they ended up in a fight one night. Dowd said he couldn't remember what started the altercation but thinks his friend Chuck jumped into the fray to help one of his friends. He recalls, "It was that protective thing—like looking after his brothers. He didn't go looking for a fight, but he didn't shy away."[4]

But life wasn't all dances on Saturday nights. Hagel continued to be an enthusiastic student leader at St. Bonaventure. His senior-year campaign for president of the student council employed some creative tactics: he tied a live rooster to the hood of his old black Jeep and drove slowly around Columbus, shouting out his positions on school-government issues while the rooster cackled away.

Hagel remembers how he came to know that rooster in the first place. He and his friend Dave Kudron were out "later than we should have been" one night and found the rooster walking across the highway. They picked it up, took it into town and, hoping to turn it into a kind of avian sculpture, proceeded to try to paint its wings gold by the light of a street lamp outside the Hagel home. The bird began to squawk, waking Betty Hagel, who put an immediate end to the episode, sending Kudron home and her son to bed. The boys let the chicken go. Next morning, though, there was the bird, sitting on the Hagels' back porch. Betty Hagel wanted nothing to do with the rooster and told her son to get rid of it. He tried to do that, but when the family returned from school and work that evening, there was the rooster, sitting on the back porch once again.

So Chuck began taking the rooster to school with him, tying it to his Jeep while he was inside the building. The bird took to sitting on the hood of the Jeep, much to the delight of the elementary school children crossing the street for daily Mass at the nearby church. The rooster on the Jeep was such a hit that Hagel and his friends incorporated the bird into their cruises through downtown Columbus on Thursday nights, the night the stores were open for business. It seemed a logical extension to make the rooster part of the student-council campaign.

But the chicken wasn't the only animal that made it into that campaign season. Hagel also found an old, moth-eaten deer head and hung it up in the school with a sign that said, "Vote for Chuck—a 'Deer' Fellow," his brother Mike said. Because of—or despite—his campaign stunts, Chuck won the election.

He also took part in the school's Model United Nations. That was not too unusual, given his long interest in current affairs, but Kudron remembers that Hagel was the only student who showed up for the occasion in a suit and tie. "Even back then, we talked with him about running for president," Kudron said. "He was knowledgeable and kind of forward. He knew what he wanted. We told him we wanted to be invited to the White House when he got elected president." Jim Micek, now an executive with Lockheed Martin, remembers that Model UN too. He said he can't recall the details, but he does remember that Hagel liked a forum in which he could talk. "He was very much a leader by nature," Micek said, "and very gregarious."

Hagel loved sports, and he loved activities like the Model UN.

Academics were not so high on the list. "To say I didn't apply myself in high school would be an understatement," Hagel said.

But he assumed that college would follow high school, and with an eye to financing his college education, Hagel tried some creative fund-raising, selling raffle tickets for his old Jeep. As Kudron remembers it, the man Hagel was working for at the time bought some tickets and won the raffle—and then gave the Jeep back to Hagel. Hagel said he never was positive who bought the Jeep and then returned it to him, but he thinks it was Tom Riley, the "wonderful, red-haired Irishman" at whose Chevron station he worked on weekends. And he thinks he made about five hundred dollars on the raffle scheme, a lot of money in 1964.

That enterprise seems to have worked better for Hagel than college itself did. He was excited to enroll at Wayne State College where he had a football scholarship. But a pinched nerve early in the season and surgery in December put an end to his football career. In fact he couldn't play any sports for a while, and he quickly lost interest in college. He said the lack of athletic discipline seemed to deplete whatever other discipline he had had. "I spent way too much time with my buddies, driving up to Yankton, South Dakota," the home of a women's college, in a state where it was then legal to drink at age eighteen.

He decided to get away from Wayne and enrolled for the following semester at what was then Kearney State College, now the University of Nebraska at Kearney, where a lot of his friends were going to school. His injury healed, and he tried football again that fall—until the damaged nerve tore once more.

But he never really got into the groove of college, he said. Even with part-time jobs to bring in some money and keep him occupied, he was unsettled. He left Kearney for Minneapolis and the Brown Institute of Radio and Television in January 1966. During the one-year program Hagel did weekend radio work in addition to selling shoes at Freeman's Department Store on East Lake Street and peddling encyclopedias door to door. He came back to Nebraska in 1967, to a job at KLMS Radio in Lincoln. He was an ad sales representative and also spent time on the air. And he loved it.

But then Uncle Sam came calling. Alma Hasselbalch was the head of the Platte County Selective Service Board for forty years. At the height of the Vietnam War in 1967, she and the rest of the board were busy people, trying to keep up with the constantly growing demand for troops. But they did their best to give vulnerable young men fair warning when Uncle Sam wanted them. The board suggested to Hagel that he reenroll in college if he wanted to avoid Vietnam.

It was perfectly legal, but Hagel declined the offer. For one thing, he had grown up with a father who had fought in the Pacific in World War II. He remembered his dad and his uncles and their friends in the VFW and the American Legion, the pride they took in their service and the respect the community gave them. Now, he thought, it was his generation's turn to serve. For another thing, college just hadn't gone well for him. "It was not an enhancement for me or for any legitimate educational institution to have me as a student right then," he said. He told the draft board he'd like to volunteer immediately for the army.

The board members were stunned. They asked him if he wanted to think it over, wanted to talk to his mother about it. He said no. He was sure he was doing the right thing.

Describing the time between his high school graduation and his enlistment in the army, Hagel used a term Winston Churchill had used. "Those were 'wilderness years' for me," he said. "I couldn't stay disciplined or focused. . . . Those were kind of lost years." Part of the reason, Hagel said, may have been the absence of a father in his family. "My mother, incredible as she was—and I've never known anyone quite like her—could do only so much with four strong, independent boys."

The young man who played the father role for his brothers needed a father himself. He recalled, "I was pretty headstrong. If I would have had a male figure or a father to kind of shape me a little bit after I got out of high school and say, 'Now, listen. These are the options, the consequences. . . .'" He had relied on the discipline of athletics to organize his life, he said, but even that structure disappeared after injuries ended his football career. "So I just wandered," he said.

In April 1967 the wandering took Hagel and five other Platte County soldiers-to-be to Omaha. A drill sergeant met their bus and took a look at the list of names. Hagel loves to tell the story of what happened next. All the others had long, hard-to-pronounce Polish names, Hagel remembers.

The sergeant asked, "Which one's Hagel?" When he raised his hand, the sergeant told him, "You're in charge." All his buddies laughed at Chuck's sudden promotion, Hagel said, and he thought it was funny, too. He thinks the sergeant picked him out not because he looked like a good leader but because Hagel "was the only name he could pronounce." Hagel's job was to make sure the group got dinner that evening and breakfast the next morning and got to the train station on time. They made it and headed off to Fort Bliss, Texas, for basic training.

Not only did Hagel have a shorter name than his fellow Platte County recruits, but he was also a few years older and had had some college education, unlike most young men drafted for Vietnam. He thinks it made a difference.

As the troops made their way through basic training at Fort Bliss, they were evaluated and rated on each step of the process: rifle range, classroom, physical training, leadership. Hagel remembers thinking that as long as he had to go through the whole process anyway he might as well "try to be the best guy" there. It worked. Hagel still has the certificate and trophy he received as the top recruit out of ten thousand in his training cycle. He also has the gold American Spirit Honor Medal. The drill sergeants, the commanders of the brigades, and the battalion commander chose the recipient of that award. It went to the individual in the training cycle who had demonstrated the most significant honor, courage, and spirit.

"It was a big honor," Hagel remembers. "I was surprised to get both awards."

Hagel remembers feeling something of a letdown as he walked

back to his barracks after the awards ceremony. All the excitement was over; he had earned the honors he had worked for. He had no immediate goals to pursue. But then it struck him: "I can really do this. That's pretty good, what I did." It was something of an epiphany.

He realized, he said in retrospect, that he needed discipline and focus. He needed goals and objectives to wake up to every morning if he was going to do more than just drift through life. He needed to keep moving forward.

When he got to the jungles of Vietnam, the goals were pretty fundamental and obvious: "staying alive" topped the list.

# 3

## Vietnam

THE TROOP TRANSPORT CIRCLED Ton Sun Hut Airbase for an hour, waiting for a Vietcong rocket attack to end so it could land. It was about 7 a.m. when the plane finally touched down and the new soldiers walked onto the tarmac. "I'll never forget, ever, the feeling I had walking off that plane," Chuck Hagel said. "It was oppressive heat like I'd never known—and the humidity and stench. . . . I was physically sick to my stomach."

And, like his comrades in arms, he was scared. "You don't get any sleep, you're afraid, it's all uncertain, the heat, the smell . . ."

Welcome to Vietnam.

It was December 4, 1967. Hagel was about to experience what he would later describe as the hardest thing he's ever done: a year as a combat infantryman at the height of America's war with Vietnam. Not surprisingly, he believes what he learned there is big part of who is he is today. Funny thing is, he wouldn't have had to be there.

*Choosing Vietnam*

When Hagel finished basic training in Texas, he had been recruited for Officer Candidate School but had declined the offer
because it would have meant a three-year commitment instead
of the two years required of an enlisted man. So he was sent to
Fort Ord, California, and the White Sands Missile Range. He was
nearly twenty-one years old, and it was the first time he had seen
the ocean. It was only the second time he'd been out of Nebraska;
the first time was for basic training at Fort Bliss.

Hagel was one of ten army privates chosen from training camps
around the country to learn how to operate Red-Eye Missiles. The
project was top secret, and the trainees and their mail were closely
monitored. Phone calls were simply off limits. Hagel isn't sure
why he was chosen for the project. He thinks it must have been
on the basis of tests the soldiers took during basic training. At any
rate, they were to learn how to operate a brand-new weapon the
army was pretty sure the Soviet Union didn't have: a heat-seeking,
shoulder-fired missile.

After their three-month training period, the ten elite recruits
were to be sent to Europe and integrated into the NATO system.
If necessary they would use their weapons to bring down low-fly-
ing Soviet MiGs over Europe. When the training ended, the ten
soldiers were sent home for a short leave, then reassembled at
Fort Dix, New Jersey, in preparation for deployment to Germany.
Compared to Vietnam, where most troops were headed those
days, Germany was a luxury posting.

But as he lay on his bunk at Fort Dix, watching his buddies
pack, Hagel had second thoughts. "I decided it was not the right
thing to do," he said. "There was a war going on. The right thing,
if I was in the army, was to go where the war was," to fight as his
father had done in World War II. So he took his orders to the
orderly's office at Fort Dix and said he wanted to volunteer to go
to Vietnam instead of Germany. The whole room fell quiet.

The soldier at the desk called the captain. The captain brought
in a chaplain. The chaplain took Hagel to his office and started

asking questions, trying to be sure this guy who wanted to trade a cushy tour of duty in Germany for the misery of Vietnam wasn't a mental case. Eventually the chaplain and the captain decided the request was legitimate, and Hagel was told to pack up his duffel bag and move to a different barracks.

When he went back to his buddies and told them he had volunteered to go to Vietnam, they thought he was joking. When they realized he was dead serious, one of the soldiers, Jerry Duvall, took off his wristwatch and gave it to Hagel, for luck. Duvall's brother had spent a year in Vietnam and never got a scratch. Hagel wore the watch until it quit.

Once he got his orders amended, Hagel had to call his mother and tell her about the change of plans. When he had left her for Fort Dix, she thought he was headed to Germany. "When I told her [it would be Vietnam], there was a pause at the other end. She said, 'Why did you do that?' I told her I just thought it was the right thing to do. She said, 'Well, I hope you've made the right decision.'" They talked some more, and Betty Hagel reassured her son that she wasn't angry with him for choosing to go to Vietnam. Before the conversation ended, Hagel's mother told him, "I'll support you no matter what you decide to do." But it was obvious she was worried, he remembers.

When his plane landed in Vietnam, he had plenty to worry about too.

Hagel and the other troops assigned to the 199th Light Infantry Brigade got the standard, army-issue rude welcome. They were marched into the chow hall, an open building where the cooks, unshaven and sweaty, laughed at the green newcomers. "The smell was unbelievable," Hagel said. Boiled lamb is the aroma he remembers best. He couldn't eat anything that morning, and he said, "I couldn't eat lamb again for a long time." The mess hall didn't even serve water, only syrupy-sweet Kool-Aid.

The troops who were leaving directed catcalls at the new guys: "You're a cute one. Charlie likes you; he'll cut your ears off"—or maybe some other body part. Hagel laughed when asked whether it was really "ears" the Vietcong were said to be interested in. "It was very imaginative dialogue," he said.

Next stop was an assembly ground where the commander of the camp gave instructions. The soldiers found their bags and their cots and got reasonably organized, then reported back to the commander for their orders. "They assigned us based just on where we were standing in the formation," Hagel remembers. Ten guys were sent off to be butt police, picking cigarette butts off the ground. Another group was sent to the mess hall to peel potatoes and empty garbage.

The group Hagel happened to be standing with was ordered to collect the fifty-gallon barrels from the latrines and burn the waste. "You can imagine that smell," Hagel said. "You'd have to pour disinfectant on those cans and then diesel fuel on top of that and then light it. "So that was my first assignment in Vietnam. . . . I didn't exactly spend my first day as a great warrior." He did learn to be careful where he stood during formation.

After about a week Hagel got new orders. The Ninth Division had taken lots of casualties and needed fresh troops to make up the difference. Before the reassigned group left Ton Sun Hut, though, they had a week of jungle school: an advanced infantry course preparing the soldiers for what they would confront in hand-to-hand combat in the jungle and in the villages of Vietnam. "I think everybody was scared," he said. "I was scared." But the soldiers learned to look past the fear, to focus on the job they had to do.

Then the Ninth Division replacements were moved to the Mekong Delta. They were assigned to different groups, Hagel to the Second Battalion, 47th Infantry, Bravo Company. Each soldier was issued an M16 rifle and battle gear: a helmet, flak jacket, web belt on which to carry a canteen, and other equipment. Bravo Company was doing bridge patrol that day in jungle owned by Michelin Tire. Hagel spent that night in base camp, then joined Bravo the next morning and was assigned a squad. Most of the soldiers' orders were for search-and-destroy missions. Based on intelligence, the officers knew the Vietcong were in certain areas, and the squad would be sent out to find and destroy them.

Sometimes Hagel and his squad patrolled bridges or roads. That meant they slept during the day, then patrolled at night, trying to prevent the Vietcong from planting mines to destroy the nation's infrastructure. Sometimes they would do night outpost work. "They would be almost suicide missions," Hagel said. "If anything happened, the base would never hear from you again."

In such a mission, a group of three soldiers would be sent into the jungle to establish a listening post, trying to discover any major enemy-troop movement and alert the company if an attack was coming. The outposts had to maintain radio silence, so they communicated with the base camp by pushing a button on the radio. For instance one squawk meant everything was OK. Two meant the outpost thought something dangerous was going to happen. Three meant "We've got a problem, and we're coming in. Don't shoot us." Four meant "They're on top of us, and we can't come in." In the pitch dark all that the troops at the outpost could do was listen. The squad could rely only on sound, not sight, to detect trouble.

"In the jungle at night," Hagel said, "you cannot see your hand in front of your face." Night-vision telescopes were available for U.S. troops in Vietnam, but soldiers were often forbidden to take them to listening posts. If the troops were captured or killed, their superiors didn't want the telescopes falling into enemy hands. So the groups of three went into the jungle with a radio, their rifles and ammunition and, usually, a pistol, Hagel said.

One of those assignments, Hagel recalled, involved an encounter that frightened him more than anything before or since. Following standard operating procedure, one of the three soldiers stood watch while the other two slept on their tarps. Early one morning when Hagel was standing watch, he heard a clang. At first he thought it was a cowbell. Then he realized what he was hearing was no herd of cows but a large group of Vietcong, moving equipment right in front him. He actually heard a whispered conversation in Vietnamese. "It was so close you could almost reach out and touch them," he said. He woke his two squad members, covering their mouths with his hands so they wouldn't cry out. "Grab your rifle, grab my boot, and crawl," he whispered.

The three soldiers slithered out in a human chain, Hagel leading the way. "We knew the VC were coming right on top of us, getting closer and closer," he recalled. The soldiers didn't dare stand up and run. So they crawled, the noise of their presence muffled by the Vietcong's own movements. Hagel had the radio with him, and once the squad was well away from the Vietcong, he called the base camp to report what had happened. Much as they might have loved to return immediately to the camp and its relative security, the three U.S. soldiers were ordered to stay outside the base camp that night, in case they were being followed.

When it was daylight, they went back to retrieve what they had left behind a few hours earlier, as they crawled away from the Vietcong. Everything was gone. "The VC had been there and had picked it all up," Hagel said. It had, indeed, been a close encounter.

## Moving Up the Ranks

Private Hagel was promoted several times in Vietnam, but he maintains that the promotions were not because of anything he did. The United States was losing so many troops in 1968, including senior people, that soldiers were often moved up the ranks. "They promoted you pretty quickly—if you could put a sentence together and knew anything about anything," he said.

Apparently Hagel qualified in both categories. Gene Bacon, who served in the same unit in Vietnam, said Hagel was not promoted by accident. "The moment I met him, I thought I was talking to a college professor," Bacon said. "And I had had two years of college at the time. I wasn't dumb. But he was very articulate, very bright. He commanded real respect from the officers right away."

Hagel arrived in Vietnam as an E3 private first class and was promoted to an E4 specialist, technically a corporal. Then he was promoted to sergeant. "It didn't really make much difference to what I did," he said. Technically sergeants were given more responsibility for squads, but in reality they mostly just kept on being soldiers.

But Hagel stood out among the soldiers in Vietnam for an unusual reason: his brother Tom arrived in Vietnam about a month after Chuck did, and the two served in the same squad for most of their tours of duty.

Tom Hagel had enlisted in the army a month after he graduated from high school and had arrived at Fort Bliss for basic training about a month after his brother got there. He, too, had declined an invitation to attend Officer Candidate School. He was sent to Vietnam about a month after his brother. Tom had also been set to go to Germany—for a six-month stint before heading to Vietnam—but he volunteered to go directly to Asia. In so doing, he and Chuck believe they must have agreed to let the army sidestep its rule against brothers serving together, the so-called Sullivan Rule enacted after World War II to prevent the draft from sending brothers to the same unit and hence the same risks. Someone had told Tom that Chuck would be sent home once Tom showed up in the same theater. He heard the Red Cross would take care of everything. But when Tom got to Vietnam and asked the Red Cross to start the procedure to send his brother home, the Red Cross workers said they'd never heard of such a thing.

So, since they were both stuck in the same part of the world, the two thought they could support each other. They didn't really think they'd serve together, but they hoped to be close enough to at least see each other once in a while. Chuck put in for a transfer to the northern part of the country, near where Tom was serving in the DMZ, the demilitarized zone. Tom put in for a transfer south, to be closer to Chuck. They figured maybe one of them would get what he asked for.

In the meantime Chuck got orders to join a different division in the central highlands, a division that had taken heavy casualties in the Tet Offensive. As the truck carrying the soldiers north was about to pull out, a military policeman called Hagel's name and told him to get out. When Hagel didn't react, the MP asked him, "Are you so dumb, soldier, that you don't know what your name is?"

Chuck said he had no idea why he was ordered off the truck, but he got out and walked back to base camp.[1] Three weeks later,

Tom was assigned to Chuck's squad, and from then on the brothers served literally side by side—not just in the same large battalion but in the same unit—until Chuck went home in December 1968, one month before Tom did. "Both of us thought it was a great idea," Tom said.

Their younger brother, Mike, said he was sort of relieved that Tom was there to take care of Chuck. When they were growing up, Tom was a hunter; Chuck barely knew which end of a rifle was which, Mike recalled with a laugh. But their mother had mixed feelings. On the one hand it was comforting for her to know her sons were in the same place, Chuck Hagel said. On the other hand losing both of them at the same time would have been devastating. And it nearly happened. Twice.

The Hagel brothers' unit was ordered to Saigon during the Tet Offensive in early 1968. They spent a month in ferocious house-to-house combat. "Both of us were very, very good at killing," Tom said.[2]

But close-up combat wasn't as frightening as those listening patrols had been, Chuck Hagel said. "When you're in a firefight, all hell breaks loose. You're not scared. You're not thinking about anything except what you're doing."

However, danger came in many forms in Vietnam. In March 1968 the Hagel brothers were on an ambush patrol northeast of Saigon. They had been walking at the front of the column until their commander rotated them to the back. Only moments later, the soldiers who had taken their place at the front tripped a booby trap. Mines full of shrapnel, planted in the trees, exploded all around them. The men walking in front were killed.

Tom thought at first that he had simply been knocked down by the force of the explosion, and when he saw Chuck lying on his back, he thought that's all that had happened to him, too. But then he noticed the blood stains on Chuck's shirt: he had been hit by shrapnel. Tom said, "I could see blood on the front of his shirt, and I tore his shirt open, and that's when geysers of blood went up."[3] He wrapped bandages around Chuck's chest to stop the bleeding.

Tom had been hit by shrapnel himself, in his back and arms, and the brothers spent some time recovering together in a field hospital. Chuck Hagel still has some of the shrapnel from one of the mines in his chest, but he insists, "Our wounds were no big deal."

A month later, after a long firefight, the brothers' unit was pulling out when a land mine exploded under their armored personnel carrier at the rear of the column. Chuck thought his brother Tom, the turret gunner, had been killed by the initial impact. He grabbed Tom and found he was "deadweight, blood pouring out of his ears."[4] He started pulling Tom and others from the carrier, trying to get everyone out before the ammunition in the carrier blew up. But he was still too close when the inevitable explosion came and set him on fire, burning his face severely.

As it turned out, Tom was wounded again but not mortally. He had simply been unconscious. And once again the brothers spent time recovering together. Chuck remembers the bandages and salve he wore on his face long after he was discharged from the hospital.

"It was so hot, and there were so many flies. The bandages would come unwrapped, and I got an infection on my face." Medics gave him salve that he was supposed to apply every day until the skin healed, but by that time his unit was involved in another firefight, and he lost all his supplies, including the salve. It took a decade for the burns to heal fully, and he still can't grow a beard. "I tried it once," he said, "and looked hideous, like some kind of goat with patches of hair here and there."[5]

Tom and Chuck's mother and brothers didn't really know the details of the injuries until after the two were home again, didn't realize Chuck had two Purple Hearts and Tom three. But the family had had a bad scare on Mother's Day in 1968. The phone rang that day, Mike said, and he answered. Someone asked if Mrs. Betty Hagel was there. Mike turned to his mother and said, "It's the army, and they want to talk to you."

"She started crying. She didn't want to take the phone," Mike said. She was sure an officer was calling with bad news. In truth it was Tom and Chuck, calling via radio hookup to wish her a happy Mother's Day.

Mike remembers how relieved his mother was but how she cried again after she hung up the phone, realizing vividly what could happen to the two soldiers in Vietnam. "She lived for the mail" that year, Mike said, for the letters from her sons as well as the Vietnamese shoes and shawls and other keepsakes they sent.

It was only a few weeks before that 1968 Mother's Day that Dr. Martin Luther King was shot dead by an assassin at a Memphis hotel. On the other side of the world, the U.S. soldiers absorbed the news.

The American troops in Vietnam were experiencing many of the same racial problems that Americans at home were experiencing, Hagel recalls. It wasn't everybody, of course. Hagel said that he and Tom had had a number of good buddies who were black. In fact, he says, one of the best military officers he's ever known was a second lieutenant named Jerome Johnson, a black officer who took over Hagel's unit after the Tet Offensive. But things were tense enough between the races that the King assassination only exacerbated the trouble.

Just two months later the troops heard the news that Bobby Kennedy had been assassinated while campaigning in California. "It kind of broke everybody's spirit," Hagel said. The soldiers were in a bad situation. They were trying to recover from the devastation of the Tet Offensive; they knew Americans' support for the war and the troops was fading. Then this—two leaders gunned down in a matter of months. "It really did have an effect on people like 'What the hell is going on?'" Hagel said. "It was like the whole world was going nuts."

The Democratic National Convention in Chicago that summer and the accompanying demonstrations and riots didn't get as much notice among the troops, many of whom paid little attention to politics, Hagel said. But he remembers betting a first sergeant in spring 1968 that Richard Nixon would be the Republican nominee and the nation's next president. The sergeant, a twenty-year veteran of the army, was an ardent Democrat. He told Hagel, who was about to vote in his first election ever, that the nation was not going to elect any Republican to the White House and, besides that, the Republicans would never nominate a has-been like Nixon. The whole idea was a joke, he told Hagel.

Of course, Nixon defeated Hubert Humphrey in November, and Hagel—who had marked his absentee ballot for a straight Republican ticket while sitting on a tank, guarding a bridge in the Mekong Delta—collected his five dollars. "That's the only time I ever got the better of a first sergeant," he said with a chuckle.

During their year in Vietnam, the Hagel brothers who served in the same squad became famous, "kind of a sideshow," their fellow soldier Gene Bacon said. *Stars and Stripes* wanted to a do a story about them, and visiting brass wanted their pictures taken with the Hagel boys. "I was always trying to get in the background of the pictures," Bacon recalls with a grin. Bacon also remembers how meticulous Chuck Hagel was about being sure the men who served under him received the medals and awards due them. Hagel himself left Vietnam with three Vietnamese Crosses of Gallantry, the Army Commendation Medal, and the Combat Infantryman Badge, in addition to the two Purple Hearts.

He also left with a new understanding of and attitude about war. He supported what the United States was doing in Vietnam—unlike his brother Tom, who came home believing the whole thing was a mistake. Mike Hagel says it always fascinated him that two men who experienced almost exactly the same things in Vietnam should come home with such disparate views about what had happened. In fact, while the brothers were still in Asia, Tom had written to Mike, "To the day I die, I will be ashamed that I fought in this war."[6] Despite Tom's words, Mike would have enlisted if he could have; a high school football injury kept him from passing the physical.

But once his brothers came home, Mike heard plenty about the war itself and the policy that drove it. "Tommy came back thinking it was total baloney, that we shouldn't have been there. Chuck came home thinking, no, we did our duty. It was the right thing to do."

Asked whether the two veterans talked about Vietnam once

they came home, Tom said, "We never talked about it. We argued about it until my mother finally said, 'Enough of this.'" Mike remembers literally pulling his two brothers apart. "That happened for three or four years," he said.

Did they ever change each other's minds? "No, I don't think so," Tom said in early 2004. He said he still thinks Vietnam was an incredible blunder on America's part. "Chuck thinks it was fought wrong" but that it was important that America step in and stop the spread of communism.

### Readjusting

Unlike many Vietnam vets—including his brother—Chuck Hagel seemed to blend right back into life in the United States. A primary reason, he thinks, is the fact that he was a little older than many of the soldiers with whom he had served.

He was twenty-one. By contrast, many American soldiers in Vietnam, like Tom, for instance, were eighteen years old, right out of high school. "They were totally involved in what was going on," Chuck Hagel remembers, unable to put any distance between their own identities and the war they'd been sucked into.

When he came back to Nebraska, Hagel said, he just wanted to get on to the next thing. He tried to pretend that readjusting to civilian life was easy: "I just kind of took the American Legion path and just said, 'I'm going to get along with my life; there's no baggage that I brought back; I'm fine.'"[7]

But in retrospect he probably should have realized and admitted to himself that Vietnam had had a traumatic effect, Hagel told a reporter. He and Tom both enrolled at the University of Nebraska at Omaha and roomed together for a year. Then Chuck decided he needed to be alone. He pretty much canceled his social life, concentrating on studying and working, trying to figure out where he'd been and where he was headed.

But he didn't agonize over his role in the war: "I never regretted it, never looked back, never thought about it. I knew it was the right decision." Maybe that's a weakness, Hagel said of his habit of not replaying and second-guessing his decisions, but it's the way he does things. "Once you've made the decision, you go forward."

Decades later, though, Hagel began to investigate the background of the war in Vietnam. By late 2004 he had read everything he could find about the history of Indochina, about the French involvement there before the Americans went in. He began to doubt his earlier faith in the American government's motivations behind the war. "I got a sense that there was just so much dishonesty in it," he told a reporter. "And it was chewing these kids up. . . . So I started connecting all the deaths and all the suffering and the chaos and wounds. I started to sense a dishonesty about it all."[8]

When he listened to tapes of the then-president Lyndon Johnson's phone calls discussing the war with Georgia senator Richard Russell, chair of the Armed Services Committee, Hagel cringed. He began to believe that the war had been waged less to defend the United States and the world from the spread of communism than to promote "an abstraction of policy" and to save face, he said.[9]

Even when he had supported the concept behind the war, Hagel had been blunt about what a horrific experience it was. Yet by being part of the military effort he had taken a big step toward rediscovering his self-worth and sense of direction. "When I came back, I was far more serious about life, about what I wanted to do." He said he seemed to have found his stride again, to have fallen back into the rhythm that had guided him through most of his life.

The war also forged a permanent bond among those who had served in Vietnam. No matter their views about the war's purpose and morality, no matter their differences in political party and ideology, the men who came back from the war in Southeast Asia share an understanding that has influenced American society and institutions.

Almost certainly, one thing that has united the senators who served in Vietnam was the negative way the nation reacted to them when they came home. Even when the soldiers didn't experience overt scorn, the feeling of disapproval was there. Randy Moody, who worked with Hagel in Washington in the early 1970s and had also served in Vietnam, said he and Hagel never talked about their experiences. "There was nothing positive to being a veteran then," Moody said. Perhaps the instant closeness felt by those veterans who were later elected to the Senate arose in part because of their shared memories of those postwar years.

In fact, John McCain, a Republican senator from Arizona, alluded to exactly that when he posed for pictures with five fellow Senate Vietnam vets in December 1996. For years, he said, Vietnam had been political poison. He recalled, "I never thought there would be six of us here. Never."[10]

Hagel said the bond went beyond personal, individual relationships. It evolved into something of a political force. That was especially true in the late 1990s, he said, when six members of the Senate were Vietnam veterans: Republicans Hagel and McCain and Democrats John Kerry from Massachusetts, Chuck Robb from Virginia, Bob Kerrey from Nebraska, and Max Cleland from Georgia.

Partisan divisions meant little to the senators who served in Vietnam. Although they may have voted against each other on some occasions, they supported each other in some high-profile cases where party loyalty would have demanded otherwise. For example, in the spring of 2004, when the Bush administration asserted that John Kerry, who by that time had wrapped up the Democratic nomination for president, was soft on defense issues, Hagel and McCain rushed to Kerry's defense. McCain lamented the negative attacks on Kerry, whom he called a good and decent man. Hagel said the charges were simply not true. He might disagree with Kerry about a lot of things, but he said, "Let's be fair about this."[11]

That incident was certainly not the first to illustrate Hagel's observation that the vets "protect each other a little bit." That protection had surfaced on other occasions. During the 2000 South Carolina Republican presidential primary, for example, charges began to circulate that McCain had been brainwashed in a Hanoi prison and was a real-world version of the fictional Manchurian candidate. His five fellow veterans in the Senate, men of both parties, quickly signed a letter denouncing the allegation.

When Kerrey, the Nebraska Democrat, admitted in 2001 that a Navy SEAL team he had commanded had killed civilians in a 1969 raid, John Kerry, the Massachusetts Democrat who opposed the war after returning from Vietnam, said a deeper inquiry into his colleague's record would serve no point. Cleland and Hagel took the same view, although McCain said he would leave the matter to the Pentagon.[12]

When Cleland was running for reelection to the Senate in 2002, ads pictured his face next to the faces of Osama bin Laden and Saddam Hussein in a campaign commercial for Saxby Chambliss, the Republican who took away Cleland's Senate seat. Republicans Hagel and McCain, along with their Democratic brethren, angrily demanded it be taken off the air. Hagel went to Senator Bill Frist, then-chair of the Republican Senatorial Campaign Committee, and told him that the ad maligning Cleland, who had lost an arm and both legs in Vietnam, was "irresponsible and disgusting." Hagel threatened to appear in commercials countering the attacks on Cleland.[13]

He remembers Cleland telling him not to do that. "He said, 'You've got a future in your party. You could be president of the United States. I don't want you to ruin yourself with your own party.'" Cleland later told reporters that Hagel had told him "some things are more important than politics." The Chambliss campaign pulled the offending commercials before Hagel had to make good on his threat.

But the Vietnam bond among the six senators, whose numbers had dwindled to three by 2004, goes beyond shared experiences and the personal loyalty that they create. It also includes a frame of reference for policy decisions. "I think each of us takes our experiences that we had in Vietnam seriously, in the sense that we may have even more of an obligation to think through these big geopolitical issues and, more importantly, ask the tough questions,"

Hagel said.[14] He added, "We try to apply those experiences in a positive way to effect change we think is important."

Neither Hagel nor any of the other senators who served in Vietnam beats his colleagues over the head with his Vietnam memories and perspectives. But the impact Vietnam had on the worldview of the senators who served is unquestionable and pervasive. A December 1996 story in the *Omaha World-Herald* noted that all six of the Vietnam vets who would serve in the Senate in 1997 were known for their willingness to argue politically unpopular positions and that none fit consistently into the ideological wings of their respective parties.

Hagel's experiences in Vietnam also made a permanent difference in how he thinks about war and its role in international relations. He remembers vividly what happened after his personnel carrier hit the land mine. He was sitting in a helicopter, his face so badly burned it hurt even to put salve on it, waiting to be evacuated. The helicopter's radio blared Armed Forces Radio, and Linda Ronstadt and the Stone Poneys were singing, "You and I travel to the beat of a different drum."

The moment is fixed in Hagel's memory. "I remember thinking, 'If I ever get out, and if I ever can influence anything, I will do all I can to prevent war,'" he recalled. He still thinks about it, saying, "Not that I'm a pacifist. I'm a hard-edged realist. I understand the world as it is. But war is a terrible thing. There's no glory, only suffering."

Some things are worth fighting and dying for, Hagel said, but going to war should be a last resort. He believes it's something his colleagues in the Congress need to understand. "Not many people up here have the view of a rifleman or look through the lens of the people who have to do the fighting and dying," he said. "We see war up here in very antiseptic terms. We see it in bright policy terms. In human suffering terms? No."

Hagel remembers how he felt when the United States finally pulled out of Vietnam: "You felt like it was all a waste, those 58,000 Americans dead and 153,000 wounded." He was frustrated that Congress just "pulled the plug" on the war, leaving behind thousands of Vietnamese who had been U.S. allies. "I still see images of a great nation running away," Hagel said, "knowing the fate of most of the people left behind. . . . I thought, 'My God, how irresponsible!'"

In 2004, looking at how entangled America had become in Iraq, Hagel began to think maybe the nation had had no good alternatives when it left Vietnam in the seventies. But when Congress voted in 1975 to cut off financial support for U.S. troops in Vietnam, effectively ending America's intervention there, Hagel remembers being "very disturbed." One of his obligations as a senator, he said, is to bring some of his perspective to the table as the Senate debates wars and rumors of wars. What he sees as an obligation some others see as disloyalty to his party and his president.

The retired *Omaha World-Herald* publisher Harold Andersen wrote in a *World-Herald* column in fall 2004 that Nebraska Republicans were getting tired of Hagel's criticism of the Bush administration's handling of the war in Iraq. Some, the column implied, saw the criticism as simply a ploy to generate publicity for a potential presidential campaign. Hagel, the Vietnam vet, struck back, writing his own column that appeared in the *World-Herald*, taking issue with Andersen's position. Hagel holds that it is his responsibility as a senator to ask the hard questions, questions that "were not asked when we sent young men and women into Vietnam. Where were our elected officials then? Eleven years and fifty-eight thousand deaths later, we lost. I don't want that to happen in Iraq." Hagel came close to being one of those 58,000 deaths. It's one reason he speaks out today. "War is not an abstraction," he wrote. "I know. I've been to war."

Vietnam is part of the reason Hagel views the world today from an internationalist perspective. "Integration of the United States in the world is key," he said. He believes war may sometimes be an ugly necessity, but it is international relationships that maintain stability and security. And the nation couldn't avoid those relationships if it wanted to, he added. The world's 6.5 billion people are all connected. They face the same threats, the same challenges, the same concerns: terrorism, weapons of mass destruction, hunger, poverty, despair. But, he said, also woven into the fabric of the international community are stability, peace, and prosperity.

Vietnam played a vital role in ending Hagel's wilderness years. It gave him his lifelong loyalty to people of all economic and political stripes. It helped shape his internationalist view of the world. When he came home, back on track emotionally, he was determined to act on what he knew and believed. He just wasn't sure how he was going to do that.

# 4

---

# Looking to Washington

AFTER LIVING HISTORY for twelve hot and humid months in Vietnam, Chuck Hagel returned to Nebraska and decided to study history at the University of Nebraska at Omaha. He knew he needed a college degree in order to keep moving forward with his life.

He and his brother Tom had served together in Vietnam and defied the odds, coming home in one piece and with their physical wounds healed. Tom enrolled at UNO, too, and his big brother is happy to tell people how Tom finished his undergraduate degree in three years with all A's while working nearly full-time and then went on to a stellar career in law school. But the same year the soldiers returned from the war, tragedy struck the family. Jimmy, the youngest Hagel boy, was killed in a car accident on November 16, 1969. He was seventeen.

Mike Hagel noted the irony: "Here these two guys had gone through what they had [in Vietnam]. It wasn't even a year since they were back—and Jimmy died. He was the athlete, the one we all thought had a future." Jim had gotten good grades in high school, which Mike remarked was more than could be said for the three older brothers. Jim had been a quarterback on the football team and a successful left-handed baseball player. And now he was gone.

Betty Hagel had remarried earlier that year, and she and E. J. Breeding, a claims adjuster for Iowa National Insurance, had moved to Hastings to start their new life together. Jim had enrolled at St. Cecilia's High School in Hastings where he was quarterback for the football team. The first weekend after the football season ended, he and a friend from Hastings went to Columbus to see some buddies there. They had apparently been drinking and were on a gravel road in Nance County when Jim, the driver, lost control of the car and crashed. The three passengers were not badly hurt.

Chuck Hagel remembers getting a phone call from his stepfather at 5:30 the next morning. He and his brothers went to Fullerton to identify the body and take it back to Hastings for the funeral. "It seemed so unfair . . . almost bizarre that Tom and I went through what we did [in Vietnam] and came back in good shape," Hagel said. "It was incredibly devastating to everybody," Tom recalled. "It hurt all of us deeply, but my poor mother. . . . It was just awful."

Chuck Hagel recalls that Jim had been in second grade when their father died. Jim and his mother were nearly inseparable for years after that, he said, and were still close when Jim reached his teenage years. After Jim's death the boys drew even closer to their mother and to each other. And, as she had when her two oldest were in Vietnam, Betty Hagel relied on her faith to get through another trauma. "Her faith was the basic foundation of her whole view on life," Tom said. "She was a true believer. That definitely helped her through all her life."

Despite the family tragedy, life had to go on. While he was working on his degree at UNO, Chuck Hagel took advantage of what he had learned from that one-year program in broadcasting at the Brown Institute. Frank Scott hired Hagel to work for the radio station KBON in Omaha. Scott still remembers the letter Hagel sent, seeking work.

"He said, essentially, 'Lucky you! Here I am!'—without sounding arrogant," Scott said. "I had to meet this guy." So he brought Hagel in for an interview and hired him on the spot. "It was the smartest thing I ever did," said Scott, who later became vice president of NBC Radio and then director of Voice of America.

Hagel was at the station when it changed its call letters to KLNG and went to an all news and talk format in 1970. KLNG was one of the first stations in the country to move away from a music format, and neither Scott nor his employees were sure it would work. To that point, talk radio had consisted mostly of what Scott called "at-your-service" shows like "ask a doctor" or "ask a lawyer." KLNG moved to call-in shows focused on current events. "It was a great experiment," Hagel remembers. No one knew whether advertisers and listeners would make the leap to the new programming.

Scott said Hagel, one of the first talk show hosts at KLNG, was good at handling people on the air. Even though the war still seething in Vietnam was a hot topic on many a caller's mind, Hagel kept his cool and managed to walk a path down the middle of the debate. Hagel said those early talk shows on KLNG were more civilized than today's tend to be, partly because the idea was new, and the broadcasters were just feeling their way along. He said, "We were more global in our thinking," and they steered clear of what he called the character assassination that typifies today's talk shows.

Besides the talk shows, Hagel covered city council meetings, fires, and whatever else needed to be reported. Scott recalled, "He had a newsman's mentality."

He also had a lot of fun. Hagel remembers reading the race results from the various horse parks in Nebraska: Grand Island in March, followed by Omaha, Columbus, and Lincoln. "I always liked to do those because I'd make horse noises and whinnies and bring in some sound effects," he said with a laugh. "Frank, the manager, would come running down the hall, yelling, 'Hagel, you're fired.'"

But the fun went on. Michael Amdor, a Creighton student and

later a district court judge in Omaha, also worked at KLNG. "He was very liberal, very Democratic," Hagel said. "I was very Republican, very conservative." But they both liked to have a good time. "We used to drive Frank crazy."

For instance, Amdor would be on the air, reading the news, concentrating on what he was doing. Hagel would slip into the news booth and throw a burning piece of paper onto the news copy, starting a minor conflagration. "And he would do worse things to me," Hagel remembers of Amdor. "Radio was a lot of fun." And the job paid the bills while Hagel was in school.

Hagel graduated from UNO in 1971 with a bachelor of general studies degree in history. "I had about six minors," he said, because he had brought so many transfer credits with him to UNO from his pre-Vietnam semesters at Wayne and Kearney.

History was a natural major for a man who had always been intrigued with the development of people and countries and governments. But Hagel wasn't sure what he would do with the degree once he finished school. He wasn't interested in studying law. He did think about teaching but never seriously pursued that option. But he felt a knowledge of history was something he could apply in any number of possible careers. "I never worried about what I was going to do or whether I would gain any real qualifications from a history degree," he recalls.

Once he finished school Hagel was ready to move on from Omaha and his radio job. He had his degree but not in a subject that prepared him for a specific career. He could have stayed in broadcasting, but it didn't appeal to him long term. He thought he'd try to find work in Washington. "I didn't have any grand plans in mind," he said. "I just always wanted to go there. I thought it would be great to work in Washington."

So he asked Scott for a week off from work at the station to go job hunting in DC. Scott not only granted the vacation request but also wrote letters introducing Hagel to the members of the Nebraska congressional delegation. And Hagel remembers Scott's inviting him to discuss his plans with Republican congressman John Y. McCollister when McCollister was at the station for an interview. Hagel was acquainted with McCollister because he had covered the congressman when he'd served on the Douglas County board.

Armed with Scott's letters, the contact with McCollister, and a lot of optimism, Hagel set out for Washington, DC. He wasn't worried that he didn't have a job lined up. It was the beginning of a pattern that would take Hagel through a variety of jobs in his lifetime. "I've always done things I thought were right," he said, "that felt good, that I wanted to do, that I thought I could do" even if the conventional wisdom suggested he was unlikely to succeed.

Hagel remembers flying into the city on a perfect Sunday afternoon in April. "You got this majestic view of the White House, the monuments, the Capitol," he said. "It almost took my breath away—the beauty, the majesty, the history of it—everything." He checked into the old Congressional Hotel and decided to spend the rest of the day walking around Capitol Hill. Eventually he sat down to rest on the steps of the Russell Senate Office Building, where he has an office today.

He remembers sitting on the steps for half an hour or so, staring across the street at the Capitol, the trees, the grounds. He thought about working in that building as an elected member of Congress. He'd never had a feeling like that before, he said, and it was a moment he would not forget.

### Climbing Capitol Hill

Hagel's immediate need, though, was to find work. He used McCollister's office as his headquarters while he called on Nebraska's other members of Congress and any other potential employer with whom he could get an interview. After a week, he went back to Nebraska with no job. A month later, he called McCollister to say he was coming back to try again. This time McCollister had a deal to offer.

McCollister's office had received fourteen thousand responses to a constituent survey, and the congressman needed someone to tabulate them. He offered Hagel two hundred dollars a week to work on those surveys in a back room in his office on a table set up in front of the office refrigerator. Whenever somebody wanted a Coke, Hagel had to move his "desk" out of the way. But the congressman added a perk that made it all possible: a bedroom in his own home, rent-free. "We had a big house," McCollister said, and only one son still living at home.

Hagel took McCollister up on the offer and started to work on the surveys, all the while continuing to look for a permanent job elsewhere in Washington. But within a couple of months, McCollister said, Hagel had made himself so useful that the congressman made him a regular member of the staff and gave him a small raise. Not many months after that, McCollister sent Hagel back to Omaha to run his district office, to be sure his constituents were getting quick responses to their questions and help with their problems. He called Hagel back to Washington in 1973 to run his office there.

By that time, Randy Moody was McCollister's press secretary, and he and Hagel shared an office in the Cannon House Office Building. Moody remembers that Hagel was always very attuned to what was happening back in Nebraska's second congressional district—both how well constituents were supporting McCollister and how well the congressman was serving them.

McCollister always solicited opinions from his staff about political issues, Moody said. Watergate was a frequent topic of those discussions in 1973 and 1974. Moody remembers that the staff helped McCollister develop his position that President Nixon should resign, even though Nixon remained popular in Nebraska. McCollister was one of the first Republicans to speak out in favor of a Nixon resignation.

Hagel remembers how disappointed McCollister and many other Republicans were in the president and the way he was handling the scandal. The White House had sent presidential aides John Erlichman and Bob Haldemann and the president's daughter Julie Nixon Eisenhower to reassure Republicans in Congress that everything would be fine. "They said, 'It's all a lie,'" Hagel said. "They blamed the press, the Democrats."

Once testimony from John Dean and others proved that the

LOOKING TO WASHINGTON

cover-up was real, people like McCollister felt betrayed, Hagel said. It was particularly appalling that the president had sent his daughter, a young woman everyone liked, to lie to his colleagues in Congress. "It really shook the party and its whole foundation," Hagel recalled.

As a staff member Hagel didn't have the investment in the party and the system that McCollister did, but he remembers sharing his boss's disappointment. He recalls telling fellow staffers that the Watergate scandal was going to transform American politics and make things very difficult for Republicans. "These guys were so selfish; they were willing to take down the whole party," he said. And take it down they did. The GOP lost seats in the House and Senate in 1974 as well as in a batch of statehouses. McCollister himself was nearly defeated. The party was bleeding from a self-inflicted wound.

Hagel said McCollister had had an enormous influence on him, more influence than anyone other than his immediate family. "I learned a lot from him," Hagel said: "how to do this business the right way, the honorable way, the honest way. Know what you're talking about. Don't take cheap shots. Study. Develop a reputation where people will respect you for what you know."

Hagel believes doing things the right way cost McCollister the election when he ran against Democrat Ed Zorinsky for the Senate in 1976. Hagel had taken time off from McCollister's congressional office to run the campaign. Carl Curtis and Roman Hruska, both of whom had been in the Senate for twenty-four years, were nearing the end of their careers. The Zorinsky campaign said it was time for a change, and Zorinsky said he would provide it. Zorinsky's campaign called McCollister "Roman Hruska, Jr."

Besides that, the post-Watergate years were tough ones for Republicans, Hagel said. Although McCollister had been outspoken against Nixon, he wouldn't disavow the entire party, "wouldn't throw his friends overboard." Furthermore McCollister may not have been political enough, Hagel said. People counseled him to stick with his principles but tone down his rhetoric for the sake of attracting voters, but "he just wouldn't play the political game." Some longtime observers of Nebraska politics remember that McCollister's style was just to charge ahead with his own ideas—and that Hagel charged right along with him. That aggressive style may not have played well with Nebraska voters.

Then, too, television was beginning to dominate politics by that time. "John probably should have sent out more press releases, done more TV interviews," Hagel said, "but in his mind it would have been for the wrong reasons: not to help him be a better congressman or do a better job but just as a political exercise."

McCollister lost the election with 47.5 percent of the vote. And Hagel was out of a job. Fortunately for him, he was not out of McCollister's good graces. Once again the congressman was to make it possible for Hagel to live and work in Washington. Originally McCollister had planned to move back to Nebraska after the election, but a friend who was retiring from Congress told him about an opening at Firestone Tire's Washington office. McCollister protested that he wasn't interested in being a lobbyist, but he agreed to at least do an interview—on his last day in his congressional office.

When he got home that Friday evening, everything was packed for the return to Nebraska the next day. Nan McCollister asked her husband how the Firestone interview had gone, and he gave her a summary of the conversation. She said, "That would be kind of fun, wouldn't it?" His wife was not ready to go home to Omaha, McCollister said. "She hadn't forgiven the voters of the second district." The McCollisters postponed their departure for Nebraska and spent the weekend talking about the possibility of John's working for Firestone in Washington. Monday morning McCollister called the firm and said he'd like to talk about the job some more. Within a few days, he had an offer.

But McCollister told his prospective bosses he would work for them only if they would also hire Chuck Hagel. Firestone agreed. The two went to work as manager and associate manager of government affairs, respectively. They lobbied on behalf of Firestone, headquartered in Akron, Ohio, and they gave the company advice on regulatory issues at both the state and federal level. Hagel took to the road, spreading Firestone's corporate message to the managers, foremen, and workers in the factories and helping show the employees how they could get involved in government. Wherever he went, radio and television stations would interview him as a representative of Firestone. "Firestone in Akron loved it," McCollister said. And Hagel made contacts all over the nation.

It wasn't an easy time to work for the company, Hagel remembers. Firestone was facing charges that failures in its Radial 500 tires were responsible for accidents all over the country. The company wanted to stonewall, Hagel said. "We said it wouldn't work. You've got a bad product. Acknowledge it and get it off the road." Frustrated and unwilling to continue to fight the battle against what he saw as an entrenched management group, McCollister left Firestone after two years, and Hagel took his place.

A year or so later, Hagel had an offer to go to work for International Harvester in Washington. When he told Dick Riley, the chairman of Firestone, that he had been offered another job and planned to take it, Riley surprised Hagel with a counteroffer that included a big salary increase. Hagel said if he were to make more money, he should have to earn it with expanded responsibilities. Riley agreed, and Hagel stayed on with Firestone.

In 1979, while he was still working for Firestone, Hagel married Patricia Lloyd, then the executive director of the National Historic Trust and now with the Johns Hopkins University's Washington program. The couple separated early in 1981 and divorced the following year. "It was a very good person I was married to; it just didn't work," Hagel said. Hagel's brother Mike said he wasn't surprised the marriage didn't last. "Patsy is a great gal," he said. "They were just two people who shouldn't have been married to each other." It was an amicable divorce, and the two remain friends.

Not too long after Hagel's promotion at Firestone, the company brought in a new CEO. He and Hagel did not see eye to eye on much of anything. As John McCollister tells it, Hagel was attending a breakfast meeting in Akron at which the new CEO carried on about how crooked everyone in Washington was. Hagel respectfully but passionately disagreed. The CEO was so infuriated at being told he was wrong that he pushed aside his grapefruit and left the table. All his underlings followed—like ducklings, McCollister said—leaving Hagel and the president of the Rubber Manufacturers Association the only ones at the table. By that afternoon McCollister said, "Everyone on K Street [home to scores of lobbying offices in Washington] knew what had happened. Chuck was sure that was it."

He didn't get fired that day, but relations didn't improve. Hagel and his boss disagreed about the role a government liaison should play, and before long the CEO simply closed the Washington office. "I think I heard about it on a Friday night at 5 p.m.," Hagel recalls. He was out of a job again. "But it was OK. It wasn't going to fit anyway," he said.

### Backing Reagan

As Hagel's job with Firestone was disappearing from under him, Bill Brock, the former senator from Tennessee, and Joe Rodgers, the chair of the finance committee for the Reagan presidential campaign, asked Hagel to join them as a consultant. Although the company had eliminated Hagel's position, Firestone continued to pay him through the end of 1980 but allowed him to work as a fund-raiser for the Reagan campaign and as the cochair of inauguration ceremonies after Reagan had been elected.

That kind of political work made him visible among Republicans in Washington, Hagel said, and he was asked to work on preparations for the 1982 World's Fair in Knoxville, Tennessee. Planning had started during the Carter administration, but the organization was not in good shape in 1981. Hagel's job was to drum up participation from companies all over the world, and he managed to do that between January and August 1981.

Then his political connections paid off again. The Vietnam veteran whom Reagan had appointed deputy administrator at the Veterans Administration withdrew before his name could be sent to the Senate for confirmation. The administration wanted to find another Vietnam vet for the position, and several people promoted Hagel as an ideal candidate.

Reagan named Hagel the deputy administrator in August 1981. At age thirty-five he was the highest-ranking Vietnam veteran in the Reagan administration, McCollister recalls. "He was very proud of that." But the good feelings didn't last long.

Hagel started work on September 1, 1981, and was officially confirmed in November. Within a few months he was convinced the VA administrator, Robert Nimmo, was steering the agency in the wrong direction.

Nimmo was trying to dismantle storefront centers put together by Vietnam vet Max Cleland, who was later elected to the Senate. The centers were designed to serve vets who didn't trust the bureaucracy and wouldn't go into "official-looking" offices. Nimmo wanted to end further testing for Agent Orange exposure, dismissing the effects of the chemical defoliant used in Vietnam as something akin to teenage acne. He used his forum as a guest on NBC's *Today* show to tell the world that Vietnam veterans were a "bunch of crybabies," Hagel said. Nimmo also did some reckless things personally, Hagel recalls. He spent tens of thousands to refurbish his office in the face of a standing order that no money be spent for such things. He requisitioned a helicopter to take him to a golf date.

Don Clarke, later to become Hagel's business partner, said it was a bad situation for Hagel. "He had greater visions of doing constructive things," Clarke said. But, as deputy, Hagel "didn't have the power to change it, hard as he might try."

Although he was increasingly uncomfortable with his job, Hagel continued to do his work and fulfill his official obligations. One of those turned out to be momentous.

Attending a Capitol Hill reception on St. Patrick's Day, 1982, Hagel met Lillian Beth Ziller, press secretary for G. V. "Sonny" Montgomery, chair of the House Veterans Affairs Committee. Ziller was named after an aunt, Lillian Phipps, and was known as Lilibet because her father liked the sound of the nickname given to Britain's Queen Elizabeth by her nanny.

Lilibet Ziller planned to attend the reception briefly, taking advantage of the free food, a time-honored practice among congressional aides. She remembers calling her youngest sister, a student at Georgetown University, and asking to borrow "that great black velvet dress of yours." She was wearing that great dress when she found herself talking to the deputy administrator of the VA. "He was just a delightful person to chat with," she remembers. "He was fun—you know: fun." By the end of the reception, Hagel had asked her to go out that evening with a group of people, but she already had other plans. When he suggested going out the following night, she was a little hesitant but told him to give her a call.

Hagel had told Lilibet he had a friend who worked at the National Theatre and sometimes gave him tickets for shows there. She was a bit suspicious, wondering whether he was just trying to get rid of tickets for his friend. He must have realized what she was thinking. The next morning at work, her phone rang. A voice said, "Is this Miss Ziller? This is the ticket office at the National Theatre." "I thought, 'Here we go,'" she remembers. But it wasn't the ticket office; it was Hagel himself, pleased with the practical joke he had pulled off.

That night's outing at the National Theatre was the couple's first date of many. The early days of their courtship coincided with Hagel's tenure at the VA. His growing unhappiness there caused some tense moments for Lilibet, still on the staff at the House committee.

But, by the spring of 1982, both Nimmo's policy trends and his personal peccadilloes had become very public. Veterans were outraged and calling for Nimmo's resignation, Hagel said. Hagel and his boss were more and more at odds. Hagel told the Reagan administration he was going to resign: "It was just dishonest to stay," he said. He submitted his letter of resignation on July 1, 1982, ten months after he had started at the VA.

"My friends thought I was crazy," Hagel remembers. McCollister remembers that a headline over a newspaper piece about Hagel's resignation read: "Wrong man quits."

Helene Von Damm, who had been Reagan's secretary when he was governor of California, was then on the president's staff and had a lot of influence in the White House. She offered to find Hagel another job in the administration, but he said no thanks. "She said, 'Your record will be blemished. And you don't have a job.'" "I said I'd find something," he recalled.

By this time Nimmo had become a high-profile problem for the Reagan administration. Hagel remembers that TV news shows and newspapers wanted to interview him about his resignation and his views on Nimmo, but he declined to talk about it publicly. "I didn't think that was the right thing to do," he said. Even so, Nimmo couldn't survive. He resigned on October 4, 1982, and left Washington. "Things turned out just the way I told the White House they would," Hagel remembers.

When Hagel was running for Senate in 1996, Nimmo told reporters Hagel had been part of the problem at the VA. "He's a personable guy," Nimmo said, "but the most passion I saw in Chuck Hagel was self-promotion. We had some major differences."[1] Hagel didn't deny the differences, but he said Nimmo brought on his problems himself. "He left in disgrace," he said. "It wasn't my doing."[2]

When a person resigns from a political appointment, he doesn't receive severance pay. Hagel had some money in savings and cashed in one of his three insurance policies to get by for a few months. And he started looking for a job. Nobody was knocking down his door, begging him to come to work. Leaving what had become a high-profile political appointment made Hagel, in some eyes, disloyal. "I was radioactive" for a while, Hagel remembers. Some of his friends advised him to leave Washington, predicting that Reagan's people would prevent his getting another job there.

"It was a tough time for me, but I wasn't afraid," Hagel said. He said he was less bothered by the difficulty of finding work than by the fact that he felt forced out of a job he had really liked and believed in.

### Teaming Up with Dick Tracy

By the end of the summer of 1982, Hagel had heard from his friends Don Clarke and Dave Smith, who were then in the cable television business. He'd gotten to know them when McCollister was running for Senate in 1976 and Clarke, Smith, and their partner Bill Collins were working for the Republican Senate Campaign Committee. They had talked to Hagel several times about his joining their cable TV firm, but now they were thinking about starting a new company: they wanted to get into cellular telephones. Hagel had no idea what those were.

Collins and Clarke explained the basics of wireless systems and gave Hagel some materials to read. He read all of that and more, then went to see some friends in New York who were involved with telecommunications. They told him more about the new technology. "We were talking about Dick Tracy stuff: It will be no wires. It will be video. It will be everything," Hagel recalls. It sounded like science fiction. Not many people believed it was likely to be successful.

But after he did his research, Hagel thought differently. He went back to Clarke, Collins, and Smith and said he wanted in on the cellular business. His problem, he told them, was that he had no money to invest. Hagel sold his 1979 Buick and cashed in his remaining two insurance policies to come up with an investment of about five thousand dollars. The partners decided to start a new company and, in September 1982, incorporated as Collins, Hagel, and Clarke. Smith went off on his own.

Hagel got 35 percent of the firm—and a two-thousand-dollar-a-month salary when the company had enough cash for salaries—and set out to find investors and raise money, preferably from people living in the markets for which the company wanted to compete. Because the FCC emphasized local ownership when it awarded licenses to broadcast stations, the partners thought the same mind-set might hold true in the cell-phone process, Don Clarke said.

At that point, the connections Hagel had made while working in Congress and, especially, for Firestone, became an important asset. "I knew a lot of people," Hagel said, people from all over the country, people who might be willing to put money into the new technology.

Clarke said, "He would go to a potential applicant city and try to find investors from that city." The partners wanted local investors whenever possible. The money had to come quickly because the new company wanted to apply to the Federal Communications Commission for cellular licenses in 1983. That meant they needed engineering plans, demographic studies, financial plans, and legal documents to support the entire package. It didn't come cheap.

Hagel was also out on a financial limb, living on the hope that cellular phones were the next big thing. It was a risk, and it kept him awake some nights, but he stayed with it. "I see risk as opportunity," he said in 1996 about his leap into the cell-phone milieu.[3] He still marvels at the way things played out. "We went into areas we didn't know anything about," he said. "But business is a matter of common sense; if you want to do something, and learn about it, you'll be successful."

Lilibet Ziller Hagel remembers those years when she was dating the cell-phone entrepreneur as a "topsy-turvy time. It was unlike anything I had ever seen," she said. "Watching from the sidelines was pretty neat." She remembers that she would have friends over for backyard picnics, and Hagel would start telling the other guests about his ventures into cellular phones. "He'd say it's going to be like Dick Tracy, and he'd take off his shoe and hold it up to his head," she said. The skeptical guests would just roll their eyes.

Collins, Hagel, and Clarke were breaking new ground. People from all backgrounds and with a variety of motives were attracted to the business, and the rules were changing every day. Those changing rules proved to be a hurdle for Hagel's company, a hurdle that would eventually make them defendants in a lawsuit.

When the FCC prepared to begin licensing firms to use part of the radio spectrum for the new technology, the commission planned to award two licenses in each of more than seven hundred markets. One license would automatically go to the local phone company. The others were open to competition from companies like Collins, Hagel, and Clarke. The FCC asked applicants to prepare detailed proposals including engineering, demographic, and financial plans, and Collins and Clarke were already working on those when Hagel came on board in 1982. The FCC planned to analyze each application and award licenses to the firms on a comparative, competitive basis.

The process began with franchises for the thirty most populous cities in the United States, and the FCC's plan worked pretty well, Hagel said. Not many people were yet aware of cellular technology's potential, and relatively few applications were sent for review. Some of Collins, Hagel, and Clarke's proposals were among those accepted. In some cities their firm was among three successful applicants, each of which received a license to serve one-third of the potential customers. As a result, license holders started trading licenses in order to acquire contiguous territories large enough to justify the expense of building a cellular network. "We went ahead and started borrowing money, started building," Hagel said.

Collins, Hagel, and Clarke's applications earned franchise awards in fifteen cities in the next thirty-city draft, Clarke remembers. But then the FCC had changed horses in midstream. By the time the agency was ready to award licenses for the next thirty cities, word had gotten around that cell phones might be a good way to make a quick buck. This time "the FCC had thousands of applications for tens of licenses," Clarke said. Realizing it would be impossible to analyze each application, the FCC put the entire process on hold for about a year while it figured out how to handle the flood.

Ultimately the agency turned to a modified lottery process. Applicants were asked to provide basic information about engineering, demographics, and financing. If they met the minimum requirements, applications were put into a pool, and the FCC drew numbers from among the qualified to determine who would actually receive a license.

The whole thing still irritates Hagel, and the usually calm storyteller sat forward in his seat when he took up the subject. "People like us were in it for the long term," he said, already building systems and customer bases. Too many others, he said, wanted to win a license only to sell or trade it away and make off with a pile of money. All were treated equally under the lottery system.

The first rounds of competition, Clarke said, involved about fifteen firms that had gotten into the business early and were actually operators of wireless or wired communications systems. But by the third round, scores of people were jumping into the pond, people and groups with no expertise in telecommunications or in the application process.

Collins, Hagel, and Clarke expanded their focus and, in addition to preparing their own lottery entries, used the technical expertise they had developed to produce and sell prepared applications to their competitors for several thousand dollars each. That brought in so much money so fast that the firm started spinning off its earnings into other investments. They bought Wendy's restaurants in London and Los Angeles, a tennis club in suburban Virginia, and an agency to represent professional athletes.

Late in 1984 Collins, Hagel, and Clarke and a group of North Carolina investors rolled all their cellular operations into a new company they called Vanguard, dedicated to the telecommunications business. While the three original partners all initially served on the Vanguard board, Hagel was the only one of the three who became a Vanguard employee. He was an executive vice president until 1987. Collins and Clarke went into other ventures, and Hagel sold them his interests in the Wendy's restaurants and other investments when they parted professional company.

In the face of the new licensure system, Vanguard—with Collins, Hagel, and Clarke all on the board—also took another tack. After working for years to line up investors to support one competitive application in each market, they found themselves facing a new reality. They disbanded their investment groups and had each investor file a separate lottery application.[4] Then they formed individual investors into alliances that called for sharing each franchise won by any one alliance member. Vanguard was to be the controlling partner in each case.

But the arrangements weren't all sweetness and light. "Some guys played all kinds of games in this," Hagel said with irritation. "Some partners would say, 'We want you to give us another 10 percent . . . or we won't let you borrow money to build a new system,'" he said. "They were essentially blackmailing you."

Clarke said the FCC process had gone so badly off course that the result was dozens of different owners with shares of the license in any particular market. It made economic sense, he said, to trade those fractions until one company got majority control of an area and was able to create a functional cellular system there. But the complicated buying and selling led to legal charges and countercharges. Lawsuits proliferated during the mid-1980s in the cell-phone world. "Everybody was sued," Hagel said, large and small investors alike—even people like Mark Warner, later to be Virginia's governor. "He had more lawsuits than he had suits," Hagel said. "It was so complicated, and there was so much going on." In fact a 1986 *Wall Street Journal* story quoted one participant in the licensing process and the ensuing frenzy of trading who said it was "a cross between Monty Hall's 'Let's Make a Deal' and the baseball trading sessions."

When it was sued in 1986, Vanguard hired the attorney Reed Hundt, who specialized in communications law, to defend it against the lawsuits filed by losing lottery applicants. The plaintiffs asked the FCC to deny Vanguard the licenses it had won, accusing the company of skewing the lottery process by negotiating advance cooperative agreements with several applicants for each license. What that did, Vanguard's opponents said, was increase the chances that Vanguard would win a license in any given market.

Vanguard said Hagel had cleared the procedure with the FCC ahead of time. "I wanted to ensure that everything we were doing was legal," Hagel said.[5] "I laid it all out. They could have killed it right there." The FCC may not actually have blessed Vanguard's plan, but neither did the agency stop the company from going forward.

Accused of wrongdoing, Vanguard maintained its innocence but was afraid the FCC would hold protracted hearings that would prevent the company from receiving its licenses for three or four years. Vanguard's attorney convinced the commission that hearings on the case would harm the public interest by delaying the FCC's goal: to be sure each market was subject to competition between the local phone company and the lottery winner. The case was later dismissed, and the commission took no action on the complaints. It did, however, change its policies to prevent license applicants from using similar tactics in future lotteries.

Hundt was the perfect attorney for the job, Hagel said.[6] "We needed someone . . . with a reputation as pristine and clean as you could possibly get in the Washington DC communications bar." Furthermore, Hundt could hardly be accused of being a crony of the partners, who had all worked for the Republican Party. He had roomed with Al Gore at St. Alban's school. "He's a big liberal Democrat," Hagel said, "and he'll tell everybody who asks him that Vanguard did nothing wrong."

Haynes Griffin, the first president of Vanguard, said the proof is in the pudding: the fact that Vanguard was granted the licenses. "On the face of it, it's not credible to say that things were done improperly. That would have been self-defeating; the FCC would not have granted the licenses." That's not to say the process wasn't complicated, Griffin said. Nor is it to deny that the way the system was set up encouraged competitors to attack the first identified license recipient in hopes of knocking somebody out of the running and improving their own prospects. But, bottom line, Griffin contends that the FCC was thorough in its analysis and that Vanguard was completely exonerated.

The company went public in 1987, the same year Hagel resigned from the firm. He continued on the board of directors until 1991 and held stock in the company until moving back to Omaha in 1993. AT&T bought Vanguard in 1999.

It took a lot of work—sometimes he got only two hours of sleep a night—but Hagel said he was glad he had been involved in building the cell-phone business. "My partners and I were the first wave of cellular-telephony pioneers," he said. "We were at the front end" of an industry that revolutionized the communications business. And their success made Hagel a millionaire several times over, something he said he had not expected. "I had never sought to make a lot of money," Hagel said. It wasn't even something he dreamed of as a kid. "My focus has always been to make an impact, to do things," he said.

But the money wasn't unwelcome. For one thing, it gave him a chance to share his new wealth with his brothers and his mother. He gave each of them ten thousand dollars and also bought his mother a car. In response she wrote a note the senator still has. The note was prompted by something that happened in 1982 when the son had sent his mother a check for twenty-five dollars for her August 29 birthday. He had just left the Veteran's Administration and had no job and no money other than what he had raised by selling his car and cashing in his insurance policies. His mother told him she wasn't going to cash the birthday check. In 1985, after he sold his Vanguard stock and shared his largesse with his family, his mother sent the twenty-five-dollar check back to him. On it she had written "Paid in full many, many, many times over." The accompanying note said, "I told you when I received this check on August 29, 1982, that I would not cash it until you made it big with your new company. Now, thanks to you, I don't ever have to cash it. . . . What a nice son you are and have always been! How proud I am."

His new wealth gave Hagel not just the opportunity to share his riches but also the freedom to do things he might not otherwise have been able to attempt, including running for office. "I don't think I'd be sitting here in the U.S. Senate if I hadn't had that economic independence," he said.

## Serving the United Service Organization

Throughout the excitement and chaos of his years in the world of cellular phones, Hagel and Lilibet Ziller continued to date, but things were in such turmoil that the couple didn't even think about marriage early on. Finally things calmed down a bit, and Charles Timothy Hagel and Lillian Beth Ziller were married in April 1985 in the Ziller family's backyard in Meridian, Mississippi.

"It was a beautiful afternoon after it had rained like crazy the night before," she remembers. Their honeymoon in Costa Rica was unconventional, mixing business with pleasure. "It was somewhat crazy," Lilibet recalls. "He had to have these business meetings before we could take off—in a crazy car without an air conditioner."

After the honeymoon the couple returned to the Washington

area and Hagel's job as an officer with Vanguard. But it wasn't long before he was looking at another opportunity, which turned out to be a chance to rescue an organization nearing its death throes.

"The USO essentially imploded in 1986," Hagel said. The World United Service Organization, designed to provide help and comfort to U.S. military personnel all over the world, couldn't even meet its payroll. Founded in 1941, at the request of President Franklin D. Roosevelt, the USO had grown exponentially during World War II. At its high point in 1944, the USO had more than three thousand clubs, staffed almost entirely by volunteers. The clubs offered troops a place to dance and meet people, a place to see movies or find religious counsel, a quiet place to talk or write letters, and, of course, a place to go for free coffee and doughnuts. And the USO sponsored the camp shows, both in the United States and abroad, that Bob Hope and other entertainers had made famous.[7]

The organization's fortunes fluctuated over the years as America found itself in and out of wars around the world. Eventually, though, the USO became a chartered private charitable organization whose mission was to serve U.S. troops and their families, even when the nation was not involved in a "hot" war.

The USO moved its headquarters from New York to Washington DC in 1977. In 1979 the six agencies that had founded the USO—the YMCA, YWCA, Salvation Army, National Catholic Community Service, National Jewish Welfare Board, and Traveler's Aid Association—pulled out, leaving the organization entirely independent. Seven years later the USO was broke and floundering.

Hagel, who had been a member of the organization's board of governors while he was at the VA, served on the search committee to find a new USO president. After a day of interviewing candidates, Hagel gave Bill White, a former USO president and the retired president of U.S. Steel, a ride back to his hotel. On the way White made a suggestion. "He said, 'What would you think about being president of the USO?'" Hagel remembers, "I said, 'But I have these companies—and we're doing a little business . . . '" White said, "I know, I know. But you need to do this. I've been asked by two or three former [USO] presidents before me to ask if you'd do this."

White asked Hagel to bring Lilibet to join White and his wife for dinner in their hotel suite. The next day other USO board members talked to Hagel about taking the job, and he started seriously considering it. He talked to his Vanguard partners about it, and they agreed he could stay on as a board member and still play a role in the business. Hagel told the search committee he would take the job on two conditions: he wanted Denny Long, retired president of Anheuser Busch, to stay on as chairman of the USO's board, and he wanted three years to turn the organization around; then he'd be off to something new.

Those three years were "three of the greatest years of our early married life," Lilibet Hagel said. She had been working as a marketing researcher at the American Society of Association Executives. Chuck was flying all over the world for the USO, and she tried to go along whenever she could. "I would run to Dulles Airport on Friday after work; we'd fly to Paris and stay with Chuck's dear friends Joe and Honey Rodgers." Rodgers was ambassador to France; Hagel had gotten to know him when they worked together on the World's Fair in 1981.

Finally, Lilibet said, her husband's travel plans got to be more enticing than her job, and she threw in the towel and joined him in his USO endeavors. "We traveled all over the place: Korea, Japan, France, Germany" for fund-raising events Hagel organized, she recalled. "We met so many successful, interesting people who really cared" about the USO and its mission.

The couple wanted children, but Lilibet had had several miscarriages in the first years of their marriage. Looking back, she said, "Everything happens for a reason." Had they had a baby during the USO years, she would never have been able to travel the world with Chuck.

Part of Hagel's job was simply to raise money for the organization both from individual donors and from host governments. But another part was to diagnose its business operations and recommend improvements. After visiting USO facilities around the world,

Hagel concluded that the organization had too many managers and staff, so he decided to eliminate an entire layer of management.

The chairman of the board was opposed to a move that would result in job losses for so many people, and he and Hagel had what Hagel recalls as "an energetic disagreement" at a board meeting. When the board voted, Hagel's position prevailed, and the USO became a more streamlined body.

Not that it was easy. Hagel's trimming started with the board of directors itself. The USO had about a hundred board members, Hagel said, and no enforceable rotation policy. People tended to come to the board and just stay. It had become sort of a social thing with few real responsibilities, Hagel said. The sheer size made the group unwieldy, and, besides, he concluded, "We needed new energy."

So he went through the roster of board members, noting how many years each had served. Then he wrote to about twenty-five of those who had been around longest, thanking them for their service. "I didn't say they were off the board—but I made it pretty clear they were off the board," Hagel said. He did the same for another twenty to twenty-five members over the following year and got the remaining members to pass a resolution clearly defining the length of terms and the number of consecutive terms members could serve.

Then Hagel began cutting in other places. He fired about a third of the headquarters staff. And he closed a number of USOs abroad, including eleven in Germany alone in his first few months at the organization and about twenty-five total over the first few years. "I didn't like to do it," Hagel said, but he had little choice. "I had to look at things I thought were drags on our budget."

Gladys Gordon, who worked at the USO when Hagel took over, remembers one of Hagel's first moves after restructuring the organization and laying off a number of employees. "He gave everyone who was left a raise," Gordon said, the amazement still echoing in her voice. "We just went, 'Who is this person?'" The raises lifted morale and told the staff Hagel was serious about rebuilding the organization. Hagel said he kept the employees he considered the strongest, and those people needed an incentive to stay and work hard. Knowing the organization was struggling, most employees were looking for work elsewhere. "The last thing I needed was to have some of the best people leaving," Hagel said.

Once he had his staff in place, Hagel started calling friends and acquaintances around the world, Gordon said, telling them the USO was in trouble and asking them to send contributions. Gordon worked in the finance department, and she saw the money start to pour in. "I remember holding one check in my hand," she said, "the most money we'd ever seen at one time." The check was accompanied by a note from the donor, apologizing that fifty thousand dollars was all he was able to send at that time. Hagel, Gordon said firmly, was an extremely successful fund-raiser. She attributes his success to the fact that he's a generous person himself. Furthermore, "he makes a convincing argument, and he's very sincere about a cause," she said. "He never talks down to anyone. He can talk to my children, my parents, a farmer, an ambassador or a president. He's the same person all the time." Gordon said potential donors found Hagel's approach appealing and believed they could trust him. "If he says it's a good thing, then you do it."

The board chairman Denny Long said one of Hagel's strengths at the USO was his ability to go to major corporations and ask not only for money but also for key executives to help the USO. "Chuck had the character and the credibility to make it work," Long said.[8]

The USO went from deep debt in February to financial solvency by December. Hagel suggested the organization celebrate its success with a gala event, Gordon remembers. The staff's first reaction was: "We don't have any money." Hagel decided to do it anyway and to have the gala in Germany, at one of the remaining USO centers. Because Hagel knew so many people and was so well liked, Gordon said, he was able to raise money to support the gala—and then some. "I think we made about five million dollars" to support USO centers overseas. "It was just amazing," she added.

Richard Henry said Hagel had succeeded at the USO because he is a born leader. Hagel knows what he wants to do and is willing to work as hard as it takes to make his vision into a reality, said Henry, who was Hagel's executive assistant at the USO and who went on to become an associate executive director for the American Association of Retired People. Hagel is passionate about what he wants to accomplish, Henry said, and that passion is contagious: he was able to persuade USO staff and board members and donors large and small to support a restructured and stronger USO. Hagel said his work leading the USO was the best job he ever had: "Every day connected you with a noble cause, a great effort that really affected and changed the lives of people." Besides that, it was just fun, he recalled.

It was also a risk. If he had failed to solve the USO's problems, Hagel's personal and political stock would have taken a big hit. But his recent success in the cell-phone business probably exponentially boosted his already strong belief that he could do whatever he wanted if he were willing to work hard enough and smart enough. He welcomed the challenge and the risk.

Hagel's tenure at the organization resulted in a trimmed-down and restructured USO with a healthy bank account. When he left in February 1990, he wasn't sure what he was going to do next. "I didn't want to go back to Vanguard," Hagel said. After the excitement of starting the fledgling company and then traveling the world to oversee the installation of cell-phone systems in places like Costa Rica, Saudi Arabia, and Great Britain, the idea of doing mostly maintenance sounded downright boring to him.

Then he got a phone call from Fred Malek, a businessman and prominent Republican. President George H. W. Bush had asked Malek to organize the 1990 Economic Summit of Industrialized Nations, known as the Group of Seven or G-7, to be held in Houston later that year. Malek said he couldn't work full-time on the project, and he wondered if Hagel would serve as his codirector or deputy. Hagel agreed. "It sounded like fun," he said.

But, about two weeks later, Malek called back and said the situation had changed. He and his partners had just bought North-west Airlines, and the company's management had walked out, leaving Malek as the new president. Malek told Hagel he would have to carry the load himself. So that's what Hagel did, through August 1990—for no salary. "I volunteered my time," he said, one of those occasions on which his financial success allowed him the freedom to do what he pleased.

In the meantime the Hagels had bought a house in McLean, Virginia, and prepared to welcome their first child into the family. They named their daughter, born in October 1990, Allyn Elizabeth, the middle name being the name of Chuck's mother. The Hagels had taken a vacation after he finished his G-7 work, and Chuck had stayed around the house to help with the baby. But by then, he said, he was getting restless and wondering what to do next.

At that point he got a call from Mike McKevitt, a former Colorado congressman and an old friend. McKevitt told Hagel the Private Sector Council (PSC) was looking for a new president; he suggested Hagel apply. Hagel said he knew about the PSC and its work and was excited about the possibility of being involved. He flew to Pittsburgh to interview with some of the board members, and they hired him. He took over in late fall 1990 and stayed the better part of two years.

The council helps link federal departments and agencies with member companies to give the federal officials access to ideas and methods used in the private sector. Departments or agencies can request help in any part of their operations: finance, human resources, information technology, or management. The member companies contribute their employees' expertise at no cost for a limited time.[9] Hagel recruited additional companies to be part of the PSC and said he enjoyed his time there. As was true in every job he'd had, he said, "I learned a lot: new relationships, new friends—it just expanded me and expanded me."

Once again, Hagel was ready to move forward. This time he did it by moving back—to Nebraska.

Senator Hagel speaks during the 2004 Republican
National Convention in New York City.

(*Opposite Top*) The Hagel brothers pose for the family's Christmas card in 1953. *From left*: Chuck, Tom, Mike, and J.m. The Hagel family lived in Ainsworth, Nebraska, at the time.

(*Opposite Bottom*) Brothers Tom, *left*, and Chuck Hagel take a moment for a photo during the months they served together in Vietnam in 1968.

(*Above*) Chuck Hagel helps President Ronald Reagan with a book of memorabilia from Reagan's inauguration one year after the event. Pictured in the Oval Office in January 1982 are, *from left*: Charles Wick, President Reagan, Hagel, and Bob Gray. Wick and Gray served as chairmen of President Reagan's inauguration, and Hagel was vice chairman. At the time the photo was taken, Hagel was the deputy administrator of the Veterans Administration.

(*Above*) Hagel and his daughter, Allyn, then five, greet the crowd at his election-night rally in Omaha on May 14, 1996, the night Hagel won the Republican nomination for the Senate.

(*Opposite Top*) Senator Hagel talks with his children at the Vietnam Veterans Memorial following his Memorial Day speech in 1995. His son, Ziller, is in the foreground, and his daughter, Allyn, is behind Ziller.

(*Opposite Bottom*) The Hagel family was photographed following the senator's Memorial Day speech at the Iwo Jima Memorial in 2003. *From left*: Allyn, Senator Hagel, Ziller, and Lilibet Hagel.

(*Opposite*) Betty Hagel Breeding and her sons celebrated the Fourth of July together in 2001 at her home in Hastings. Pictured with her are, *from left*: Mike, Tom, and Chuck.

(*Above*) Senator Hagel meets with Nebraska soldiers at Camp Fallujah in Iraq on December 15, 2004. *From left*: Cpl. Jenna Vaughn of Lincoln, (USMC); S.Sgt. Ismael Tejeda of Central City (USMC); Senator Hagel; SK2 James Salmons of Pilger (U.S. Navy); and Maj. Doug Hinkley of Lincoln (U.S. Army).

Senator Hagel speaks with children at the
Crete Middle School in Crete, Nebraska,
in October 2004.

# 5

## Embracing a Political Future

WHEN CHUCK HAGEL WAS IN HIGH SCHOOL, he thought about being a governor, a senator, or a representative—or a priest or a teacher or any number of other things. "I could have died a happy man, a fulfilled man without ever running for office," he said.

Unlike some people who grow up knowing exactly what they want to do and spend their lives pursuing that career, Hagel has never had a highly focused long-term goal. He just wanted to do something interesting, something to which he could apply his energy and enthusiasm.

He had had plenty of opportunities to do that when he worked for Representative McCollister and then at Vanguard, the USO, the G–7, and the Private Sector Council, but by the early 1990s he was ready to move on again. He was independently wealthy. He had connections all over the nation—all over the world. It was then that elective office became a realistic possibility.

It started when some friends and acquaintances in Virginia

asked Hagel to consider running for governor from that state. He had lived there for twenty years by that time and might have been as much a Virginian as a Nebraskan. Hagel was mildly interested but never pursued the option, he said.

Instead, he began to think about going home to Nebraska and, eventually, launching a campaign from there. At about the same time, he was being offered a chance to join the McCarthy Group, an investment-banking firm in Omaha with which he was already connected. The business opportunity and the potential political opportunity seem to have been intertwined.

Hagel weighed all the options. On the one hand he and his family had a great life in Virginia and no compelling reason to leave the area. A move would take him out of the Washington milieu where he had countless contacts and would probably have plenty of future opportunities in private business or appointed public service.

On the other hand he was excited about the offer to join the McCarthy Group and the potential to get involved in electoral politics from Nebraska. "I knew the only way I'd have an opportunity to run would be from Nebraska—and I'd have to be there to do it," he said. That wasn't the primary reason he decided to move, he said, but it was one of the reasons.

## Moving Home

The move didn't come as a surprise to Hagel's family. His brother Tom recalls that he, Mike, and Chuck had been visiting several years earlier when Chuck, in general terms, outlined what he hoped to do in the future. The plan included a run for elective office.

Mike remembers that discussion, too. Besides, he said, he always thought his brother would eventually run for office. He recalled, "That's just the way he is. He loves a challenge, the opportunity to change things." Hagel's high school friends had seen the same thing in him decades earlier. "He was kind of a natural politician," Larry Dowd said. "He's good on his feet in front of a crowd." Dowd sort of expected Hagel to come back to Nebraska and run for Congress or governor.

EMBRACING A POLITICAL FUTURE

But Lilibet Hagel didn't want to move to Nebraska and dragged her feet every step of the way, she said. She had lived in the DC area since she was twenty-one. Two of her sisters lived there; her friends were there. She didn't want to leave, but finally her husband talked her into it.

Once they made the decision to move, the Hagels bought a $1.1-million, 8,500-square-foot home in west Omaha and moved in with their children. Allyn was three and Charles Ziller Hagel less than a year old. Once she settled in, Lilibet said she grew to love Nebraska.

"It's more relaxed," she said, "and the people are not quite as self-absorbed with where they're going and how fast they're getting there." And she discovered that Nebraskans are not isolated from the world, either. In fact, the people in the smallest towns seem to be most aware of the big issues, she said, noting, "People take time to really think about things and to see their place in the world."

Chuck threw himself into his work as president of McCarthy and Company. Hagel and Mike McCarthy had become acquainted in 1988 when John Gottschalk, president of the World-Herald Company and a member of the USO board of directors—and a boyhood acquaintance of Hagel's in Rushville—invited them on a fishing trip to Wyoming. McCarthy had just moved to Omaha from Iowa and founded the McCarthy Group in 1986. The Democratic former Iowan and the Republican former Nebraskan hit it off.

"It was one of those things that happens with friends," Hagel said. "The chemistry was just right."

Shortly after they met, Hagel accepted McCarthy's offer to serve on the board of American Information Systems (AIS), a small Omaha firm that made electronic voting machines and in which the McCarthy Group had invested. When he went to work for the McCarthy Group full time in 1993, Hagel served as president of a subsidiary, the McCarthy Company. In that role, one of Hagel's first jobs was to raise money to develop cellular-phone systems in places like Egypt and Costa Rica. His work was similar to what he had done at Vanguard.

Later, because of Hagel's background in cellular phones and his contacts around the world, the McCarthy Group, along with the Thompson family in Lincoln and the Hunt family in Blair, Nebraska, developed a private telephone system in Hungary as the Cold War melted down. "We would never have attempted that without Chuck," McCarthy said. "He helped expand our horizons, our credibility. And he's very much about getting something done," a crucial quality in the investment business.

During his time at McCarthy, Hagel agreed to become chairman of the board at AIS, which was about to go bankrupt. He didn't have an office at the firm's headquarters but did spend time with the senior management, trying to guide them to more solid financial ground. Under Hagel's leadership, the firm, which developed vote-counting technology similar to that used to score tests, turned around and became successful. Now known as ES&S, Election Systems and Software, it has become the largest election-service company in the world, Mike McCarthy said.

As successful as it may have been, Hagel's association with AIS and ES&S was later to haunt his political career.

McCarthy expected Hagel to run for office before he'd been back in the state too many years, he said. Hagel was open about his ambitions. "Chuck is one of the few patriots I've met," McCarthy noted. "He truly loves his country. He thinks it's more important than any of us are individually." He believes the nation needs to be protected and that it is the citizens' obligation to do that, McCarthy said.

But McCarthy was surprised at how fast his associate became involved in the Nebraska political scene. Hagel's first shot at a high-profile position would have been in 1994, when Bob Kerrey was up for reelection to the Senate. Nebraska Republicans approached Hagel "out of desperation," the senator said in retrospect, looking for someone to oppose the popular Democratic senator. Many saw him as a good match for Kerrey, Hagel recalled: both had served in Vietnam; both had made millions as successful businessmen.

Lou Ann Linehan was executive director of the Douglas County Republican Party in the early 1990s, and John Y. McCollister had introduced her to Hagel when the Republicans were looking for potential candidates to run for Senate in 1994. She remembers waiting to hear what Hagel had decided to do. She was sitting on a soccer field in Omaha, watching one of her children play, when Hagel called her cell phone and said he had decided not to enter the race. "It was October 4, 1993," Linehan remembers, "his birthday." Hagel told Linehan he hadn't been back in the state long enough to run for a statewide office. Linehan said she thought it was the right decision.

Lilibet Hagel said she had thought all along that the idea was ridiculous. Those urging her husband to run in 1994, she said, were "just diehard Republicans who wanted to oust Kerrey" and really didn't know much about Hagel. She said the possibility of a 1994 Senate race "came and went in our house without much discussion at all." Instead of getting on the ballot himself, Hagel worked with Linehan and others in the Douglas County and state party organizations to get Republicans elected in other races—county board, city council, and sheriff, for instance—getting to know and be known by Nebraska's Republican stalwarts.

About a year later Hagel was willing to think about running for Senate. The Republicans won big in the 1994 congressional elections as well as in gubernatorial races across the nation. The tide seemed to have turned in the party's favor, and within months, Hagel had gotten serious about making a bid for the Senate seat held by the Democrat James Exon, Linehan said.

The climate may have been better, but the decision still was not an easy one. Lilibet Hagel said she remembers one night when she was up with the couple's young son, Ziller, who had an ear infection. She was headed back to bed about 5:30 in the morning and was surprised to find her husband sitting in the kitchen, drinking coffee.

"Both of us love to sleep," she said, and she was amazed to see him up before dawn. She asked him what in the world he was doing at that hour of the day: "What are you thinking about?"

Ten years later she said it still made her teary-eyed to remember his answer: "He said, 'I'm thinking about what this decision means to all of you.'"

But after considering all that, Hagel was ready to go forward and do battle with Exon, a former Nebraska governor and three-term senator. Mike McCarthy, who was then Hagel's business partner and who became his campaign treasurer, remembers telling Hagel he thought he was being unrealistic, that the battle would be too tough and that he might not win. But the advice didn't stop Hagel. "When he fixes on accomplishing a goal, he's very difficult to deter," McCarthy said. "He's very determined."

In this case, Hagel was, indeed, determined. He resigned from his position with McCarthy and enlisted Linehan and others to help him start planning his campaign against the incumbent. But everything changed in March 1995 when Exon announced his decision to retire and not seek another Senate term. The Hagel camp's focus shifted to the Republican primary race against the Nebraska attorney general Don Stenberg, who was very popular with the state party's conservative base.

## Primary Considerations

Linehan said Hagel was firmly aware that he didn't have the name recognition or party structure Stenberg had established. So when the campaign's first poll showed Stenberg with more than 60 percent of likely votes and Hagel with a rating somewhere in the single digits, it didn't faze Hagel.

"He said, 'Put that in a drawer. We're never going to talk about it again,'" Linehan said. "Then we just went to work: raising money, setting up county organizations, making phone calls." Hagel's campaign philosophy, Linehan said, was "Do it well, do it right and do as much as you can do in a 24-hour period seven days a week."

Looking back, Linehan said the race reminded her of the tortoise and the hare. Stenberg, the front-runner with the name recognition, barely moved while Hagel and his campaign went out and enthusiastically recruited new people to politics and converted party loyalists to their camp. Dick Robinson, the president of Norfolk Iron and Metal in Norfolk, Nebraska, was one of the recruits. He said he was pretty jaded about politicians and politics and wasn't too excited about meeting Hagel in spring 1995.

"I thought I'd throw him every hot-button issue I've ever thought of . . . and see what he's made of," Robinson said. "He never blinked. He gave me honest answers." That was true even when they disagreed, Robinson said, and he appreciated it: "I'd rather have a guy just tell me when we disagree and be honest about it."

The skeptic was so impressed with Hagel that, by the time they parted, Robinson had agreed to do whatever he could to get Hagel elected. He became an enthusiastic fund-raiser in northeastern Nebraska, sponsoring events where potential contributors and supporters could meet the candidate. "When you introduce Chuck Hagel to other people, that's all it takes," Robinson said. "His personality is such that . . . people want to help."

Hagel campaigned in person across the state throughout 1995 and into early 1996. "He really connected with the people of Nebraska," McCarthy said. "He worked very hard."

Not that campaigning was all glamour and excitement. Hagel tells the story of his very first campaign trip, which he made with his Omaha neighbor, David Solberg. Solberg, a successful businessman, had access to a twin-engine plane, and he and Hagel took off on a Sunday afternoon for Scottsbluff. The plan was to hold a press conference there the next morning, then hop back east across the state, stopping in communities along the way.

The men arrived in Scottsbluff late on Sunday afternoon and checked into their hotel. A young man who worked at the hotel offered to give them a ride to a restaurant about five miles away in Gering, and Hagel and Solberg enjoyed a leisurely dinner there.

When it was time to return to the hotel, the men decided to call a cab. They soon discovered that there were only two cab drivers in the community, and both were asleep and not taking calls. The hotel employee who had brought them had gone home, and the only person on duty was a night clerk who could not leave her post.

The restaurant was empty except for the hostess and someone

in the kitchen. The employees were waiting for their last guests to leave. Hagel explained the problem to the hostess and asked whether a busboy might still be around, someone they could pay to take them back to their hotel. No, the hostess said, the busboys had gone home long ago. She herself was in a hurry to get home to her kids. That left the person in the kitchen. The hostess said she would see what she could do.

"Five minutes passed," Hagel remembers. "Then seven." Finally, he noticed the kitchen door opening a crack and two faces peeking out at him and Solberg. The women were deciding whether it was safe to get involved with the two men. Finally the women came out into the dining room. "Which of you boys is running for Senate?" asked the elderly woman who had been working in the kitchen.

Hagel started to explain, but the woman cut him off: "Where are you going? Where do you live?" He told her he had lived in nearby Terrytown when he was growing up. "Who was your dad? What school did you go to?" she asked.

Eventually, Hagel and Solberg passed the test, and the woman said she would drop them off at the hotel on her way home to nearby Minatare. The three went out to the parking lot to a car that Hagel remembers as a "boat." When Solberg opened the back door to climb in, he was greeted with some flapping and rustling. It turned out the woman had chickens in a cage on the backseat. "Solberg sat in back with the chickens. I sat in front," Hagel recalls.

Their driver took off with the pedal to the metal, in the sway-backed car that hadn't seen new shock absorbers in years, Hagel remembered. When they approached the hotel, the woman ignored the driveway and, instead, just drove right over the curb, the grass, and some bushes to deposit the men at the front door. "Here we are, boys," she announced.

What was the lesson of that experience? "That it was a people-oriented campaign," Hagel said with a laugh, a campaign that involved shaking a lot of hands, meeting a lot of Nebraskans, and spreading the word about who he was and what he wanted to do.

It was not until March 1996 that Hagel appeared in a series of sixty-second television ads. Linehan said he proved to be a natural on TV, and viewers responded positively. "Our [poll] numbers started climbing," she said.

Mike McCarthy said he thought the ad campaign was effective because it was upbeat and positive in a year when negative advertising was becoming the norm. "He distinguished himself from the ordinary," McCarthy said, and the people of the state seemed to like what they saw.

About two weeks before the election, polls showed the candidates in a dead heat. At the same time that Stenberg realized Hagel was threatening to overtake him, Ben Nelson, the front-runner on the Democratic side, realized it, too, Linehan said. Both Stenberg and Nelson—two years into his second term as Nebraska governor—began running TV commercials to counter Hagel's. They reminded voters that Hagel had lived in Virginia most of his life, and painted him as an outsider, not someone Nebraskans would want representing them in the Senate.

The commercials were effective, and Hagel began dropping like a rock in the polls, Linehan remembers. One adviser predicted the race was over. But Hagel declined to answer the commercials in kind. He had insisted from the start of the campaign that he would run a race of which he and the voters of Nebraska could be proud.

Hagel's insistence on positive campaigning worked on two levels, reflecting the candidate's commitment to high principles as well as his sense that Nebraskans would be turned off by negative campaigning. No matter what the motivation, Hagel's demand that his campaign keep to the high road made him "a nightmare challenge for political operatives," Linehan said.

What to do? Forbidden to go negative, Linehan and Doug McAuliffe of McAuliffe Message Media drove around Omaha for a couple hours that spring, trying to figure out how to counter Stenberg's and Nelson's ads. Finally, McAuliffe had an idea. Why not tape some commercials featuring regular Nebraskans, volunteers working on Hagel's campaign? They could tell everyone how angry they were about the negative ads being directed against their candidate.

So the two lined up about twenty volunteers and began making commercials. After they had finished two, Linehan began debating with herself whether her boss would consider the ads negative. So she showed the two finished commercials to Rob Owen, a campaign staff member who had told her he'd quit if the campaign ever went negative.

"He was the test case," Linehan said. Owen said the commercials didn't look negative to him. In fact, he said, they ought to be on the air as soon as possible. So Linehan and McAuliffe made twenty-five copies of the TV commercials and a similar radio spot. She remembers how eight staff members drove through pouring rain to deliver the tapes to radio and TV stations and get the ads on the air right away. The deliveries were accomplished, the commercials went on the air, and almost immediately the tide began to turn.

"And we beat Stenberg by about twenty points," Linehan recalls with satisfaction. In just a couple of weeks, she said, "We went from 'It's over' to a landslide by going to the people of Nebraska and asking what they thought."

## Moving toward November

Hagel's comeback performance drew a lot of attention far beyond Nebraska. "Everybody loved this guy," Linehan said. The first poll pitting Hagel against Nelson showed Hagel trailing—but not so far that he couldn't make up the difference—and the campaign moved enthusiastically ahead.

Hagel's platform proposed a major tax cut, including a major reduction in the capital-gains tax and elimination of the estate tax, to be offset by reducing the budgets of federal regulatory agencies. The platform also included shifting funding and control of welfare and Medicaid to the states, cutting the projected increase in Medicare spending and trimming the federal bureaucracy by eliminating the Energy, Commerce, Education, and Housing and Urban Development departments.

In late October Hagel sent a mass mailing to Nebraskans, asking for their votes and outlining his political philosophy. Underlined in the first paragraph was this sentence: "I will work with Democrats and Independents and fight for the common-sense changes we need." In the letter Hagel said he supported major tax relief for Nebraska families, a balanced federal budget, eliminating the federal Department of Education, and returning more control to local voters.

In a later paragraph, these words were underlined and boldfaced: "We need to return our culture to the values that have made America great." The values listed were personal responsibility, hard work, self-discipline, honesty, and respect for others, part of Hagel's Nebraska legacy and a nice fit with his conservative political philosophy.

On the stump, Hagel backed school choice, opposed racial quotas and preferences, and backed the Freedom to Farm Act that many Nebraskans opposed. He said Nelson would be lost in the Senate. He said Nebraska needed a senator with the guts and the leadership ability to take on the status quo in Washington. He promised to work to make government smaller and more responsive.

The Republican National Senatorial Committee was eager to help the party reclaim one of Nebraska's Senate seats, and New York senator Alfonse D'Amato, chairman of the committee, came to Hagel bearing offers of help. He wanted to give money and assistance to the Hagel campaign, but he made it clear Hagel would have to get rid of most of his campaign staff and bring in national consultants. D'Amato advised Hagel to forget the positive ads and emphasize the negative instead.

Hagel wasn't buying it. He told D'Amato the political world of Nebraska was far different from the political world of New York. "I know my world," he said. "Your guys don't." Hagel said he refused to fire people who had helped him win the primary and in whom he had confidence.

Furthermore, Hagel refused to allow the committee to spend huge sums on negative TV commercials. The response offended

D'Amato, Hagel said, and things went downhill from there. "At the end of the meeting, I said, 'To hell with you! Keep your damn money and your people. I don't want any help. I'll win without you."

Eventually, Hagel did receive some money from D'Amato's committee. Thad Cochran, who had served as a Republican congressman from Mississippi when Hagel was working for McCollister, came to Nebraska to campaign with his old friend. When he went back to Washington, he told a few key senators that he'd been working for Hagel and thought he could win—even though polls showed him twenty-five or thirty points behind.

That encouraged several Republican senators to come to Nebraska and campaign for a day. Large, enthusiastic crowds at Hagel's rallies convinced them Cochran was right, and they pressured D'Amato to provide money and help, help that was to prove controversial in the days right before the general election. D'Amato eventually got over his disagreement with Hagel. In fact Hagel said D'Amato loves to introduce his Nebraska friend as "Senator My Way." Hagel breaks into a dead-on imitation of D'Amato's New York City accent, calling out, "Hey, Chuckie, babeee! You gotta do it all your own way?"

During the summer of the 1996 campaign, the Democrats advertised hard against Hagel, echoing the primary-campaign theme that painted Hagel as a carpetbagger who was simply using the state to fulfill his own political goals. Hagel and the Republicans responded by accusing Nelson of reneging on a 1994 campaign promise that, if he were reelected as governor, he would serve out a full second term. That would have taken him to 1998, but here he was, running for Senate halfway through his second term. Hagel called for Nelson to resign as governor while running for the Senate.

Deb Fiddelke, who was the communications director for the Hagel campaign, remembers a time that summer when Hagel was twenty-one points down in the polls. Fiddelke and Linehan were the only two staff members who had worked on a campaign before; the rest were young people, many just out of college. They

EMBRACING A POLITICAL FUTURE

were frustrated and depressed. Hagel gathered the staff in a conference room and "gave us a pep talk I'll never forget," said Fiddelke, who went on to be Hagel's communications director in the Senate before leaving for a job in the Bush White House. "He refused to let us believe we wouldn't win," she recalled.

The candidate told his staffers: "We're doing the right thing, and the people of Nebraska will respond. . . . Stay focused, and when November 5 rolls around, we're going to win." He inspired the group, Fiddelke said. They kept working, and polls showed the gap between the candidates shrinking. By the end of October, Hagel and Nelson were neck-and-neck.

Then, less than two weeks before Election Day, the Nelson campaign dropped a bomb. The staff began airing a TV commercial implying that Hagel had attempted to "rig" the FCC's cell-phone license lottery. Actually Nelson was careful to say he was not accusing Hagel of breaking the law. He was simply pointing out the complaint some of Vanguard's competitors had filed with the FCC, the lawsuit later settled out of court.

Nelson said the issue was legitimate because of Hagel's campaign claims that he had built companies and created jobs during his years in the private sector. "He won a lottery he and his partners are accused of rigging in apparent violation of the law," Nelson told reporters.[1]

At a press conference, Hagel responded vehemently: "What he's saying is a lie, L-I-E, lie."[2] Hagel said all the complaints against Vanguard had been dismissed and that the company had never even been prosecuted. He suggested taxpayers might want to look at Nelson's previous business background, including his association with First Executive Corporation and other failed companies he had presided over.[3] It was a subject Hagel said he had declined to bring up earlier in the campaign, despite suggestions from some of his advisers that he do so.

But Nelson said the Republicans had started the mudslinging. He said his assertions about Hagel's past were simply a counterpunch prompted by the National Republican Senatorial Committee's ads blaming him for higher property and income taxes in Nebraska and a 31 percent increase in state spending. Calling the ads lies and half-truths, Nelson said Hagel should be held accountable for the ads, even if the national committee had produced them.

When Nelson complained about the ads, Hagel said in an October 24 statement that he hadn't known in advance about the GOP committee's ads and couldn't control what the national group decided to run. He added that he had said in the past that he would denounce any ads that grossly distorted or lied about an opponent's record. Implying that the ads in question didn't meet those criteria, Hagel said, "Ben Nelson doesn't have a problem lying in his own ads. Why should he complain when someone else tells the truth about his record?"[4]

A week later, as Nelson complained that Hagel was standing on the sidelines while the Republican Party attacked, Hagel insisted he would not respond by lying about the governor or his business dealings or his character. He continued to lament the Nelson campaign's commercials. "This is why good people don't run for office," he said.[5]

Years later, thinking about the commercials Nelson ran still makes Hagel angry. "It was a lie," he said about the ad's implications. He had told reporters in November 1996 that the FCC ruling gave Vanguard a "clean bill of health" and that he and Vanguard had done nothing wrong.

Eric Bernthal, the lead attorney who represented Vanguard in 1996, said Vanguard's actions during the mid-1980s lotteries amounted to "an aggressive interpretation of what was permitted under the commission's rules." He said the FCC never ruled formally whether or not the approach was consistent with its rules.[6]

But he said Hagel's meeting with FCC officials showed that he acted in good faith, and that helped Vanguard's case. Bernthal offered language from a 1987 FCC document that said the commission "believes that Vanguard and the pre-filers made good-faith judgments based on legal advice that they independently sought to verify at the commission. They did not attempt to manipulate or skew the lotteries."[7]

Elliot Greenwald, the attorney who had represented the competitors who filed the complaint, said he didn't doubt that Hagel had gone to the FCC and laid out his company's plan to enter each of its investors separately in the lottery or that Hagel was sure he had the FCC's blessing.

"I suspect he heard what he wanted to hear," Greenwald said. "He may not have given enough detail. A lot of the wrongdoing was in the detail."[8]

Although the FCC had decided not to act on the petition to deny Vanguard the licenses it had been awarded, some of Vanguard's competitors, including some former partners, had gone to court to challenge the firm's winning licenses in several areas. Hagel was not one of the Vanguard officials named in the complaint, and Vanguard eventually negotiated settlements with the challengers.

The campaign commercials that raised the Vanguard issue caused a stir, coming about ten days before the 1996 election. The first one aired on a Friday, which meant the Hagel camp was unable to mount a media response until after the weekend. "You get pounded for three days straight before you can address the charges," Hagel said.

Chuck and Lilibet Hagel were scheduled that night to attend a fund-raiser for the Pope Paul VI Institute for the Study of Morally and Professionally Acceptable Reproductive Health Services as guests of some of the candidate's supporters. Hagel decided he'd better warn Lilibet about the ads before they were confronted by people talking about them. "She knows the truth. We were married when all that happened," he said.

When they arrived at the dinner, Lilibet made conversation with the people at their table while her husband did meet-and-greets elsewhere in the room. Eventually the subject of the commercials came up, and it became obvious the Nelson accusations had raised doubts in at least a few minds. A man across the table asked, "Well, Mrs. Hagel, if it's not true, why would Nelson say it?"

Hagel recalls that his wife responded with a few well-chosen words in her husband's defense. She herself remembers that the encounter was uncomfortable but not really painful. The pain was more intense when she learned that one of Chuck's business partners had gone to Mike McCarthy and asked whether the implications were true. "That really brought me up short," she said. She realized that even friends and acquaintances might doubt a candidate's integrity. "That's the only time I said, 'Ouch, that hurts,' Lilibet remembers. "The rest of it seemed like gutter politics, pulled out at the eleventh hour."

Thinking back on it, Hagel said, his brush with the FCC in the 1980s made him "kind of a sitting duck for Nelson." He surmises that Nelson's advisers told him he should use whatever he could find against Hagel. But Hagel said running the last-minute commercials was a desperate act, a despicable act.

Linehan said the Hagel camp was "very lucky that the *World-Herald* wrote an editorial that basically said Nelson had crossed the line" and that the charges were false. The editorial appeared on the Sunday after the Friday ads, a little more than a week before the election. It was a ringing defense of Hagel.

The traditionally conservative paper said the Democratic Party had paid for mudslinging ads against Hagel during the primary campaign and that the Nelson campaign had now done the same in the days before the general election. Nelson, the editorial said, "has descended into the negative campaign tactics that are used all too often in our nation today."[9]

The paper was a lot easier on Hagel's Republican backers. It said the Republican committee's ads charging Nelson with raising taxes were open to debate, and it lamented the intrusion of outside groups into the state race. But no matter the circumstances, the editorial said, "Nelson's vehement attack on Hagel's personal integrity was unjustified." The attack was an attempt to try to "deceive Nebraskans into thinking that Chuck Hagel is untrustworthy. . . . If the governor thinks that stooping to unsubstantiated personal attacks will enhance his campaign, he's wrong."

Over that weekend the Hagel campaign produced a series of commercials similar to those it ran before the primary election, featuring Nebraskans who supported Hagel and expressed their anger at the Nelson campaign's commercials. Once again, Hagel said, he wanted to run a clean campaign. He admits some negative ads were directed at Nelson but says his campaign didn't endorse them. Hagel said in 2004 that he didn't know who paid for the ads, although newspaper accounts from 1996 indicated Hagel was aware the ads were coming from the Republican National Senatorial Committee.

The day after the election Bob Kerrey, chairman of the Democratic National Senatorial Committee that year, said that "Ben got caught in a big TV advertising campaign against him," the commercials sponsored by the Republican National Senatorial Committee.[10]

The Nelson campaign's ads about the cell-phone licenses, though, hadn't been effective, Democrats said. Tim Becker, then-governor Nelson's chief of staff, said, "In retrospect, it was too complicated an issue to explain. There wasn't time to fully develop it."[11]

Nelson blamed his defeat partly on what he called "a million dollars in attack ads misrepresenting [his] record as governor."[12] In speeches Hagel had accused Nelson of raising taxes in the process of shifting the tax revenue from one source to another. But it was the ads paid for by the Republican National Senatorial Committee that made the accusations of tax hikes explicit.

Some observers thought there was plenty of campaign blame to go around. In an editorial shortly before the election, the *Lincoln Journal Star* had taken both candidates to task for the brouhaha. On the one hand, the paper said, Nelson was trying to taint Hagel's business record, although no one had ever proven Hagel or his partners had done anything wrong. On the other hand, the paper said, the Republican ads bashed the governor for following state law and forcing county assessors to equalize property valuations—which did result in some individuals' paying more in property tax.

While the paper noted that Hagel was not responsible for the ads attacking Nelson's record, it added, "We don't have candidate Hagel standing up for the truth" or telling the national committee to pull the ads. Turning to Nelson, the paper said the governor himself was responsible for the shabby ads attacking Hagel's business dealings. In the process of going after each other, neither candidate, the paper added, had seriously grappled with important issues facing the state and nation.[13]

Looking back at the mudslinging that marked the end of that 1996 campaign, Bill Avery, a political science professor at the University of Nebraska–Lincoln and a leader in the state's Democratic Party, said the GOP's ads that tried to pin higher taxes on Nelson were misleading. Yes, many Nebraskans were paying more in total taxes, but the increase had come largely through the changes in property evaluations and increases in property taxes; property taxes in Nebraska are assessed only by counties, cities, and school districts—not by the state. Attacking a political official's record is fair, Avery said, "but not if you make it look like what it's not."

On the other hand, Avery said the ads that the Nelson campaign ran in response were "not the best." It was not a mistake to respond to the GOP's ads about taxes, Avery said, but the ads raising questions about Hagel's business dealings looked like negative campaigning to many Nebraskans, and they backfired.

Hagel has consistently continued to proclaim his opposition to negative political advertising. In February 2000 he told reporters the negative advertising in the presidential campaign that year was some of the worst he could remember. "It's degrading to the process and to the American people," he said.[14] More recently, he said keeping campaigns on the high road is important because the strength of the democratic system is based on the integrity of the nation's people and its institutions: "When you debase the political process and define it down to the lowest common denominator, there will be a price paid for that."

The American democratic process was intended to enhance debate and improve dialogue about the important issues government faces, Hagel said. "Americans should hear different points of view" and then make up their own minds what they agree with. "If you so degrade [the process] that there's no confidence in any of it, democracy will pay the price," he said. "Then the whole system collapses, and then what are the American people left with?" "I don't worry about my opponent," he said. "I worry about me:

EMBRACING A POLITICAL FUTURE

whether I'm up to the task, what I'm going to say. Do I have something to say?"

"The people of Nebraska needed to know what kind of senator I would be, what I believe in," he said of the 1996 campaign. "It's irrelevant who I was running against and what that person said."

Hagel sees political campaigns deteriorating into character assassinations. "You seek to take his character and integrity by whatever means you can to win—just completely destroy it. It's not good enough just to win and, God forbid, to win honestly."

Nasty campaign tactics are another of the subjects on which Hagel has spoken out loudly, even against members of his own party. Hagel criticized Republican Jon Christensen four days before the Nebraska gubernatorial primary in 1998 when Christensen sent out a direct-mail attack on his opponent Mike Johanns. Hagel said Christensen's mailing was trash and would cost Christensen the nomination. That public rebuke earned Hagel "a lot of negative feedback from right-wing Republicans," he said. Some of Christensen's supporters were still not speaking to Hagel six years later.

He also protested in 2000 when Senator John McCain was running against George W. Bush in the Republican presidential primary. Before the South Carolina primary election, the Bush camp produced ads implying that McCain had been brainwashed as a prisoner of war in Vietnam and, thus, would be dangerous in the Oval Office. "And then to have him [Bush] say he didn't know" the commercials were running, Hagel said, his voice rising: "That crosses the line."

And Hagel vehemently took on the Republican Party for its attacks on the Democrat Max Cleland of Georgia in the 2002 Senate race where Cleland's photo appeared in ads alongside pictures of Saddam Hussein and Osama bin Laden. Hagel threatened to make commercials of his own, defending his Democratic colleague, if the offending spots weren't pulled.

During the 2004 presidential race, Hagel criticized his party's campaign tactics again, defending Democratic presidential candidate John Kerry against the Bush campaign's accusations that

Kerry was soft on defense. Publicly criticizing members of one's own party for campaign tactics is not common, and some would consider it politically risky. But Hagel has no qualms: "For me there's no risk at all in it because it's so outrageously wrong for this country," he said. "I will go down fighting every time against that kind of thing."

Ultimately, in the 1996 Senate race, Nelson's last-minute questions about Hagel's cell-phone dealings appeared to have little direct effect on the election's outcome. A Gallup poll for the October 23–25 period showed voters giving Nelson 49 percent of the vote to Hagel's 44 percent, with 7 percent still undecided. A poll for October 30 to November 1, five and six days after the ads appeared, showed Nelson and Hagel even at 47 percent each, with 6 percent undecided.[15]

But some voters told reporters after the election that the negative ads worked against Nelson. "I feel that Nelson was doing negative campaigning. That hurts," said Bob Schultz of Lincoln, who changed his mind late in the campaign and decided to vote for Hagel. "I'm tired of it," he said.[16]

Ads or no ads, when the voters actually hit the polls on Election Day, November 5, 1996, they gave Hagel a 14-percentage-point victory and a majority in eighty-seven of the state's ninety-three counties. In 2004 the Associated Press in Nebraska compiled a list that named the top story for each of the previous ten years. Hagel's "out of nowhere" victory was the winner for 1996.

*From Nowhere to the Senate*

How did that happen? How did someone relatively unknown in Nebraska manage to defeat a popular sitting governor, someone who had won reelection in 1994 with 74 percent of the vote? Hagel said the day after the election that he attributed the victory to his consistent message—less government, lower taxes, less regulation, and a transfer of power away from the federal government—and to his strong statewide organization. He also credited nineteen months of full-time campaigning in 165 Nebraska communities.[17]

Hagel's image seems to have squared with what many Nebraskans want in their leaders. He came across to most voters as someone who was candid and straightforward, earnest and direct. "He looks you right in the eye," John Y. McCollister said. "If he's asked a question, he answers that question instead of something else." University of Nebraska–Lincoln political scientist Brian Humes said Hagel had qualities Nebraskans look for in a candidate: born in a small Nebraska town, Hagel had pulled himself up by his bootstraps. If he'd been nothing more than a successful businessman who moved to Nebraska to run for office, he'd have been seen as a carpetbagger. But he didn't come off that way, Humes said.

Of course it didn't hurt that Hagel was a successful businessman with money of his own to spend on the campaign. "He had the resources to tell his story," said Randy Moody, who worked with Hagel in McCollister's office. The fact that Hagel could put nearly a million dollars of his own money into the campaign gave him a big megaphone to spread his message.

But personal contacts also mattered. Mike Hagel said his brother had the advantage of knowing people all over the state, even though he hadn't lived in Nebraska for two decades. And, he added, "You have to understand something about Chuck: he loves a challenge."

Lilibet Hagel talked about her husband's methodical approach to campaigning. He would get up every day and get to work on the campaign trail, just as he had worked in every previous job he had held. "I always figured he'd win," she said. "I just knew." She thought Nebraskans were ready for somebody with a positive message. "Chuck would say campaigns are about hope," she said, and the Hagels and the campaign staff could feel people responding to that.

During the campaign, someone would occasionally ask Hagel what he would do if he lost the election, Tom Hagel recalls. "He said, 'I've gone through a war. If I lose this, I'll move on. It's not life and death.'" Tom added, "Chuck is the type of person who is incredibly disciplined and single-minded. He's been this way since he was a kid. He sets his mind on something, and that's it. I don't think it ever entered his mind there was a possibility he would lose."

That was true. "It never crossed my mind," the senator said. That kind of assuredness is not arrogance but is a matter of disciplining the mind, he said, and not getting dragged down by the unknowns, the risks involved. Dwelling on the "what ifs" skews one's perspective and leads to bad decisions, he said.

But Hagel and many observers say all his personal efforts would have fallen short had he not had an outstanding campaign organization and staff. "He had so many good people behind him, every step of the way," Lilibet Hagel said. Many observers point especially to Linehan as a political wizard.

Tom Janssen, a member of the campaign staff, said Linehan was able to show Nebraskans who Hagel is and what kind of vision he had for the state and the nation. It wasn't just the advertising but also the people who were recruited to work for the campaign and the way the workers' time was scheduled that made the campaign so effective, Janssen said. Linehan shaped a bunch of political neophytes into an efficient campaign team.

Mike McCarthy said Linehan may be the only person he knows who has more energy than Hagel himself. And Linehan brought a valuable balance to the campaign, McCarthy said. "It's very difficult to maintain your perspective when you're shaking hands eighteen hours a day," he said. "Somehow Lou Ann was always able to find time for Chuck to know what was going on in the world and to stay in touch with policy, which is what keeps him grounded in his decision making." As the senator's chief of staff, Linehan still helps her boss find that balance between process and substance, McCarthy added.

Linehan said the campaign's success rested on building an organization from the bottom up, covering every one of Nebraska's ninety-three counties. The campaign enlisted thousands of volunteers who put in thousands of hours of work. People will do things for an election they would not otherwise do, Linehan said, because they know they have only one chance to make it work. "If

EMBRACING A POLITICAL FUTURE

you don't do everything you can [to prepare] for Election Day, you can't go back and replay it," she said. "The calendar helps get people motivated."

But Hagel never asked his paid staff or his volunteers to work harder than he did himself, Linehan said, and that kept workers going. "People don't want to disappoint him," she said. And the election victories were not just about Chuck Hagel, she said, but about "all of us winning." At the victory celebrations after both the primary and the general election, every staff member was on stage with the candidate and his family, she added.

But that staff doesn't come free. Neither does the advertising or the travel or the brochures and balloons and signs associated with rallies and campaign events. Both Hagel and Nelson spent plenty on their campaigns against each other. Both candidates had amassed small fortunes in business, and both were able to lend money to their campaigns. Hagel lent his fund almost one million dollars, the highest personal loan in the history of Nebraska elections to that point.[18]

The Center for Responsive Politics, a political watchdog group, said Hagel's campaign took in $3.6 million during the 1991–1996 election cycle. Fifty-six percent of that money came from individuals, about 13 percent from political-action committees, and almost 30 percent from Hagel himself. It took two years and many fundraisers after the election to pay back the money he had lent the campaign, Hagel said.

As for campaign promises, Hagel admitted that, after one-and-a-half terms in the Senate, he had made good on few of the specifics. He hasn't moved the Congress to make the 25-percent cuts in twenty-nine regulatory agencies or to eliminate several cabinet-level departments. All the departments he said he wanted to abolish continue to function and grow. Hagel has taken the opportunities he has had to vote in favor of tax cuts, but he hasn't taking a prominent role in attempting to wipe out the inheritance or capital-gains taxes, which he had said he wanted to do.

The health of that multitude of government agencies still riles Hagel. "I've always believed we have a bloated bureaucracy—way too much government," he said. He would like to see more authority devolve to state and local governments. So the threat to eliminate or downsize some of the federal departments should always be on the table, he said.

Agencies like the Occupational Safety and Health Administration (OSHA) and the Environmental Protection Agency should be redirected, he said. When they were created decades ago, the idea was that they would work with businesses to improve working conditions and protect the environment. That has changed entirely, he said. When OSHA inspects a workplace today, it is less intent on working with the management to fix potential dangers than on imposing fines for every possible infraction. "The intent is to punish" rather than help, Hagel said. "That needs to be fixed."

Hagel would like to move as many regulatory functions out of Washington as possible. But it's not likely to happen, he said, because members of Congress are so intimidated by the special interests that can and do run hundreds of thousands of dollars' worth of advertisements against them. "They pick out one or two inconsequential votes," he said of those single-issue groups, and frame them to make the message fit their purposes, a tactic he knows could easily be used against him if he runs for higher office.

Irritating as it may be, Hagel said he tries not to let attacks like that bother him. "You have to do what you think is right. You're here to try to accomplish something." All any politician—liberal or conservative—can do is be honest about his or her positions, defend and explain them, and try to show the reasoning behind the decisions, he said.

Whether or not his campaign promises had been realistic, Hagel was on his way to the U.S. Senate in November 1996.

Dick Robinson of Norfolk said everything came together in the election: an articulate, intelligent, driven candidate; a Republican state that hadn't elected a Republican senator since 1972; a campaign staff primed to succeed. "It was the perfect storm," Robinson said.

And it swept Hagel into Washington riding a wave that would give him prominence and access to influence in the Senate.

# 6

## Moving Forward in the Senate

"OUT OF NOWHERE" was the phrase that kept coming up in conversations and in newspaper headlines in the days following the 1996 Nebraska Senate election. Chuck Hagel, a political unknown in Nebraska until he announced he was running for Senate, had beaten one of the best-known politicians in the state, the sitting governor.

The junior senator from a state known to many as "the middle of nowhere" followed his election victory with some plum Senate committee assignments. The combination of those committee positions, his boundless energy, and his willingness to speak his mind put Chuck Hagel's political rocket on a steep trajectory as he ventured into elected office.

### Fitting In

Scores of friends and relatives gathered in Washington in January 1997 to celebrate with Hagel as he was sworn in as one of a hundred U.S. senators. With tears in her eyes, Betty Hagel Breeding sat in a front-row seat in the Senate gallery, a seat offered to her by Senator Trent Lott's wife, and watched her oldest son take the oath of office and take his place as a senator. It was a long way from that modest house in Ainsworth, Nebraska, to the U.S. Capitol.

Senator Christopher Dodd, a Democrat from Connecticut, remembers meeting Hagel on the day of the swearing in. The ceremony is usually followed by parties in the offices of each new member, Dodd said, and the practice is for the other senators to make the rounds to say hello.

"I can't recall any other conversation I had that day," Dodd said, "but I remember the one with Chuck. We got into a conversation about the value of international institutions," a topic well beyond the usual social patter expected on such occasions. Dodd had heard how Hagel "came out of nowhere" to get elected to the Senate, and he was impressed by his first encounter with the newcomer. "He is a conservative," Dodd said, and the two disagree on many policy matters. "But on international affairs I thought I'd enjoy doing business with him, and I have," he added.

Hagel went to Washington intending to get involved in foreign relations. He wanted to serve on either the Armed Services Committee or the Foreign Relations Committee. By the time he actually took office in January, Hagel was, indeed, a member of the Foreign Relations Committee as well as the Banking, Housing, and Urban Affairs Committee and the Committee on Aging. He explained how the process worked.

The Senate Republicans make committee assignments purely on the basis of seniority. Hagel was one of nine new Republican senators in 1996, four of whom had previously held other elected offices and got a bump in seniority because of it. Hagel was one of five with absolutely no previous experience in office. In fact, he said, he was the only new Republican senator who had never even run for office before.

The five without experience drew straws to determine their seniority standing in the Republican caucus; Hagel came in second, behind Susan Collins of Maine. That established the order in which they would make their committee selections—at the end of the list on which Ted Stevens of Alaska and Pete Domenici of New Mexico, the Senate's senior Republicans, held the top spots in 2004.

The process of getting senators onto committees, then, works something like the professional football draft, Hagel said. The senators choose their standing committees—their "A" committees—in order of seniority in two, or sometimes three, rounds.

Each senator gets at least two major "A" committee assignments, although for those at the end of the list, the two may not be their first choices. And then the leadership assigns each senator to a "B" committee, a select committee. That was how Hagel ended up on the Committee on Aging.

His first choice from the "A" list, reflecting his lifelong fascination with international affairs, was Foreign Relations. "I was lucky because very few people wanted to be on Foreign Relations," he said. The committee had come to be seen as a dead end by many senators, largely because of its leadership during the previous two decades, Hagel explained. Claiborne Pell of Rhode Island had been the chairman for years, but because of his failing health in latter years, he hadn't given the committee his full attention. Pell was succeeded by Jesse Helms of North Carolina, who was "not particularly enthusiastic about foreign policy," Hagel said.

That history meant that a lot of senators with far more seniority than Hagel were eager to leave the committee for slots on more active and more prominent committees, and few others wanted to take their places on Foreign Relations. "When the dust cleared," Hagel said, he was the fourth-ranking Republican on the committee, "and I hadn't even been to a meeting yet." One of eleven Republicans on the committee, Hagel was outranked only by Helms, Richard Lugar of Indiana, and Paul Coverdale of Georgia.

Hagel said he wanted Foreign Relations "because within that jurisdiction is almost everything" he thought mattered for America's future: confirmations of treaties and of administrative appointees who work in international relations, oversight of multilateral banks, and a reach into business and commerce and trade issues and into military security and intelligence. "I just felt as the world is growing closer together and becoming even more interconnected, this was the committee that would give me most significant reach and the most opportunities to play a role long term," Hagel said.

Hagel also got his second "A" committee choice: Banking. "I felt it was a good balance with Foreign Relations, and besides I knew something about it," he said.

He was pleased with his first assignments. "I thought I could learn wherever I went," Hagel said. He said he felt a particular lack of expertise on the Committee on Aging but found it an excellent opportunity to learn about Medicare, Social Security, and other issues that affect the elderly.

### Looking beyond the Borders

The boy who subscribed to *Time* when he was in grade school had become a senator who is an ardent internationalist. He said he sees the world as "completely interconnected . . . one large fabric where all our interests are interwoven."

Three years before the al-Qaeda attacks on the World Trade Center and the Pentagon, Hagel said in a speech at Harvard University that "borderless threats abound, including terrorism." The world, he said, should meet those threats with borderless efforts to build consensus on political and economic matters.

It's a view he has developed over time. The senator remembers being fascinated listening to his father and his father's friends, World War II veterans, talk about Italy, Germany, Japan, the Philippines, and Australia. He recalls vague thoughts about how the United States must have sent its troops to fight in those faraway places for some reason in its own interest. "I was in no position to be able to sense that international relations are the great umbrella that everything fits within or under" at that point, he said, but hearing those veterans' stories planted the seed.

Hagel's experiences in Vietnam and with the World USO watered that seed and made it grow. So did the influence of his first wife, Patricia Lloyd, who had traveled abroad more than Hagel had at that point and had "a very wide and positive sense of the world." Now, Hagel said, he believes America must internationalize its role in the world in trade, political alliances, science, health, and the environment. "We are all interconnected," he said.

Hagel has little patience with the "straw man" argument some critics advance against his internationalist view: that the United States should never have to ask the United Nations for permission to defend itself. "Of course we won't," he said. Nations will continue to respond to events in their own self-interest, but they must also realize they have common interests. Notably, he said, collective security offered through institutions like NATO and the UN contained the Soviet Union for forty-five years and eventually contributed to its implosion. "Internationalism and sovereignty are not mutually exclusive," Hagel said. "They enhance each other."

Hagel displays "an almost fierce internationalism that has set him apart from others [in the Senate] who either aren't interested or take a more protectionist view or predictable position," said *Washington Post* reporter Helen Dewar. Hagel's perspective has given him some stature in the Senate, she said, and quickly made him one of the leading lights on the Foreign Relations Committee. When reporters have questions about foreign affairs, she said, "You call [Senator Richard] Lugar or Hagel. They know what they're talking about."

Foreign policy is where Hagel hopes to leave his mark. He said if he has any legacy in the Senate, he hopes he'll be remembered as "someone who fought to bring back a bipartisan leadership effort in foreign policy, trade policy, and national security."[1]

Ever since he arrived in the Senate, Hagel has consistently supported U.S. cooperation with other nations through coalitions like NATO and the United Nations. When some members of the Senate in 2000 were urging that the United States set a deadline for withdrawing its peacekeeping troops from Kosovo, Hagel fought the proposal. He said it would send a signal to NATO that the United States is not a reliable ally.

Hagel is a skeptic about the use of U.S. force, said the *National Review* in August 2002. In April that year Hagel had said, "America must be about enhancing its relationships in the world, not just its power." The magazine commented, "It's not that he isn't willing to unleash the military (he was an early backer of action against Serbia, for instance), but he believes everything must be done in consultation with other countries and with the approval of international organizations."

In a 2003 speech Hagel said America's foreign-policy strategy should focus on redefining and strengthening its global alliances and its ties to multilateral institutions. That would expand, not limit, the nation's power, he said: "Alliances must be built on solid foundations to handle both the routine and urgent challenges of our times."

Because of his position on the Foreign Relations Committee and his internationalist creed, Hagel deals regularly with representatives of nations around the world, sometimes three or four ambassadors, foreign ministers, or finance ministers in a single day, a good dozen in a week. He said he has built a reputation in the Senate as someone who is interested in other nations and who is not timid about speaking out on international issues. He's not the only senator who meets with a lot of foreign leaders, Hagel said, but he is sure he is among the top five.

"To do my job, I have to do that," he said. He and his visitors may not necessarily agree, he added, "but I need to reach out and hear what's on their minds," see things through their eyes. "We've not done that very well in the United States."

Rutgers political scientist Ross Baker worked for Hagel one semester while he was collecting material for his research on Congress. He said Hagel has taken very well to the world of international diplomacy. Baker remembers accompanying Hagel to a conference of foreign defense ministers. Senator Joe Lieberman, a Connecticut Democrat, introduced Hagel as one of the rising stars of the Republican Party. The Democratic senator didn't have to give Hagel a boost like that, Baker said, but the fact that he did indicates that Hagel is not an ideologue who can't or won't work with people whose political views may be different from his own.

Sandy Berger, national security adviser under Bill Clinton, worked often with Hagel and said he found him to be "a well-informed, thoughtful, and principled man who truly believes politics stops at the water's edge."

The idea that politics should be put aside when the nation is under threat was a frequent refrain after the terrorist attacks on the United States on September 11, 2001. Hagel was at a Capitol Hill restaurant that Tuesday morning, hosting a breakfast for members of his Sandhills Political Action Committee. Shortly after the event began, Deb Fiddelke, then his press secretary, handed him a note saying that a plane had hit one of the World Trade Center towers in New York City. Hagel remembers thinking it must have been some private plane with a disoriented pilot, and he simply went on with the meeting.

A few minutes later, though, Fiddelke interrupted the proceedings to say the second tower had been hit. Hagel told all those at the meeting to go back to their offices, and he ran to his own, a block and a half away. Not much later the windows in the Russell Building and all the buildings on Capitol Hill rattled as the third jetliner hit the Pentagon, several miles away. At that point, alarms began to sound, and the police began to clear the Capitol and surrounding buildings. Hagel and his staff moved to the park across the street from the Russell Building where people were listening to radios and using cell phones to call friends, trying to piece together what was going on.

The police took the senators from the lawn to a nearby precinct house, where they briefed them about the attacks in New York and on the Pentagon, told them President Bush's whereabouts, and tried to explain the situation. The police asked the lawmakers to come back in a few hours for an update; in the meantime, they were to stay out of the Capitol Hill office buildings.

Hagel said he happened to be sitting at the briefing next to Senator Pete Domenici. Domenici and his wife had an apartment on Capitol Hill, and the New Mexican invited Hagel to go home with him until things could be sorted out. Hagel sent his staff home and called his wife in suburban Virginia who had, by that time, picked up their children from school and was safe at home.

After the senators returned for their second briefing at the precinct house, Hagel remembers doing dozens of interviews with reporters for broadcast and print media. Everyone was trying to make sense of the attacks on an America that thought it would never be attacked. Everyone wanted to know whether Hagel thought the carnage could have been avoided, whether better security might have stopped the terrorists before they reached their targets.

Interviewed on the PBS's *NewsHour* three days later, Hagel urged the American people and their leaders not to see all of Islam as responsible for the terrorism. "Islam is not about this kind of terror," he said, adding that the United States would need the cooperation of all Muslim nations in tracking down the terrorists and preventing further attacks.

On September 30, Hagel told CNN's Wolf Blitzer it was essential that the United States assemble and maintain a coalition of nations in the fight against Osama bin Laden and terrorism in general. "This is a long-term effort," he said. "[It's] going to require a very significant international coalition. No one is safe from this."

A year later, he was still urging cooperation among nations—not only military cooperation but also diplomatic, humanitarian, and economic cooperation in trade, law enforcement, and intelligence. He said collective security agreements and multinational organizations, which he praised for having maintained international stability since World War II, must continue to be strengthened and nourished. The cooperative institutions, he said, "have represented common-denominator self-interests through coalitions of common interests." It was another reflection of his internationalist perspective.

Hagel acted on his internationalist views in July 2002 when he introduced a bill to provide up to $300 million a year—a total of $3.3 billion—in military and economic aid to Afghanistan through 2005. Afghanistan was in chaos in the summer of 2002. After years of war with the Soviet Union and then a civil war, after the viciously backward rule of the Taliban and then the military attacks by the United States in the wake of the September 11 terrorism, Afghanistan was barely a nation at all. The United States had begun to send aid for rebuilding, but Hagel thought it was not enough.

"There was no focused program out of the White House to address the aid that was going to be required for Afghanistan," he said. "There were pieces but no focus." His bill was designed to aid in Afghanistan's recovery by supplying economic, political, humanitarian, and security assistance. It designated funds for basic food, shelter, and medical assistance as well as funds to strengthen the new Afghan government's capacity to meet the needs of its people and avoid long-term reliance on international aid.

The bill also called for a greater role for Afghan women and provided for removal of land mines and for assistance to orphans. Hagel said at the time that the aid would also help "assure the security of the United States and the world by reducing or eliminating the likelihood of violence against the United States or allied forces in Afghanistan and . . . reduce the chance that Afghanistan [would] again be a source of international terrorism." The aid wouldn't solve all of Afghanistan's problems, Hagel said, but without it, Afghanistan's future would have been bleak indeed, and a country left in shambles would have been fertile ground for terrorists. The money was essential if the world were to have any hope that a stable, functioning civil society be restored in the battered nation.

The Senate passed the bill in November that year, and the House of Representatives soon followed. President Bush signed it into law in early December. "In some ways," Hagel said, "I think the White House was grateful we had done it," because it took the issue out of the administration's hands.

Hagel said Senator Joe Biden, a Democrat from Delaware, and Senator Richard Lugar, a Republican from Indiana, fellow members of the Senate Foreign Relations Committee, helped him shepherd the bill through the legislative process. It's a piece of work Hagel counts among his best in the Senate.

Hagel had another chance to drive home his belief that international alliances and cooperation should be at the foundation of U.S. foreign policy when he wrote an article for the July/August 2004 issue of *Foreign Affairs*, a magazine published by the New York–based Council on Foreign Relations, of which he is a member. "A Republican foreign policy must view alliances and international institutions as extensions of our influence, not as constraints on our power," Hagel wrote, adding that it should work to strengthen groups like NATO and the United Nations. "At times, the United States can and must lead," Hagel said, "but it would be wise to share the authority for—as well as the burdens, costs, and risks of—such operations with others."

One operation that appears to demand involvement from the international community is the global environment, and it's an operation in which Hagel has become deeply involved.

## Warming to the Environment

In August 1997 Hagel was a featured speaker at an Australian conference on the international treaty on the environment, commonly known as the Kyoto Protocol after the city in which it had been developed. The international conferees had scheduled the treaty to be signed in December.

Making good on a campaign promise to oppose Kyoto, Hagel had been a cosponsor, with the Democrat Robert Byrd of West Virginia, of a successful Senate resolution to oppose the treaty. It would have required industrial plants—but not automobile manufacturers—to cut pollution from burning fossil fuels to 2000 levels by 2010. Hagel said the treaty would hurt U.S. businesses, reducing economic growth by 1 percent in the first year alone and costing up to 1.5 million jobs as well as raising energy prices for consumers, farmers, business, and industry. The July resolution put the Senate on record as opposing any treaty that would bind industrialized nations to reductions in greenhouse gases without requiring similar commitments from the developing world.

At the Australia conference, Hagel said he wanted environmental protection as much as anyone but that the Kyoto Protocol was not the way to achieve that goal. He said conflicting opinions among scientists over the causes and effects of global warming as well as over the seriousness and immediacy of the threat were reasons the nations of the world should not rush to sign a treaty in December. Furthermore, he said, any problem that did exist would not be solved by excusing the world's 130 developing nations from any controls on emissions because the 130 included some of the world's most rapidly developing economies, economies that use more fossil fuels each year.

"By the year 2015, China will be the world's largest producer of greenhouse gases," Hagel said. "And China has made it very clear that it will never agree to binding limits on its emissions of greenhouse gases." The Kyoto Protocol was fatally flawed, he said, because it excluded from its mandates nations that are increasingly large contributors to worldwide pollution. He said greenhouse-gas emissions would continue to rise under Kyoto, while the economies in the United States and other industrialized nations would suffer from the treaty's severe restrictions.

Worry about the environment may have been the right problem, but the Kyoto agreement was the wrong solution, Hagel said. Hagel's view prevailed in the Senate, which voted against the Kyoto Protocol in December 1997. In fact not a single senator voted in favor of the agreement.

Two years later Hagel sponsored a bill to support development of new technologies to reduce greenhouse gases. He said it was a better alternative to a treaty like Kyoto.

In spring 2001 Hagel returned to the topic, testifying before the Senate Commerce Committee hearing on climate change. He said he was still not convinced that science had unequivocally identified the right environmental problem. He cited research that indicated most of the warming that occurred in the twentieth century came before 1940, even though most of the man-made carbon-dioxide emissions came after 1940. He cited other studies that, taken together, made it impossible to conclude that greenhouse-gas emissions were the sole or even the primary cause of global warming or that global warming was an imminent danger, despite other research to the contrary.

But, Hagel said, the United States should not ignore climate change. He recommended that the nation develop its own domestic policy before getting involved in any international agreements and that the policy be based on voluntary compliance by business and industry "without the heavy hand of government mandates."

Hagel opposed a 2003 bill, cosponsored by John McCain and Joe Lieberman, to reduce emissions of carbon dioxide and other greenhouse gases much as the Kyoto treaty would have done. The bill would have required U.S. industrial plants—but not auto manufacturers—to cut pollution from burning fossil fuels to 2000 levels by 2010.

Hagel continued to believe voluntary compliance was the right approach. He said in 2004 that he liked what the Bush administration had done: putting billions of dollars into scientific research to develop technology that would prevent greenhouse-gas emissions and to apply that technology in the United States and in developing countries—"so every new power plant has it." He said that kind of action would truly help slow the emissions and would also have a positive influence on stability, terrorism, hopelessness, and radicalism in the developing world.

Late in 2004 Hagel warmed even more to the idea of some sort of global action on climate change and pollution. He announced he would make the nation's response to global climate change one of his priorities in the coming Congress, and he traveled to London to meet with the British prime minister Tony Blair, who had heard about the bill Hagel planned to introduce and wanted to talk to him about it.

Blair was interested in creating a new international treaty on global warming that the United States would support. The new initiative would seek to develop the technology needed for renewable energy and the reduction of carbon emissions.[2] That was in line with Hagel's goals of promoting the development and sharing of clean-energy technology and giving tax incentives to businesses that adopt environmentally friendly practices.

"He [Blair] wants to try to engage us in some common ground so the United States can be seen in the world as helping lead this effort rather than obstructing it," Hagel said after his trip to London.[3] Hagel said he felt obliged to offer an alternative agreement on the environment since he helped lead U.S. opposition to Kyoto. "If Kyoto was the wrong solution, what is the right solution?"

Hagel said he was not yet convinced that global warming was due primarily to greenhouse-gas emissions from industries and automobiles and said he wanted to see more scientific investigation of the causes. But, he added, "Obviously something's going on out there."[4] The senator said he and Blair agreed that the Kyoto accord was flawed because it did not include developing countries. But they also agreed that the issue of climate change was important for the environment, the world's energy resources, its security, and its politics, Hagel said.[5]

The science behind the assertions of global warming may not have convinced him to act, but his internationalist position seems to have done the trick. The senator said a global response to climate change is "a big deal to our allies, and it's time we reconnect with them." The issue deserves attention not only on the merits but also because America's record on the environment has become one of many image problems for the United States, Hagel said: "Here's the U.S., the biggest polluter, the wealthiest nation, pushing everybody around unilaterally." He believes that needs to change.

Besides that, he added, "It's just smart for us to reduce greenhouse gasses, to pay attention to improving the environment. It's smart to find alternative sources of energy." The nation can't deal with dwindling energy resources without connecting that issue to the environment, he said.

## Taking Up Taxes

Early in his first term in the Senate, Hagel turned his attention to one of the themes of his campaign: lower taxes. He spoke out for reducing the estate tax, saying the change would benefit farmers.

Not everyone agreed with that assessment, even some senators from states with as many farmers as Nebraska has. Democratic senator Tom Harkin of Iowa, who opposed the move, said the tax affects only 6 percent of U.S. farmers.

Showing his colors on taxes and spending, Hagel voted for the balanced budget amendment to the U.S. Constitution in March 1997. His fellow Nebraska senator, Democrat Bob Kerrey, voted against it. The proposed amendment failed, 66 to 34.

The first bill Hagel introduced in the Senate was related to taxes and allowed self-employed Americans to deduct 100 percent of their health insurance costs for tax purposes. The Senate passed the bill, 98 to 0, in June 1997.

Throughout his Senate career, Hagel has consistently supported lower taxes. He spoke enthusiastically in favor of the Bush administration's tax cut proposals in 2003. If the purpose of the tax cuts was to grow the economy, Hagel said he was in favor of the biggest cuts the Congress could muster.[6]

When billionaire investor Warren Buffett made headlines in March 2003 by charging that businesses don't pay their fair share of taxes, Hagel was quick to disagree. He asserted tax breaks for businesses were good for the economy. People who own stock in large companies make money when those companies do well, he said. "More than half of American households today are invested in the stock market, and the stock market is invested in businesses."[7]

Furthermore, Hagel said the tax cuts that Congress passed in 2003 should be made permanent "because growth and opportunities come from the private sector." If more capital is available, more can be applied to new developments in industry and more will go to small business entrepreneurs who generate new products, Hagel said. And that means economic growth, and economic growth means jobs.

Asked whether that philosophy could be described as "trickle-down economics," a term coined by David Stockman, an official in the Reagan administration of the 1980s, Hagel said, "I've never liked that term. I think it's a buffoonish, simplistic way to describe

MOVING FORWARD IN THE SENATE

something." Instead, he said he thinks it is a simple truth that when people are allowed to keep more of their own money and make their own decisions about where to spend it, much of that money goes into investments in the stock market, investments that promote new research, lead to new consumer products, and earn money for investors to put away and save.

"Does that help everybody? Of course, it does," Hagel said. Because tax cuts generate additional income for people in the upper and middle classes, he said, they also generate new tax revenues that go to help those at the bottom who need extra help.

"I'm a strong supporter of tax cuts," Hagel said, not just because they're good for the wealthy or even the middle class. He thinks citizens also need to have some confidence in the fairness of their government. He said politicians need to do a better job of explaining the underlying foundation for cutting taxes and not just allow the debate to devolve to the lowest common denominator: the rich against everybody else.

Politicians also need to be more careful about spending, Hagel said. He believes national security is the government's paramount responsibility, but he doesn't believe defense spending is untouchable. Every dollar should be defended and accounted for. But looking at the big picture, at a total budget getting close to $2.4 trillion in 2004, Hagel said the government and the nation were going to have to return to fiscal discipline that was lost during the economic boom years of the late 1990s. His record shows that he has voted against increased spending, and he believes a lot of current spending could be frozen.

"You never have enough to spend. I know that," he said. "I have legions of constituents in here all the time—conservative Republicans—saying we're not spending enough for farmers or teachers or policemen or the military or contractors or bridge builders. You name the area. We're not spending enough," he said. It's a constant debate.

When they debate bills that are going to require funding, members of Congress need to keep the big picture in mind, he pointed out. If they vote in favor of a program, how will it affect the budget overall? If they are going to add this piece to the budget, what are they willing to give up in return?

And the legislators need to be realistic, Hagel said. The government's budget was showing surpluses in the recent past, surpluses Hagel said were mostly conjured by including the Social Security reserve in the total calculations. In fact, he said in 1999 that his colleagues in the Senate should abandon the "cute technical finessing of numbers" that was building a dishonest 2000 budget because playing games like that robs the American people of the opportunity for legitimate public debate about national priorities, choices, and directions.[8] But the numbers games continued. When the Congress itself starts to believe that kind of manipulated picture, it means "we've lost all common sense around here," Hagel said. By 2004 the budget was running badly in the red again.

Hagel worried about the deficits the nation was accumulating: $130 billion for the first four months of the 2004–05 budget. Matters were likely to get worse when the baby boomers began to retire and collect Social Security and Medicare benefits, he said in February 2004: "The obligations that the United States government has to these future generations right now are overwhelming."[9]

Those were the reasons he gave for voting against the administration-backed Medicare reform bill in late 2003. Hagel had introduced his own version of reform, what *Washington Post* reporter Helen Dewar called "a slimmed-down alternative . . . that sidestepped ideology and picked up considerable support as a lower-cost alternative." However, that plan didn't serve the political needs of either the administration or the Democrats, she said.

But the failure of his own plan didn't stop Hagel from attacking the administration's bill. In a column he wrote for the *Omaha World-Herald*, Hagel said the measure wouldn't strengthen Medicare and did not responsibly address the need for prescription-drug coverage for the elderly. Instead, the senator wrote, the new plan would add trillions to Medicare's $13.5 trillion in unfunded liabilities. He pointed out that 75 percent of Medicare beneficiaries already had some prescription coverage and said the administration's plan was simply a payoff for special interest groups. Rather than messing with drug benefits, the government should have concentrated on making reimbursements for health care in rural areas more equitable, Hagel wrote.

Hagel so strongly opposed the Medicare bill that he supported Democratic senator Ted Kennedy's filibuster to try to block its passage. Hagel's good friend, Senator John McCain of Arizona, was the only other Republican to break ranks and support Kennedy's efforts. Ultimately, the filibuster attempt failed, and the bill passed. Hagel's sniping did not stop.

The senator said the bill's priority should have been to lower the cost of prescription drugs, not simply to hand over more payments for commodities whose prices continue to increase. "We should have some mechanism for Medicare to negotiate drug prices with pharmaceutical companies and instead we have a specific provision in this bill preventing negotiation," Hagel contended.[10] Furthermore, instead of adding an across-the-board benefit, Medicare reform "should have focused on those most in need" of drug coverage, the senator said.

Speaking to high school students in Columbus, Nebraska, in February 2004, Hagel said reforming its entitlement programs like Medicare and Social Security was one of the biggest challenges facing America. He himself is at the front end of the baby boom's seventy-six million people, all of whom will become eligible for programs like Medicare and Social Security in the next decades. "We'll need thirty-five trillion dollars over thirty years to pay for the baby boomers," Hagel said. "I don't know where we'll get it."

The nation was facing two choices, Hagel said. The first option was to let the system crash and then increase taxes on the younger generations still in the workforce when that happens—or make the hugely unpopular decision to cut benefits to the retirees. The second choice was to get busy and fix the system before it collapsed. America could not continue to run up huge budget deficits, he said, without losing the confidence of world markets. "It will catch up with us."

Hagel's concern about spending and deficits dovetailed in this instance with what appeared to be a growing concern for the disadvantaged. He said government must be concerned about people at all socioeconomic levels. The middle class, he said, is crucial in a free society. It is the largest segment of the country and includes the bulk of the workforce, the productive capacity of the nation.

Politicians have to be sure the middle class has an opportunity to prosper, Hagel said, and must be careful not to overburden that group with regulation and taxes. "The upper class has the resources to take care of itself," he said, adding that big corporations can handle more regulations but small businesses can't. But America must also stay tuned to the lower socioeconomic class, he said, and be sure a safety net is in place to catch them if they fall.

It's that kind of rhetoric that makes Tom Hagel, the family Democrat, think his brother has changed. When Chuck Hagel was elected to the Senate, Tom told the *Washington Post* he was worried the new senator would listen only to the rich and powerful and would forget his own humble roots and the people still struggling to make it in America. When the Congress passed tax cuts in 1999, Tom Hagel told the *New York Times* the bill his brother had supported would benefit the richest Americans most: "I've never seen him express any overwhelming concern about poverty in America, and I think a good example of that is the tax-cut bill."

In an interview five years later, though, Tom said that when he watched his brother on television in 2004, "If I close my eyes he almost sounds like a Democrat—which in my mind is progress." He thought his brother had continued to learn during his years in office. "I think he has developed an appreciation for the less fortunate," he said. "I think he's moved in a positive direction in that regard."

But taking care of the people at the bottom levels of the economy also costs money, also requires government intervention. How much government is enough? How much is too much? That's the great debate surrounding the budget each year, Hagel said. And underlying even those questions is another: what is the role of government? America's two major political parties can be distinguished on the basis of their answers to that question. In general Republicans want less government than Democrats do. And, in general, it is in policies regarding taxes and spending that Hagel looks most like a typical Republican, most like a typical conservative.

## Nurturing Agriculture and Trade

Setting aside any evidence to the contrary, Nebraskans still consider their state a farm state. The overall number of farmers may make up only 3 percent of the population, and the state's economy may be diversifying, but farms and ranches still use more than 90 percent of the state's land, and Nebraska's psyche is still nurtured by agriculture.

One might expect, then, that a senator from Nebraska would be an ardent and undiscriminating proponent of anything that looks as if it might benefit farmers and ranchers. Wrong. Not that Hagel has ignored agriculture or failed to champion some of its issues. But he hasn't taken the most expected route. Instead, his stand on agricultural policy has reflected his conservative philosophy and his enthusiasm for free markets and free trade.

In May 2002 he criticized the farm bill making its way through Congress for giving two-thirds of all farm support monies to just 10 percent of farmers. "This farm bill is a glorified carbon copy of market-distorting legislation that will accelerate the vicious cycle of overproduction, low crop prices, and soaring land values," he said. "The winners will be large agribusiness, big landowners, and large farm operations."[11]

Hagel voted against the farm bill.

Not everyone in Nebraska was happy with that vote. The Nebraska Farmers Union (NEFU), an organization that says it is dedicated to protecting and enhancing farmers' economic well-being, had fought for a number of provisions included in the bill: higher marketing-loan rates; a larger income safety net for dairy farmers; mandatory country-of-origin labeling on meats, fruits, vegetables, fish, and peanuts; increased cost-share funding for conservation practices; and others.

Contradicting Hagel's assertion that the bill benefited the big farmer at the expense of the small, the NEFU said the bill set a limit on payments to the wealthiest landowners and Fortune 500 companies. John Hansen, head of the NEFU, wrote in a 2002 press release that the organization was disappointed that Hagel had voted against it.

Writing for an online publication, Hagel said the bill was a step backward into an antique farm policy of more government command and control. "These lopsided payments," he wrote, "encourage and subsidize overproduction, keep commodity prices low, drive up land prices, and allow large farms to outbid and buy up other producers with taxpayer dollars." In fact, under the provisions of the bill, two-thirds of all farm support money would go to just 10 percent of farmers, he wrote: "Unlimited government payments will only encourage large farm operations and wealthy, absentee landowners to buy more ground, no matter how low the commodity prices drop." And that would push up rent for the majority of producers, who rent at least some of the land they farm.[12]

The Concord Coalition, a nonpartisan organization founded to advocate balanced budgets and the future viability of Social Security, Medicare, and Medicaid, said the 2002 Farm Bill was "a textbook example of an entitlement that survives because it is politically attractive, not because it is good policy." The bill reversed the attempt made in the 1996 Freedom to Farm Act to get away from Depression-era farm subsidies that distort markets, burden taxpayers, and harm the environment, the coalition said. Instead, the bill extended existing subsidies and created new ones.[13] Obviously the 2002 Farm Bill had both enthusiastic supporters—including the Bush administration—and ardent detractors.

Rob Robertson of the Nebraska Farm Bureau Federation (NFBF), which calls itself a voice for agriculture and the competitive-enterprise system, said he thought Hagel took the long-term view on the farm bill. It was tempting to do the politically palatable thing, Robertson said, and vote for the increased subsidies, but that would lead to farmers' being more dependent on the government in the long run. Like Hagel, Robertson thought that was a bad idea.

MOVING FORWARD IN THE SENATE

Robertson said the NFBF appreciated Hagel's stand on agricultural issues in general. Hagel believes the government should not make farmers wards of the state, Robertson said. Hagel has supported emergency aid for farmers stricken by drought or floods, has pushed to hold back the growth of regulations on pesticide use, and has promoted affordable crop insurance and the production of ethanol, a grain-based fuel. Although some farmers may not have agreed with Hagel's vote on the farm bill, Robertson said, most of them seemed to think that Hagel had done what he believed was best for Nebraska farmers' interests. Most farmers see the senator as a friend of agriculture, Robertson said.

That's true, said Dennis Richters, who farms near Utica, Nebraska. Richters said he thinks most farmers have a generally good impression of Hagel. "I think his positions are pretty valid," Richters said.

University of Nebraska political scientist Brian Humes said Hagel has been smart to frame his opposition to agricultural subsidies as opposition to a welfare program. That resonates with independent Nebraskans who don't like the idea of being forced to rely on government, Humes said.

But calling agricultural subsidies "welfare" drives John Hansen of the Nebraska Farmers Union nuts. The subsidies are not welfare, Hansen said. The payments are money that came out of farmers' pockets in the first place. Every major commodity in the nation is sold for far less than the full cost of production, Hansen said; all the subsidies do is return some of the money farmers lose and make it possible for them to pay their bills. Removing the government from the equation, he said, would allow agribusiness to decrease commodity prices even more and put farmers out of business.

"I think Hagel genuinely has concerns about farmers," Hansen said, "but every problem that farmers face, he has kind of a free-trade answer for." Everything comes back to getting rid of government red tape and getting government out of farming, Hansen observed. "That isn't going to cut it."

Hansen contends that Hagel "hasn't even remotely begun to

connect the dots between theory and reality." But, Hansen said of the senator, "He's a bright guy, and I think he's even well intentioned."

Steve Wellman, an Otoe County, Nebraska, farmer, said he doesn't agree with Hagel about everything, but he appreciates the senator's candor. "With Hagel you know when you first talk with him what his stand is. He's up front about it, and he has his reasons." Furthermore, Hagel is a strong leader, Wellman said, someone who will stand up for what he believes in and not necessarily follow party dictates.

John Dinkel of Norfolk, Nebraska, who owns a farm implement company with his brother, said he heard no complaints when Hagel voted against the farm bill. "Most farmers realize there's not an unlimited pot of gold in Washington," Dinkel said.

But Rob Heyen, who farms in Seward County, said he was disappointed Hagel didn't support the 2002 Farm Bill. Heyen said he thought Hagel was honest and straightforward but seemed less interested in agriculture than in international affairs. Nebraska's junior senator, Ben Nelson, seemed more attuned to agricultural concerns, Heyen added. Heyen said the fact that Hagel had lived out of the state for so long before running for office from Nebraska also bothered him. But Heyen said he thought the members of Hagel's staff who dealt with agricultural issues—three full-time and one part-time—did a good job, and he considered them a direct arm of the senator.

It wasn't politically easy to oppose the farm bill in the year he was running for reelection, Hagel admitted. But he said he went to his constituents and told them that he voted as he did because, in his judgment, the bill was not in their best interests. "You just do it straight," he said, and listen to what people have to say in return. He said he thinks most Americans value that approach.

Wellman and Richters said they like Hagel's support for free trade. The agricultural industry needs to find out the true value of what it's producing, Richters said. "You don't do that if you play a lot of games" with protectionist policies.

John Hansen of the Farmers Union thought differently. Hagel, he said, is a hard-line free-trade ideologue who judges everything according to its relationship to trade. The senator, Hansen said, is aligned with big business, including businesses that process agricultural products, more than he is aligned with the farmers who produce the products.

Hansen is right that Hagel favors free trade. The senator has said repeatedly that he believes free trade is a benefit to Nebraska farmers and said one reason he wanted to be on the Foreign Relations Committee was so he could play a role in trade policy. Trade is in everyone's best interest, Hagel told a meeting sponsored by the U.S. Chamber of Commerce in 2004. Yes, free trade may sometimes result in job losses, he said, but the markets will always work in the long run. "Trade is about opportunities, not guarantees," he added.

In a speech on the Senate floor in March 2004, Hagel said he sympathized with American workers who lost their jobs when manufacturing operations moved overseas but added that, on the other hand, free trade and outsourcing have also increased productivity, led to technological advances, and created high-tech jobs. The loss of manufacturing jobs in America, he said, is part of a worldwide trend. In fact, the percentage of job losses in America has been lower than the percentage lost in Japan, Brazil, and China, he told his colleagues. Preaching his belief in free trade, Hagel told the Senate that the United States must continue to lead in trade in order to maintain its leadership in the global economy. But America must also retrain workers who lose their jobs and must educate the next generation of Americans to compete in the world economy, he said.

In a 2004 interview Hagel gave an example of the way he believes America benefits from free trade. He said Nebraska exported close to three billion dollars in products in 2003. That kind of trade is possible because of security, stability, open markets, tax treaties, and trade treaties—all of which fall under the large umbrella of foreign policy. He said it all connects, and it all benefits Nebraska.

Something else that would benefit Nebraska and the United

States in general would be an end to boycotts and economic sanctions, Hagel said. He has been a vocal opponent of unilateral trade sanctions against Cuba and Iran and, in early 1999, got the Senate to approve a measure removing food and medicine from the list of items to be used in any economic sanctions. Hagel was furious when a group of Republicans in the House of Representatives stripped the ban from the larger agricultural appropriations bill that September.

Hagel has been outspoken in favor of ending the United States' boycott on trade with Cuba, saying it would not only be good for Nebraska producers but would also be the best way to undermine Fidel Castro's dictatorship. "If you opened that economy by trading with us—free trade—I don't know what he would have to say about the United States," Hagel said.[14]

That's a viewpoint that farmer Dennis Richters shares. The boycott hasn't driven Castro out of power even though it's brought the Cuban economy to its knees, he said, and renewing trade with the island nation would help U.S. farmers sell their products and would develop a political relationship that would benefit both sides. The Nebraska Farm Bureau Federation also likes Hagel's position. Rob Robertson pointed out that each individual trade agreement creates winners and losers, but he asserted that the positives far outweigh the negatives when markets are opened with countries like Cuba.

On one agriculture-related topic, sources from all sides seem to agree: Hagel has been a staunch and effective proponent of bio-diesel fuels. Farmer Steve Wellman said Hagel had worked hard in 2003 to get tax credits for renewable fuels into the energy bill. The measure was predicted to double production by 2012. However, the bill never made it out of the Senate because of controversy over what some called an unfair provision to give makers of MTBE, an additive intended to make fuel cleaner, immunity from being sued over leaks that may have contaminated groundwater. "But he's done what he could," Wellman said.

Richters agreed that Hagel was headed in the right direction with bio-diesel fuels. Not only would increased ethanol production benefit Nebraska farmers, Richters said, but it would also help ease the nation's dependence on foreign oil. "It's safer to be dependent on ourselves than on somebody else," he added.

Robertson of the Farm Bureau said Hagel was instrumental in getting "an impossible coalition" of Republicans, Democrats, and petroleum, environmental, and agricultural industries organized to include the ethanol tax credits in the bill.

Even the Farmers Union likes Hagel's position on renewable fuels. "His work on ethanol has been useful," John Hansen said. "He gets very high marks on that." "The good thing about Hagel," Hansen continued, "is that if you can actually get him engaged, he has lot of personal courage and is very effective. He's not afraid to take risks, not afraid to be aggressive, not afraid to shake the powers that be."

## Reforming Immigration Policy

Hagel stepped across party lines again in 2003 and 2004 to cosponsor immigration legislation. This time he was working with Democrat Tom Daschle of South Dakota, then the Senate's minority leader. The two began working on a plan in late summer 2003 and introduced the bill in January 2004.

Hagel had argued publicly against the anti-immigration sentiment that had swept the nation after the terrorist attacks of September 11, 2001. He said the United States' contradictory and punitive immigration policy was working against its own interests, and he welcomed the immigration reforms President Bush recommended in fall 2003. But those reforms didn't go far enough to suit Hagel. Hagel and Daschle came up with a plan that would have tied work to the prospect of legal residency for millions of people living in the country illegally.

In order to qualify, undocumented immigrants must have lived in the United States at least five years and have been employed at least three of those years before reforms were passed. Then they would be required to work one more year after the legislation was enacted before they could apply for legal status. Applicants would also have to pass national security and criminal background checks and would be required to have paid federal taxes, know English and U.S. civics, and pay a thousand-dollar fine for having lived in the country illegally.

In addition the proposal would remove limits on the number of dependents of legal permanent residents who could get visas to come to the United States and apply for residency, treating them instead like the spouses and minor children of U.S. citizens.[15]

Hagel said one of the big problems with immigration law as it stood in 2004 was that it forced families apart.[16] Too often, one or several members of a family come to the United States, find jobs, and send money home, but the rest of the family is forbidden to join them. Hagel and Daschle said the proposal was not intended to offer amnesty to undocumented immigrants. "Amnesty is: we forgive, we forget, and we move on," Hagel said. "These are earned rights, earned green cards, and earned status."[17]

Furthermore, Hagel said immigration was, essentially, a national-security issue. As many as eight to twelve million undocumented immigrants were living in the United States, he said—thirty thousand in Nebraska alone. Authorities had no idea who all those people were or where they were, Hagel said. If most of those people could get into the pipeline toward citizenship, law enforcement could concentrate on the smaller group, the ones more likely to break the law. Another reason to push for reform, he said, was that current immigration law was a patchwork of rules that sometimes conflicted with each other. And, furthermore, the U.S. economy always needs immigrant workers.[18]

When they introduced their bill, Hagel and Daschle said they didn't expect it to pass during the 2004 session—and it didn't— but predicted it would eventually be the backbone for immigration reform.

Hagel told a group at Omaha's Chicano Awareness Center in February 2004 that the reforms would require a lot of presidential leadership. Bush is from a border state, he said, and he understands immigration problems. But, Hagel cautioned, "That doesn't necessarily translate into leadership." Daschle and Hagel got good marks for leadership from members of Mexico's congress. Mexican congressmen who deal with foreign relations were pleased with the U.S. senators' bipartisan work on the bill and said it would help advance the dialogue on a highly polarized issue that has kept many lawmakers quiet for fear of political repercussions.[19]

By March 2004 the Bush administration had given little attention to its own plan or other plans for immigration reform, and senators were getting restless. Senators expressing frustration were a bipartisan group that included Hagel, McCain, and Republican Larry E. Craig of Idaho as well as Democrats Dodd, Richard J. Durbin of Illinois, and Barbara Boxer of California. The senators accused the administration of ignoring the potentially divisive issue during an election year.[20]

At a hearing that month, Hagel noted that Bush's 2003 plan had laid out a set of principles but no details about how to flesh out those principles and that nothing more had been forthcoming from the administration. "That only takes us about 5 percent of the way," the senator said.

Hagel talked about immigration reform at a meeting of the United States-Mexico Business Committee in March 2004. Asked about the nature of the immigration debate within the Republican Party, Hagel said part of it was driven by economics—some states had lost jobs in the economic turndown—and part of it was philosophical. Some people simply think immigration is dangerous, he said. They have an insular sense of the world and would like to establish "Fortress America." September 11, 2001, should have dispelled the idea that sheer American power can overcome any threat, he said, and he predicted that, eventually, the currents of change would overcome obstacles to reforms.

One group that considered immigration dangerous attacked Hagel and Daschle through a series of April 2004 TV commercials that aired in Nebraska. "Senator Chuck Hagel thinks it's a good idea for American corporations to send our jobs overseas," the ad said. "Well, now he's introduced a bill to give away jobs here at home, too. . . . His bill offers American jobs and amnesty to more than six million illegal aliens." The ads were sponsored by the Coalition for the Future American Worker. The coalition, based outside Nebraska, called itself an umbrella of groups that want to protect American workers.

Hagel launched a series of counter-ads, accusing the coalition of being on record as supporting sterilization as a means to reduce U.S. immigration, a charge the coalition denied. Hagel said the coalition included among its affiliates a group of racists and bigots headed by a white supremacist. Their focus, he said, was to kill all immigration, and their strategy was to intimidate politicians by making the topic a political hot potato. "They tap into a Rush Limbaugh insecurity in this country that I think is dangerously intolerant and essentially un-American," he said.

Hagel said he decided to run the counter-ads, paid for by his campaign fund, because charges like those made by the coalition should not go unanswered. Nebraskans have a lot of common sense, he said, but some folks are tempted to think that if the accused doesn't respond, the accusations must be true.

Any furor the coalition ads might have raised in Nebraska seemed not to make much progress. However, the Hagel-Daschle bill made no progress either, and languished in the Senate Judiciary Committee at the end of the 2004 session. Because Daschle lost his bid for reelection, Hagel would be forced to find another cosponsor if he wished to go forward with the bill in subsequent sessions. Hagel continued to push the initiative, though, telling reporters that reforming immigration and making the United States more accessible to immigrants was part of the war against terrorism, a terrorism based in hatred for and suspicion of the United States. He promised to make immigration reform one of his priorities in coming years.

*Reforming Campaign Finance*

Although he has been less prominent on the domestic-policy front than in foreign affairs, Hagel got into a high-profile dispute over campaign finance reform in 2001, a dispute that put him at odds with his friend Senator John McCain.

The Senate devoted two weeks in March 2001 to the debate over campaign finance reform. Hagel and McCain, along with Democrat Russ Feingold of Wisconsin, introduced opposing bills. Hagel said he thought the bill that became known as "McCain-Feingold" would gut a regulatory system that needed only some fine tuning.

Hagel was philosophically opposed to severe controls on political donations, as he made clear in 1998, when the Senate had considered an earlier round of reform proposals. The bill up for discussion that year, he said, would do nothing to strengthen the democratic system and would, instead, simply limit people's free-speech rights. He said the best way to deal with potential corruption in campaign financing would be to require full disclosure of every dollar given and every dollar spent.[21]

In 2000 Hagel had said he thought the Congress should reform campaign financing but not because money in politics was inherently evil. Instead, he said, the problem was that the flood of soft money meant candidates could lose control of their own campaigns. "Then there's no accountability," he said.[22]

When the senators got down to serious consideration of the issue in 2001, they looked at Hagel's bill, written and introduced the previous year. It would have tripled the limit on "hard money" donations to candidates from one thousand to three thousand dollars per year and capped "soft-money" donations—those made to political parties—at six thousand dollars per year per donor rather than banning those soft-money donations entirely as McCain-Feingold proposed. Hagel said banning soft-money donations would weaken the political parties and simply drive donations to "darker, unaccountable forces."[23]

Looking back on the issue, Hagel said those forces had materialized in a big way. They were the "so-called 527s," independent political-action committees entirely outside the party system. "Parties are the only transparent, open vehicles we have" for political debate and activity, Hagel said. Why weaken parties and strengthen the unaccountable outside groups?

But in 2001 McCain said he couldn't buy the Hagel bill because of its soft-money provisions. Putting a cap on the size of contributions would only enshrine in law something that had "been illegal since 1907, as far as corporate contributions are concerned, and since 1947, as far as labor unions have been concerned," McCain said.[24] Common Cause, a citizens' lobbying group, also opposed Hagel's provision to protect soft money. And Common Cause argued that Hagel's proposal to increase the limits on hard-money contributions from individuals meant a single person could legally contribute $270,000 in hard and soft money combined in an election cycle.

Hagel said in 2004 that hard money was already required to be reported, and he had proposed that soft money be subject to the same disclosure rules. "Why not focus on what's reportable?" he asked. Why not raise the limits so that corporations and unions wouldn't be looking for ways to make undisclosed donations?

In 2001 Hagel said McCain-Feingold would limit people's ability to get involved in politics. "Democracy is messy," Hagel said shortly before debate on the bill began. "We're going to hear a number of examples of how messy and unfair democracy is over the next two weeks. The answer to reforming our system is not to shut people out or diminish the ability of our people or institutions to participate in the process." If soft-money donations were banned, Hagel argued, donors who could afford to would find a way to circumvent the system, while those with limited funds would find themselves further locked out of the process.[25]

The media made a great deal of the fact that the two opposing bills were introduced by men who were close friends, but a story in *Time* magazine said Hagel played a central role in the debate as someone that the hard-nosed true believers on both sides of the question could talk to while the Senate worked toward a compromise. The story observed, "Hagel is that highly evolved political creature: principled but open for business."[26]

Finally, Hagel abandoned his bill in the face of certain failure and set about trying to incorporate his hard-money and soft-money provisions into the McCain-Feingold proposal. Even that attempt failed when the Senate voted to table the proposed amendment on March 27.

The one section from Hagel's bill that did make it into the final measure strengthened the disclosure requirements of the McCain-Feingold proposal, making it harder for donors to hide their contributions. Eventually, the amended bill passed both the Senate and the House, was signed by Bush, and became law. But its effects and defects are still debated.

"Even today, McCain is upset with a lot of what's happened" under the new provisions, Hagel said, and has asked the Federal Election Commission (FEC) to rework its campaign finance directives. "I told him you can't write a law and give it to the FEC and then blame them, the regulators," if things don't turn out as you had planned, Hagel noted.

## Supporting Special Education

Some lawmakers champion a particular cause because of some personal connection: a family member killed in a car wreck, a close friend injured on the job, a child born with a birth defect. Certainly, his own experiences in Vietnam explain a great deal of Hagel's involvement with veterans' affairs and veterans' welfare.

But no close personal experience seems to explain his interest in special education and education for people with disabilities. The first learning-disabled person he remembers encountering was a classmate in Ainsworth. He was a big kid, Hagel said, too big for a second-grader. It was obvious he had been held back several times. "Everybody made fun of him," Hagel said.

He recalls having the boy over to play a time or two. The boy wasn't a troublemaker, but "he was hard to communicate with," Hagel said. "I didn't understand it. I just assumed he wasn't very smart." Hagel remembers being confused. All he knew was that something wasn't right.

When he was a high school student at St. Bonaventure in Columbus, Hagel noticed that some nuns were trying to give extra help to students with learning disabilities. By and large, though, nobody paid much attention to the students. "Those kids were just marginalized," he said. They had no hope and no future, and some of them got into trouble as a result.

The next step in his education on the subject came when he was in basic training for Vietnam. Thousands were being drafted in the late 1960s, including some who "just couldn't get it. I saw what the drill sergeants did to them," he said, and it made him uncomfortable. At that point, though, he was consumed with his own worries and interests and wasn't particularly burning with desire to change the status quo. But as he got older and saw friends whose children had disabilities, he started "putting it back together," he said. "Then you get to the point that you're in the United States Senate. And you think, 'What do I want to do with this privilege? Just go vote, get my picture taken, do interviews?'"

He said he doesn't want to look back on his years in the Senate and wish he had done more to use the power he had to make something better. He decided early on that special education was one of the issues he should take on. Hagel counts his modest but hard-fought successes in that arena as among his biggest contributions in Congress.

During his first term in the Senate, Hagel pushed successfully to increase federal funding for special education from 9 percent to 16 percent of total costs and promised to keep pushing until he got Congress to agree to fund the 40 percent originally included in the 1975 Individuals with Disabilities Education Act (IDEA).

He and Iowa Democrat Tom Harkin cosponsored a bill to do exactly that in 2001. Approved in the Senate, the measure was eliminated when the Senate-House conference committee met to reconcile the two chambers' versions of that year's education bill. Hagel said the Republicans in Congress had generally steered clear of the issue while Democrats had pushed for more funding. When he began working with Harkin, some Republican friends warned him he shouldn't be aligning himself with one of the Senate's most liberal members. Hagel ignored the warning. He said the fact that he, a conservative Republican, would get behind the funding bill moved others of his party to reconsider their positions.

Hagel returned to the issue in 2003, sponsoring with Democrat Christopher Dodd of Connecticut and Independent Jim Jeffords of Vermont an amendment to increase funding for IDEA to

$2.2 billion, about 18 percent of the total. Hagel noted he'd been working on the issue for five years and that, gradually, Congress was moving closer to meeting its original funding promise.

In April 2004 Hagel and Harkin tried a new tactic. Instead of proposing, again, simply to increase the funding by some percentage, they introduced an amendment that would mandate funding increases of two billion dollars each year in addition to whatever other funding the Congress provided. This time eleven Republicans were listed as cosponsors of the bill. While the Senate approved another increase in funding, it rejected the amendment to make it mandatory.

Hagel said he was disappointed that the federal government had failed to live up to its part of the special-education bargain for nearly thirty years. The result had been a huge unfunded mandate upon the states, he said, meaning that school districts were required to spend money on special education that they would otherwise be able to spend on teacher salaries, new computers, and other improvements.

But he said he was happy that, at least, the Senate agreed to authorize full funding for IDEA in coming years. That would put billions of dollars into the program and begin to fulfill the federal government's obligations. "We've made tremendous progress here," he said, "and we'll stay at it."

## Moving Quietly

More than one Republican politician in recent decades has hung his or her political hat on social issues, making every campaign into a referendum on abortion or gun control or gay marriage. Not Hagel.

Although the conservative Republican takes typically conservative Republican positions on the topics that have become so dear to many in his party, he has not made them his signature issues.

For instance, Hagel did not receive an endorsement from Nebraska Right to Life when he ran in 1996. But he voted with the majority in Congress in 2003 to approve a government ban on so-called partial-birth abortion, and he was a cosponsor of the Senate's 2004 Unborn Victims of Violence Act, which would have made a person convicted of killing a pregnant woman guilty of two murders, a measure pro-choice groups said was a prelude to equating abortion with murder.

When a Nebraska district court judge ruled the state's ban on partial-birth abortion unconstitutional, Hagel said he was deeply disappointed. "The ban on partial-birth abortion reflects the will of the majority of Nebraskans and Americans," Hagel said. "It is a commonsense ban on an uncommonly inhumane procedure. I am hopeful that when this decision is appealed to the Supreme Court, it will be overturned."[27]

But Hagel is not likely to lead the parade to get that done. He said he is against abortion but doesn't think the Supreme Court's 1971 *Roe v. Wade* ruling that made abortion legal is likely ever to be reversed. "And I don't know if it would be good for this country to undertake the effort to do that," he added. The issue has so split the American people, he said, that a legislative effort to ban abortion entirely would probably make things worse. But because he believes abortion is wrong, he said, "In my world of laws changed and laws enacted, I would like to see it gone."

How does he live with that dichotomy? First of all, he said, abortion is a personal issue, a philosophical and religious issue, not a political issue: "You believe what you believe." He doesn't impugn the motives of those who support abortion as a woman's right to choose, "but this is where I am." He said he tries to explain where he stands and then move on.

Even though some news stories have characterized him as a strong foe of abortion, he said he has never used his stand on abortion as a campaign issue because campaigns should be about debating foreign policy and tax policy and other things that truly are political issues. Some pro-choice voters have challenged him, saying, in effect, "You're a conservative Republican, and you don't like the government telling people what to do. So why do you favor government intervention in matters of pregnancy and abortion?"

Generally, Hagel said, it's true that he opposes government intervention, but he says "fundamentally, I believe that [a fetus] is a child, a human life, and it deserves protection. It's a pretty deeply held philosophical point with me."

As for gun control, Hagel said he believes the Second Amendment, with its guarantee of the right to bear arms, is important, but he doesn't base his arguments on that alone. The problem with gun violence in America goes deeper than the guns themselves, he believes. "It's a behavior problem. It's bad people doing bad things—using firearms." Banning guns is not going to stop the problem, he said.

On the other hand, "You don't want to make them so easily available that anyone" of any age and with any background can buy as many guns as he pleases—"and we don't," Hagel said. Hundreds of gun-control laws are on the books in city ordinances, state laws, and federal laws—and should be there, he said—but the problem is more complex than either side in the gun debate wants to make it out to be.

Regarding gay marriage Hagel tells those who ask that he supported both the 1996 Defense of Marriage Act passed by Congress and Nebraska's constitutional amendment barring gay marriage. But while he believes marriage is a sacred oath between a man and a woman, Hagel said he does not favor amending the U.S. Constitution to include a ban on gay marriage.

"I am a conservative, and I think amending the Constitution should be used only for very important issues that can't be handled any other way," Hagel said early in 2004, soon after President Bush had called for an amendment banning states from recognizing unions of gay men or women as marriage.[28] When the Senate debated the matter that July, Hagel was overwhelmed with mail, phone calls, and e-mail from Nebraskans—11,128 in ten days.[29] The vast majority of the messages urged him to vote in favor of the amendment. But in the end there was no showdown.

As it became obvious to Senate leaders that they didn't have the votes to pass the amendment and send it to the states for ratification, the leaders opted to take a procedural vote—a motion to end debate and move to a vote on the issue—hoping to get at least a simple majority to declare a moral victory.[30] But only forty-eight senators voted to end debate, not even a simple majority and far short of the sixty-vote super-majority needed to move forward.

Hagel voted with the leadership on this one, casting his vote to stop debate, keep the amendment alive, and head to a final vote. He and Nebraska's Democratic Senator Ben Nelson both said they wanted to see whether federal courts would strike down the Defense of Marriage Act and whether a federal judge in Omaha would rule the state's law unconstitutional. Ultimately, if the courts rule to curb the states' ability to govern on the issue of same-sex marriage, Hagel said, a federal amendment may be needed: "But not today." Amending the Constitution should always be a final recourse, he said, used only if every other option has been exhausted.[31]

Furthermore, in July 2004 Hagel said he believes the federal government should not interfere in states' decisions to allow or ban gay marriages. His emphasis on states' rights puts him squarely in the conservative camp.

Every public-policy issue he confronts as a senator, Hagel said, brings out special interest groups on both sides, and although the pressure may be particularly heavy on hot-button social issues, "that's life in the big city." He said he has never worried about an interest group telling him that if he votes against their viewpoint they will run ads against him. Threatening people is not a good idea, he said, and most members of Congress will react negatively when it happens. Hagel said his solution to handling controversial issues is to work hard, understand the matter, come to a conclusion, say it straight, and vote. "The rest of it you just deal with," he said.

## Remembering the Veterans

Even before he got out of the cell-phone business, Hagel took on a leadership role in a project involving veterans. In 1984 U.S. District Court Judge Jack B. Weinstein asked Hagel to serve as chair of a program to compensate Vietnam veterans who been injured by exposure to Agent Orange. The herbicide, which the

MOVING FORWARD IN THE SENATE

U.S. military sprayed as a defoliant in Vietnam between 1965 and 1970, was suspected of causing injuries and disabilities to servicemen exposed to it. Hundreds of those servicemen joined a class action lawsuit against the companies that made the chemical, and those companies settled out of court for $180 million, the largest settlement on the record to that time. Weinstein asked Hagel to put together a board that would decide how to spend the money.

Hagel asked four other Vietnam veterans to serve with him, and over the next ten years they devised a program, sanctioned by the courts, to distribute the money. What they developed had two parts: a payment program that provided cash compensation to disabled veterans and survivors of deceased veterans, and a class assistance program that provided funds for social services organizations for the benefit of all parties to the lawsuit, according to a State of Virginia Web site. "It was a complicated and detailed assignment," Hagel said.

The judge said he'd selected Hagel as chair because he wanted someone who had a good reputation among veterans' groups and someone the various groups could agree on. And he wanted someone credible and competent. The judge figured Hagel's experience as deputy administrator at the VA, the man who was responsible for the day-to-day operations of the agency, stood him in good stead. Also, Hagel said with a chuckle, the judge told him he didn't want to put a lawyer in charge.

Even before his days at Vanguard, Hagel had taken a role in veterans' affairs. While he was at Firestone, he helped raise money for the Vietnam Veterans Memorial constructed on the National Mall near the Lincoln Memorial. When he worked at the VA, he continued to encourage people to give to the project, and he was one of two main speakers at the groundbreaking in March 1982. The memorial was dedicated in November of that year. In 1992 Hagel served as chairman of the committee that planned a tenth anniversary observance.

Hagel has taken up military and veterans' issues in the Senate, too. Some legislation was designed to improve pay and retirement equity for members of the armed forces, to improve health care benefits for members of the military, and to improve veterans' access to health care.

In fact the Vietnam Veterans of America chose him as legislator of the year in 2000 for his "leadership in securing meaningful legislation for veterans' preference, championing of homeless veterans, assisting in business opportunities for Vietnam veterans, and for his steadfast advocacy to assist veterans and educate young people about the Vietnam War." That same year, Hagel introduced legislation to authorize construction of an underground visitors' center near the Vietnam Veterans Memorial on the National Mall in Washington. The bill cleared both houses of Congress in late 2003, and President Bush signed it into law. A design team was selected in fall 2004, and construction was to begin once private money had been raised to finance the project.

### The Nebraska Brethren

When Hagel took his place in the Senate alongside Bob Kerrey, Nebraska became the only state in the union to be represented by two senators who had served in Vietnam. Although they were of opposite political parties, the two men clicked, and they became a formidable pair.

Their Vietnam background first brought them together when both served on the commission examining the effects of Agent Orange on U.S. veterans. It was the late 1980s, and Hagel was head of the World USO; Kerrey was about to run for Senate. After that initial acquaintance, the two fell out of touch, Kerrey said, although they had a few dealings when Kerrey was in the Senate and Hagel was head of the Private Sector Council.

Then Hagel contributed a thousand dollars to Kerrey's brief 1992 bid for the presidential nomination. Hagel said he was pleased to have "an attractive, articulate individual from Nebraska in the hunt." He was also pleased to see a Vietnam veteran running for the presidency. He added, "And I liked him personally." If the idea of presidential primaries and campaigns is to find the best people, narrow the race to the best candidates, and choose the best president, the process should transcend simple partisan politics, Hagel said. "Why should we be afraid of competition?"

Kerrey knew that Hagel had been urged to run against him in his bid for reelection to the Senate in 1994, a prospect Hagel said he never seriously considered, but the men didn't really have much contact with each other while Hagel was living in Nebraska. But once Hagel joined Kerrey in the Senate, they began to work closely together. It may have been their common Vietnam background that brought them together in the 1980s, Hagel said, but it was their compatible personalities that made theirs such a good partnership in the Senate. "We had a chemistry that worked," he said.

The two men are similar in many ways, Hagel observed. Both of them tend to say what they think and to say it in what, for Washington, are pretty blunt terms. Their experiences in Vietnam may be one reason behind that, Hagel said. Vietnam vets aren't easily buffaloed. "What are they going to do?" he asked rhetorically. "Send you back to Vietnam?" By comparison, political risks are no big deal. "We're not afraid of being threatened. We're not afraid of losing."

Kerrey, who left the Senate to become president of the New School University in New York City, agreed that he and Hagel have similar values and a similar approach to problems. "We just hit it off," Kerrey said. "Chuck is a very honest, straightforward person who typically tells you what's on his mind. He's not a loose cannon, but you don't feel he's trimming when he gives you an answer." Yes, the Vietnam bond may have had some influence on their relationship, Kerrey said, but he thinks popular lore has made too much of it. "If Chuck had been a conscientious objector and gone to prison, I'd still have liked him," Kerrey said.

Hagel returns the sentiment. He enjoyed the four years the two worked together in the Senate. Although they differed on many issues, each of them knew where the other stood, and they were always able to work together, Hagel said. "We have a tremendous relationship."

Allison Stevens, a reporter for *Congressional Quarterly*, a Capitol Hill publication, remembers attending some of the weekly Ne-

braska Breakfasts, hosted by the Nebraska congressional delegation for visiting constituents each Wednesday when Congress is in
session. The senators and representatives introduce guests in the
audience, make a few announcements, and banter among themselves to the general amusement of the gathered Nebraskans. The
members seem to make an effort to be entertaining, but Stevens
said Kerrey and Hagel took the sessions to a new level: "Kerrey
and Hagel would stand up and do their morning routine. They
were just hysterical."

Lilibet Hagel said her husband was very sorry to see Kerrey step
down from Congress in 2000. The two had worked well together
for a number of reasons, she said. The shared Vietnam experience
was part of it, but "they're both mavericks, too. Both are sort of
change agents." The two men seemed to understand each other
well, "but they're both secure enough that they wish each other
well rather than resent each other's success, which is rare in this
business and in this town," she said.

Hagel was host for the official farewell party when Kerrey left
Congress in 2000, and the two still talk regularly. "I miss him,"
Hagel said.

Things are not the same between Hagel and Ben Nelson, elected
to Kerrey's Senate seat in 2000. The frosty relationship between
the two men was the subject of a story in the *Omaha World-Herald* in spring 2004. The story laid out four sources of friction between Hagel and Nelson: they're from two different parties; they
have different personalities; they have different political styles;
they fought a bitter election battle against each other in 1996.

It's not that unusual for senators from the same state to have
trouble getting along. The caustic relationship between Frank
Lautenberg and Robert Torecelli, Democratic senators from New
Jersey who served together before Torecelli left the Senate, is part
of Capitol Hill folklore, for example. Nelson and Hagel don't get
even close to that level, observers said.

Sometimes friction is worse when a state's senators are both
from the same party, according to several Capitol Hill reporters. In those cases *Congressional Quarterly*'s Allison Stevens said,

"They're fighting for the same attention and the same money from the same donors."

But in the case of Hagel and Nelson, the 1996 campaign could be the source of much of the friction. The criticism the candidates leveled at each other on the campaign trail and, especially, the dramatically negative last-minute ads on both sides may have left bad feelings that just can't be remedied. Hagel still bristles when he thinks about the Nelson campaign's eleventh-hour accusations that Hagel and his company broke the law during the cell-phone licensing rush of the 1980s. "It made me mad as hell," Hagel recalled.[32]

The two men also have different personalities and take different approaches to their work. In the Senate, Hagel and Nelson often take conflicting positions, despite the fact that Nelson is considered a conservative Democrat. "The fact is we are of different parties, we believe different things," Hagel said. "Of course, there's going to be some tension there, but it's not personal."[33]

Hagel has criticized Nelson's positions on the farm bill, tax policy, and homeland-security policy. Nelson's common reply has been, "I've gotten over losing in 1996. I don't know if Senator Hagel has gotten over winning."

But the root of the uncomfortable relationship may go deeper than party or personality or even a nasty campaign, congressional scholar Ross Baker said. "In a funny way . . . I think it's more a product of Hagel's disappointment at Bob Kerrey's leaving the Senate." Hagel and Kerrey had a special relationship, one that Hagel is unlikely to develop with whoever else may hold Nebraska's other Senate seat.

Hagel plays down his differences with Nelson. He and Nelson are both professionals, he said. "We don't have to be buddies" to work together on behalf of the state. But Ben Nelson is not Bob Kerrey? "No, he's not Bob Kerrey," Hagel said solemnly.

No one seems to disagree that the two senators do, indeed, work together on behalf of Nebraska. They have cooperated on campaign finance legislation and rural issues, and they've worked together to get federal money for the state's rural hospitals, highways, and waterways, and for research.

Observers and the members of the delegation themselves say the Nebraska congressional delegation works well together in general, as do the members' staffs. Doug Bereuter, former representative from Nebraska's First District, said he thought part of the reason is the small size of the delegation—two senators and three representatives—that has to try to cover all aspects of policy making. And the weekly Nebraska Breakfasts keep them cooperating. "We know we'll be sitting together every Wednesday," Bereuter said.

But the comity all the members seem eager to preserve was put to the test in March 2004 when President Bush announced he was about to appoint a Nebraskan to a new post as assistant secretary of commerce for manufacturing and services: a manufacturing czar. Hagel knew nothing about the nomination until the morning of March 10 when he read a press release from Nelson's office congratulating Behlen Manufacturing's head Tony Raimondo of Columbus on the appointment that was to be announced the next morning. Hagel wasn't happy about the surprise.

Common practice in Washington is that the president informs members of Congress from his own party when someone from their state is about to be anointed with a high-level position. In this case neither Hagel nor any of the Republican leaders in Congress had been told.

In fact Raimondo himself had sidestepped an opportunity to tell Hagel his appointment was in the works. Less than a month before the matter became public, Hagel had spoken at the chamber of commerce luncheon in Columbus. Raimondo was in the audience, and during a question-and-answer period, Raimondo asked Hagel whether he knew when the administration might announce its choice for manufacturing czar. No, Hagel responded, adding that he really couldn't see a reason to create the position. He and Raimondo visited face-to-face after the meeting, but even then Raimondo didn't tell Hagel he had applied for the position the previous November and had been interviewed by administration officials in early 2004.

Complicating matters further, Nelson and Raimondo, a Republican, had close connections. The Columbus, Nebraska, manufacturer had donated to both Hagel's and Nelson's campaigns, but Nelson was an unpaid adviser to the board of Raimondo's Behlen company.

When Hagel read the Nelson press release announcing Raimondo's appointment and realized what was going on, he was astounded. "This is all very bizarre," Hagel told reporters, noting that Nebraska's Republican governor Mike Johanns had not been consulted either.

Then things got really interesting. By the afternoon, Senator John Kerry, the presumptive Democratic nominee for president, said Raimondo's firm was setting up a manufacturing operation in China, taking jobs out of the United States. Raimondo responded that Behlen, which makes farm equipment and building materials at four U.S. plants, was not shipping any jobs overseas. Instead, he said, the new plant in China would manufacture buildings for use only in China. But Kerry had raised enough questions that, by the next morning, the White House said the announcement was being postponed for scheduling reasons. On Friday Raimondo withdrew from the whole process, saying he didn't think his appointment could be confirmed in the Senate.

Then the finger pointing began.

Democratic Party leaders in Nebraska said it was less Kerry's fault that Raimondo withdrew than Hagel's. Barry Rubin, the state party's executive director, said Hagel had blocked the nomination in retaliation for being left out of the appointment process. Hagel said that wasn't true: "I don't have any power to hold anything up. How am I going to hold it up? I didn't even know about it."[34]

Hagel wondered how it was that John Kerry knew about Raimondo's nomination before it had been officially announced, and suggested Nelson's communications director may have leaked the news to the Democratic candidate. Nelson took umbrage at the aspersions cast on his staff member.[35]

Hagel said he thought Behlen's plant in China would have been "a huge problem" for Raimondo if he had been nominated and faced a Senate confirmation battle.[36] Hagel said "senior Republicans" in the Senate told the White House they might not be able to get Raimondo confirmed. But, he added, he was all in favor of Behlen's plans for a plant in China, plans that fit right in with the senator's position on free trade.

Eventually a White House official said the nomination was scuttled because of Nebraska politics: tensions between Hagel and Nelson. The story reported that Raimondo also blamed Hagel. "I can't imagine why a Nebraskan would stop another Nebraskan from getting an appointment," Raimondo said. "All [Hagel] had to be is neutral, and it was done."[37]

Hagel said he was not responsible for the nomination's collapse. "By the time Senator Hagel, or any other Republican senator, knew about this nomination, John Kerry had already defined it" as a jobs issue, Mike Buttry, Hagel's communications director, said at the time. "The White House so mishandled this there was nothing left to do, there was nothing left to support."[38]

That position got some support from syndicated columnist Marianne Means, who said the White House completely flubbed the nomination process.[39] Columnist Robert Novak blamed the mess on sheer incompetence in the White House. Novak suggested the Bush administration decided not to keep Hagel in the loop in retaliation for his frequent, public opposition to administration policies.[40] A few weeks later Hagel declined to talk any further about the entire fiasco. He told a reporter for *Roll Call*, a Capitol Hill publication, that he had said what he was going to say and didn't want to talk about it anymore.

Examining the relationship between Hagel and Nelson once more, the *World-Herald* concluded that the two senators rarely displayed any ill will toward each other in public and that, by all reports, they continued to work together on matters that affect their state. Indeed, in early May 2004, only a few weeks after the *World-Herald* story examining their differences, Hagel and Nelson introduced a bill together to create a fourth permanent district judge position for the state, a move designed to ease the crowded dockets facing Nebraska courts.

*Living the Life of a Senator*

As skeptical as she had been about leaving the Washington area to move to Nebraska, Lilibet Hagel had mixed feelings about returning to the nation's capital after her husband was elected to the Senate. "It was a bittersweet move," she said.

Part of the problem was that, for a political spouse, a campaign is much more fun than the job it leads to, she said, "because you're part of the team." Campaigning is exciting and ends in a decisive result. "So it's a great journey," she said. "This is a long slog. It's got its own high points, but it's different."

Lilibet had spent some time on the campaign trail with her husband, attending events, greeting supporters and potential supporters, and walking in a lot of parades. But she had also spent time at home with the couple's young children during those months and had liked the balance that gave her. "It would be hard to listen to the same speech every day," she said with a smile.

The campaign was hard work, she said, for the candidate, for his staff, and for her—"just like a job, really." But it was fun, too. Lilibet said she and her husband try to face new challenges with the idea that they are going to enjoy them and make them fun. After the election, she found herself back in a part of the country she knew well but in a role that was different from any she had had before. She remembers attending a luncheon for Senate spouses at the beginning of the 1997 session of Congress. All the new spouses were introduced, she said, and then all the returning spouses introduced themselves and gave a word of advice to the newcomers.

Ann Simpson, wife of Wyoming Republican Alan Simpson, was the first to speak, Lilibet said. Simpson told the congressional spouses to expect scores of people from their home states to call and want to stay at their houses during a Washington visit. "My advice is 'just say no,'" Simpson said. Most senators' families don't need a lot of extra people underfoot. When her husband came home from his job, sometimes even family was almost too much for him, she said.

Lilibet remembers another piece of advice, one that frightened her. Linda Daschle, wife of South Dakota Democrat Tom Daschle, said she and her husband made their health their priority, and she recommended the new senators and their spouses do the same. When her husband came home that evening, Lilibet asked him, "What have you gotten yourself into?" Considering Linda Daschle's advice, Lilibet had begun to think being a senator could be hazardous to a person's health. "Now I know exactly what she meant," she said eight years later. The demands on a senator's time are endless, and maintaining one's health and stamina are an essential part of the job.

Both the Hagels have tried to follow that early advice. Lilibet runs almost every day near the family's home in suburban Virginia. And she bicycles enough to be ready for the June Bike Ride across Nebraska each year. Chuck used to run with her, until the motion and impact started to bother his back. Now he swims regularly—outdoors when the weather is good and in the Senate gym during the winter. And he takes the steps instead of the elevator, walks from his office in the Russell Senate Office Building to the Capitol instead of taking the tram. "You've got to look for little ways to keep in shape," he said.

As for sleep: "I probably don't get enough, like most Americans," he said. Although he usually has a staff member drive him the half hour to and from Capitol Hill, he spends the time in the car working. Only occasionally does he grab a five-minute nap. Hagel remembers John Y. McCollister, his first Washington boss, taking power naps very effectively. "He could just sit at his desk and nod off for five to ten minutes," Hagel said. "Then he'd have a whole new burst of energy." Hagel said he knows he should try something similar, but he's usually too keyed-up to be able to do it.

It's probably that same keyed-up personality, the one his Little League coach noticed in Ainsworth about fifty years ago, that prevents Hagel from enjoying golf. He said he finds it boring: "If I'm going to invest that many hours in something, I'd rather do what I want."

One of the things he wants to do is spend time with his children. Seldom does Hagel accept an invitation to attend a weekday evening reception, dinner, or ceremony. If he is asked to speak, the stipulation is that he will speak before dinner but won't stay for the meal. He wants to get home to his family. "I just happen to enjoy them," he said, and believes it is important to spend as much time as possible with his children as they are growing up.

Hagel's mother is his model when it comes to raising children, he said. His mother treated each of her boys as individuals. Each got his share of attention, but the attention was tailored to their different personalities, their strengths and weaknesses. And she never imposed her will too far into their lives, he added. Betty Hagel respected each of her sons' individuality and privacy. Even as adults, they understood exactly where she stood on things and what she expected of them, but she always told them in private, never embarrassed them in front of others. "As I get older and my kids get older, I see how difficult that is," Hagel said.

And, of course, it takes time.

Lilibet Hagel said the Hagels work hard to find that time, to watch their children play soccer and baseball and act in the school play, and to attend services at St. John's Episcopal Church across from Lafayette Park in downtown Washington. They work to maintain a balance between public and private life, Lilibet said.

"Everything is business in Washington," she said. "People here tend to take things way too seriously; it's hard to resist that." Not that senators shouldn't be serious about their work, she added. "All the issues are so important, and what they're doing is real life. But it's easy for that to consume all your attention," to the neglect of family life.

But the long slog has its rewards, too. The best part, Lilibet said, is the proximity to important events and prominent people. Even if the people aren't necessarily those she admires, "it's very interesting to see them close up."

She recalls a tour she and her husband took with a group of senators during Hagel's first year in Congress. A high-ranking person was sitting in front of her on the bus, talking with Hagel and another senator about hiring a market research company from

New York to help mold their public image on a number of political issues. "I don't consider myself a political expert, but there was something so jarring about that," Lilibet said. "I thought, 'Oh, my goodness. What have we joined into here?'" She was not too surprised to find that the person in question was soon out of a job. He was in way over his head, she said, and way off track.

Most of the time, though, she meets simply interesting people. The Hagels were invited to dinner several times at the home of Jim Wolfensohn when he was president of the World Bank. Their fellow guests were people like UN Secretary General Khofi Annan, cellist Yo Yo Ma, Federal Reserve Chairman Alan Greenspan, Vice President Dick Cheney and his wife Lynne, journalist Jim Lehrer, and other senators from both parties. The conversation is fascinating, Lilibet said. Even among those who don't always see eye-to-eye, the disagreements are polite.

One night, though, things got a bit off course. Secretary of Defense Donald Rumsfeld and his wife, Joyce, were among the guests, and Lilibet was seated next to Rumsfeld. The general discussion got around to the Middle Eastern prisoners at Guantanamo Bay and the rights they were or were not being granted.

Rumsfeld tried to change the subject, saying he had to deal with those topics all day and didn't care to rehash them over dinner. But the topic came up again, and Rumsfeld slammed his fist on the table—"Lilibet almost jumped out of her chair," her husband remembers with a chuckle—and said, "We're leaving." Joyce Rumsfeld slowed her husband down before he could storm out of the room, and one of the other guests managed to break the tension with a sardonic comment. But, a moment later, the Rumsfelds were gone.

While memorable, that dinner party was unusual, both Hagels said. Ordinarily, things are calmer, whatever the mix of personalities. Chuck Hagel said such events often bring together some liberals and some conservatives. "You wouldn't put just any conservative Republican and any liberal Democrat in there," he said. "You'd get two who can have fun with each other, who like each other. There's a little chemistry to it."

MOVING FORWARD IN THE SENATE

Lilibet Hagel said when she and her husband were on their way to their first dinner party where they knew they'd be rubbing shoulders with lots of famous and powerful people, she asked Chuck with some amazement in her voice, "How did we get invited to this?" He answered, "I don't know, honey, but it sure is fun."

That's one of their guidelines, Lilibet said. They try to attend only functions that are fun or interesting to them. They found out early on that to do otherwise is to invite exhaustion. "It's a burn-out profession," she said.

On the other hand, life as a Senate family offers plenty of opportunities. It can be a struggle to work through the scheduling and the demands on a senator's time, "but I don't know how you can complain about it," Lilibet said.

In addition to her Senate-related activities, Lilibet is involved with a laboratory school for the disabled. Another Senate spouse asked her to cochair a reception to benefit the school in the late 1990s, and she liked the people at the school so much that she's continued to work with them. "They celebrate differences," she said, and don't focus on the students' limitations.

She said she doesn't take credit for her husband's Senate leadership regarding funding for special education, but her work at the school may have helped keep it on his radar screen. She isn't sure. He's a deep thinker, she said, "and a lot percolates beneath the surface."

Lilibet also volunteers to teach English as a second language to adults. She described her class in an e-mail message. It includes a couple of young women from Germany and Thailand who are working as nannies, a chemical engineer from Columbia, "a young Vietnamese woman who wants to take the foreign-service exam and one day work for the State Department, a Chinese man who just won a full scholarship to Syracuse's MBA program, a Korean diplomat's wife, a Chinese man who owns a garage and gas station, and a young flamboyant Russian woman the likes of whom none of us have ever seen.

"They are congenial and kind and very bright—and more interested in the world than they are absorbed in themselves. They don't know what my husband does—as far as I know—which also makes it fun to talk politics with them."

Lilibet said she is hooked on current affairs and politics. "I don't see how anyone could say it's boring," she observed. "It changes every day and affects our lives so closely." She and her husband talk a lot about issues he's working on, she said. Does he ever ask her advice? "He doesn't usually have to ask. I've usually already told him," she said with a laugh. Nearly all the time, she said, their views are similar.

Is he truly conservative? The concept is hard to pin down, she said. "He's very compassionate, but I do believe he thinks the best way for people to gain self-sufficiency and to achieve is by asking more of themselves."

Is he truly partisan? "He's truer to the [Republican] principles than the party," she said. Why is he so willing to take positions at odds with his party's? She replied, "He's very good at acting within the system to get things done, but he will never put on the cloak of someone else's rigid beliefs."

That independent spirit is one reason Hagel has achieved a prominence in Washington that most members of Congress only dream of.

# 7

## Risking the Administration's Wrath

No question about it: Chuck Hagel loves his job. "Senators have the most political independence, probably the best political job in the world," he said.

He has made a virtue of that independence and has moved into the public arena as one of the most outspoken and frequently quoted members of the Senate, risking his party's wrath in the process. His willingness to say what he thinks even when that's diametrically opposed to what the Republican Party and the Republican administration are saying has made him something of a thorn in the White House's rose garden.

Not that he isn't a real Republican. He voted with his party 93 percent of the time in 2004 and in support of President Bush's initiatives 94 percent of the time—higher percentages than those earned by the other Republican members of the Nebraska delegation.[1] And Hagel espouses solid, conservative Republican principles, sticking with the party on issues that reflect its core values.

But at the same time, Hagel does not seem to be an unbendable ideologue.

Democratic senator Joe Biden of Delaware serves with Hagel on the Foreign Relations Committee, and the two have worked together on a number of foreign-policy issues. He, too, characterized Hagel as anything but an ideologue. "I think he's a committed conservative in the traditional sense of the word," Biden said. But Hagel has an open mind—which used to be expected of senators but is rare today, Biden said—and is not judgmental toward those who disagree with him. "He'll try to persuade you, but he won't judge you," Biden said. Hagel has firm views but is a pragmatist, a legislator who wants to get things accomplished.

Bill Avery, who teaches political science at the University of Nebraska–Lincoln, agreed. "He's right of center—but not far right," Avery said.

### Conservative—or Moderate?

Some have called Hagel a pragmatist, a senator who is carving out a role as a leading moderate voice in the Republican Party, particularly on foreign policy.[2] Others have labeled Hagel a moderate—or a maverick. A columnist for United Press International even called him "dovish" in December 2004 when Hagel vehemently criticized Secretary of Defense Donald Rumsfeld for his handling of the Iraq war.

Mike McCarthy, Hagel's former partner in Omaha, said he thinks Hagel believes in individual freedom and personal responsibility, less government, and less government interference in the daily lives of American citizens. If those beliefs make a person a conservative, McCarthy said, then Hagel is a conservative. But, he added, if the definition means an unwillingness to change, "I think it would be a mischaracterization to call him conservative." McCarthy believes it's that willingness to change that leads some to tag Hagel a moderate. The senator, McCarthy said, questions the status quo and is always open to other viewpoints, whether they be from Democrats in Congress or people from other nations. "He's not an ideologue in the sense that people want him to be when they give that conservative label," McCarthy said.

Hagel himself said he is a conservative, not a moderate. He finds it interesting that people sometimes call him a moderate when his voting record is so solidly conservative Republican, and he thinks the "moderate" label may be more a result of style than substance. "My style is one that would be described as more moderate," Hagel said. He tries to be thoughtful, to listen, not to overreact, to see both sides of the issue, "and if that, in the minds of some, is a projection of 'moderate,' then there's nothing I can do about it," he said.

Philosophically, Hagel is in tune with most tenets of the Republican Party. His grandfather and his father were Republicans, and he grew up inclined toward the party's point of view. When he got older and thought consciously about his political affiliation, he knew he agreed with the party's core positions: strong national defense, fiscal responsibility, individual responsibility, free trade. Parties are philosophical repositories, he said, and even those who find their philosophical home in one party or the other are not likely to agree with all the planks in a given platform.

Clearly, Hagel doesn't agree with everything his party espouses. The reasons behind his disagreements are complex. One of them has to do with the institution of the Senate itself. As is true in any institution, the Senate's structure, rules, and norms shape its members. Hagel recognizes and accepts that influence.

Hagel's respect for the Senate as an institution is relatively rare, some observers say. Norman Ornstein of the American Enterprise Institute, a conservative think tank in Washington, told the *Washington Post* in spring 2004, "The idea that they have an independent institutional responsibility, that the institution itself is bigger than the individuals or the parties, doesn't occur to the bulk [of members] for a nanosecond."

Though he may be a conservative Republican by nature and by choice, Hagel sometimes seems to feel a greater loyalty to the institutions of the Senate and of democratic government at large than he does to his party. Despite his conservative voting record,

Hagel refuses to see himself as a Republican first and a senator second.

He sounded different when he was running against Ben Nelson in 1996. In a speech to the Downtown Omaha Rotary Club, Hagel said, "When you go to Washington you line up. You're either politically anchored with the Republicans or the Democrats." But once he arrived in the Senate, Hagel said he began to appreciate the institution's influence on its members.

Despite his voting record as a loyal Republican, Hagel has had no problem speaking out when he disagrees with the party line or the party leaders. When *Washington Post* columnist David Broder wrote about Hagel after the senator had been in office about eighteen months, Hagel had already voted against his party on granting the president fast-track trade authority, replenishing the International Monetary Fund (IMF), and allowing presidential discretion on economic sanctions—all foreign-policy matters dear to Hagel's heart. "Hagel fears little," Broder wrote.[3]

But when the senator made an attempt in December 1998 to unseat Mitch McConnell of Kentucky as chairman of the Republican National Senatorial Committee, the group charged with helping elect and reelect Republicans to the Senate, Hagel's reputation for speaking his mind seemed to be a political liability.

## Bucking the Leadership

Hagel's message in that in-house campaign was a version of the campaign philosophy he had preached to Senator Alfonse D'Amato during the senatorial campaign in 1996: that the Republican candidates should stop assaulting their Democratic rivals and should focus, instead, on their own strengths. If he were chair of the committee, Hagel said, he would emphasize raising "hard-money" campaign contributions to candidates instead of unregulated and unlimited "soft money" gifts to political parties. Those groups are required by law to spend the funds only on party-building activities and not on behalf of specific individual candidates—although the latter often happens.

Hagel and Senate majority leader Trent Lott had become friends in the days when Hagel had worked in John Y. McCollister's congressional office, and the two senators had a cordial relationship during Hagel's first year in the Senate. In fact Lott, one of the Senate's most powerful Republicans, told Medill News Service in November 1997 that the Nebraska freshman had been "a star in this new class." Lott predicted Hagel would one day have a place in the Senate leadership, but Hagel said he had no higher political aspirations.

Majority leader Lott chose Hagel to lead the Republicans' side of a bipartisan deal that would replenish IMF reserves in early 1998, but at the last minute some Republican senators decided they would vote for the funds only if the IMF installed more stringent reforms than Hagel had proposed. With the blessing of Lott and other GOP leaders, Hagel's plan got rewritten in committee into a version that neither the IMF, the Clinton administration, nor Hagel could live with.

In the ensuing political free-for-all, Hagel publicly charged the Republican leadership with holding IMF legislation hostage while Asian economies that needed IMF help were spinning into chaos. Eventually Hagel hammered out a compromise and forced the matter to a vote; the Senate approved the bill by a surprisingly lopsided vote of 82 to 16. Despite the clash, Lott told the *Omaha World-Herald* that month that he didn't begrudge Hagel the tactics he used to force the matter to a vote—and a victory—against the wishes of the Republican leadership.

But in November that year, relations between the veteran and the newcomer became less friendly. Hagel's bid to unseat McConnell and lead the Republican National Senatorial Committee put him in direct opposition to Lott, who actively promoted McConnell's reelection to the position. Lott said his party needed a chairman "with the seasoned experience and proven skills to lead us to victory."[4]

"Mr. Lott got on the line, calling every member personally," Hagel remembers. "[The Republican leadership] did everything they could to stop me." He suspects the old guard saw him as a brash newcomer and were afraid he'd be hard to work with. And, frankly, Hagel said, they were probably right. He wanted the party to go in a different direction, toward more openness, more transparency, a wider sense of party. He wanted to reach out to more people and to pursue different approaches to raising money. "Most of the leaders didn't think that was what we should do," he said.

His attempt to change the party's direction may have doused any hopes he'd had for being a party leader inside the Senate, but it got Hagel some great press. An editorial in the *Washington Post* said the newspaper hoped Hagel would prevail. Normally, the paper said, it would not take sides in a party's internal competitions, but in this case it made an exception. McConnell, the paper said, had become the chief defender of "the current squalid system of campaign finance" and "the principal obstacle to its sorely needed reform."[5]

*Wall Street Journal* columnist Gerald Seib wrote that it was unlikely Hagel would win the election but added, "It would be nice if some of the Hagel message would take root."

Hagel thought he had a good twenty votes lined up to support him, but when the results were in, he had only thirteen to McConnell's thirty-nine. In retrospect he said he could see that he had taken on the Republican leadership too soon. But he thought the party was squandering some opportunities and had lost some Senate seats it should have kept in 1998. He said he thought he should do more than just carp from the sidelines. "I thought I owed my colleagues some alternative," he said. At the time of the incident, Hagel said he hadn't gone looking for a fight. But he didn't sound sorry that he had found one. If a person is honest about who he is and what he believes, he said, "you shouldn't worry about the consequences."[6]

In a 2002 editorial endorsing Hagel's reelection, the *Omaha World-Herald* recalled that Hagel had been uncomfortable with his party's leadership in Congress almost since he had arrived there. Hagel had told the paper three years earlier that Lott was part of "that crowd" that was too extremist and had vowed that he would lead the effort to drive them out of leadership positions.

His relationship with Lott and McConnell was a little tense after the 1998 showdown, Hagel said, but like good politicians, the three have since mended fences. Looking back at the fight several years later, McConnell said, "He wanted the job, and so did I. It wasn't a blood feud or anything."

Hagel said, "I was addressing my criticism to the body. It had nothing to do with personalities."

The set-to with the Republican leadership also made no difference in Hagel's willingness to disagree with his party. He went after the Republicans again in July 1999, saying the GOP's tactics in blocking the confirmation of Richard Holbrooke as ambassador to the United Nations were irresponsible.

In a September news conference that same year, Hagel berated the Republican leaders for "hijacking" the will of a House-Senate conference committee by stripping a ban on unilateral U.S. sanctions on trade in food and medicine from the agricultural appropriations bill. That made Hagel angry on several levels.

First he objected to "a small, elite cabal of Republican leaders" arbitrarily imposing their own wishes over those of seventy senators who voted to support the original amendment. Second, thanks to those leaders' actions, a bill that contained emergency relief for farmers was stalled and going nowhere. Third, Hagel had been a strong proponent of ending unilateral trade sanctions on food and medicine and wanted the ban included in the bill's final version.

In a floor speech Hagel expressed his frustration with what he called high-handed leadership tactics and the Senate's unwillingness to take on tough issues—or any issues. "I'm one senator who will continue to raise hell about this," he said.

In October Hagel criticized the way Senate leaders were handling the debate over the federal budget. With some understatement Lott told reporters he was disappointed with Hagel's criticism of his own party's leaders and positions. "I think his conduct is not helpful," the majority leader said.[7]

But the conduct continued.

In June 2000 Hagel said the Senate was nearing paralysis because of partisan maneuvering. He said he was tired of "all this nonsense," for which he said the Republicans and Democrats were equally to blame.[8]

When the Senate recessed in August that year, Hagel found himself something of a star at the Republican National Convention in Philadelphia. He met with editors from *Time* and *Newsweek* and appeared on TV news shows. He preached his policy of internationalism in a speech at a convention luncheon meeting. Cooperative engagement, he said, would "help us refine peace and prosperity in our time."[9]

The high point came under the convention's klieg lights when Hagel took to the podium and introduced to the assembled delegates his fellow senator, John McCain, for whom he had served as national cochair as McCain made a run for the presidential nomination.

After that introduction Hagel had trouble getting off the convention floor. People wanted to shake his hand, wanted his autograph, wanted to stand next to him for a snapshot. And the same thing happened in his hotel lobby and on the street. Hagel was becoming a recognized face and voice among the Republican faithful.

In fact he was said to be on George Bush's short list of possible vice-presidential running mates. Syndicated columnist Mark Shields had started promoting Hagel for the job the previous December. Shields said Hagel embodied honor and duty and praised him as an independent reformer who was "McCain without McCain"—independent and outspoken but without the cantankerous streak many saw in the Arizona senator.

During the spring, various newspapers picked up the theme, reporting that Hagel was being considered for the vice-presidential slot. Analysts said his record as a Vietnam veteran would help the ticket, as would the fact that he was conservative and plain spoken.

Lott was rumored to be politicking against Hagel, and Hagel

himself expressed no real enthusiasm for the position. When Bush chose Dick Cheney as his running mate, Hagel said he was relieved. "I'm not looking for a new job," he said. Instead he went back to his "old" job in the Senate: voting solidly Republican but speaking out loudly when he thought his party was on the wrong track.

He had another run-in with Lott that summer. Hagel had introduced a bill in July to allow Medicare to cover some of the cost of prescription drugs. Lott preferred legislation that would have Medicare and the people it served share the costs, and he wanted Hagel to support the party leaders' line. Hagel not only declined to lend his support but also declined to kowtow to party discipline. "I don't answer to Trent Lott," Hagel said. "I answer to Nebraskans and the people of this country."[10]

Once the U.S. Supreme Court settled the 2000 election and declared George Bush the winner, Hagel joined his fellow Republicans on Capitol Hill in rejoicing that the party had regained control of the Oval Office. But that didn't keep him from criticizing one of the new president's early major policy statements.

Hagel took offense in January 2002 at the most famous line in George Bush's first State of the Union Address. Referring to Iran, Iraq, and North Korea, Bush said, "States like these, and their terrorist allies, constitute an axis of evil." Hagel said Bush's remark was nothing but "name-calling" and was counterproductive and over-simplifying in a complex world. It was the first of many disagreements the senator would have with the Bush White House over foreign policy—not to mention a few over domestic policy.

## Leading an Uprising

In November 2002, soon after the election in which the Republicans gained congressional seats, Hagel led an uprising by the Senate's Republican Caucus that forced the majority leader Lott to promise to remove special-interest provisions from the homeland security bill. Hagel said the provisions had been inserted by House Republican leaders, with the knowledge of the White House, after most members of Congress thought the conference committee had worked out an agreement that eliminated those provisions.

The measures Hagel and others objected to included retroactive protection from liability for part of the pharmaceutical industry, permission for U.S. companies to benefit from homeland security contracts even if they moved their business offshore to avoid paying taxes, and special considerations for Texas A&M University's efforts to be named a national bioterrorism-research center. An irate Hagel told his fellow Republicans, "We have just been given the opportunity by the voters to lead the country. And here we go. Our first action is a dishonest, behind-closed-doors deal."

Hagel took on his fellow Republicans not only on matters of substance but also on questions of style. After the 2002 elections the Republicans controlled both houses of Congress and the White House. By the end of 2003 it looked as if the GOP had marginalized Democrats' influence in both chambers by shutting them out of negotiations on the final version of major bills. But not all members of Congress were pleased about the level of partisanship. Hagel worried about the effect it would have on the institution.

"It's almost anything goes," Hagel said. "I think we're on the edge of something dangerous if we don't turn it around. . . . It's like the Middle East. You just keep ratcheting up the intensity of the conflict."[11]

Tom Janssen, who served on Hagel's campaign and congressional staffs, said Hagel is not partisan in the sense that he wakes up each morning, reads what the Republican National Committee has to say, and then plans his day accordingly. His core beliefs may reflect Republican principles, but, according to Janssen, "he's not afraid to work with Democrats." Politics requires compromise, Janssen said, and Hagel understands that. He's willing to work with people on both sides of the aisle to get things done.

It's a fact of life that members of Congress almost have to work across party lines to get legislation passed, particularly in a Senate so narrowly divided between Republicans and Democrats. Some senators view the aisle between the parties as a sort of no-man's

RISKING THE ADMINISTRATION'S WRATH

land, a free-fire zone, says the congressional scholar Ross Baker, and view crossing it as a grim necessity. Hagel, he said, moves across that line pretty easily. "That makes for a successful senator," he observed.

It also goes over well in a state like Nebraska. Any good leader, said Dick Robinson of Norfolk, Nebraska, should not be strictly conservative or liberal. Instead, said Robinson, who worked on Hagel's 1996 campaign, a leader should look at each issue and ask what's best for the nation, regardless of the political backlash.

An April 2004 editorial in the *Omaha World-Herald* praised Hagel—as well as Nebraska senator Ben Nelson and former senators Bob Kerrey and James Exon—for putting the public good before ideological or partisan needs. "Such an approach is a welcome contrast to the to-the-death zealotry that too often characterizes the approach of many lockstep ideological warriors in Congress," the paper said.

Nebraskans like to see someone stand on substance rather than procedure, and they like it when Hagel seems to take a stand on principle rather than politics. Dennis Richters, a Nebraska farmer and Republican, said Hagel's tendency to say what he thinks might hurt him in the party hierarchy, but it plays well at home. "We Nebraskans love that, of course," Richters said.

Many political observers have commented that partisanship in Congress increased dramatically in the late 1990s and early years of the twenty-first century. John Podesta, the chief of staff in Bill Clinton's White House and now head of the Center for American Progress, was a Senate staffer in the early 1980s. The place was much more bipartisan then, he said. Staff members and senators of both parties knew and got along with each other. Now senators barely know their colleagues, especially those on the other side of the aisle, and staff members seem often to be at war with each other, Podesta said.

Doug Bereuter, who retired in 2004 after twenty-five years representing Nebraska in the House, agreed. He told the *Washington Post* that Washington had grown more and more partisan during his time in office. "Cross-party friendships—and the compromises they engender—become more difficult when extreme partisanship rules," he said.

Partisanship as such, Hagel said, is not a bad thing. In fact, it's a strength of the American system, a way to give Americans choices. "But partisanship today is dangerously raw," he said, "almost to the point of disunity in government." For instance some Republicans criticized Hagel in 2003 for appearing on the same conference program with the Democratic senator Hillary Clinton of New York. That kind of fussing is "just silliness," Hagel said.

"I deal with ninety-nine other U.S. senators every day—liberals, conservatives, Democrats, Republicans. My dear friend Paul Wellstone [the late Democratic senator from Minnesota] was probably a socialist. That's my business—to deal with my colleagues." Besides that, he said, although he disagrees with Senator Clinton on a multitude of issues, he believes she is a good senator.

He isn't interested in his colleagues' pedigrees, Hagel said, only with how he and they can work together. "We deal back here with issues, facts, and policy, and we vote on that basis." Too many people forget that, Hagel said. "Almost everything is based on a partisan appeal: 'Do this because it's the Republican thing to do or because the president needs it.' I think that's irresponsible and mindless."

Hagel's opinion would be no surprise to Judy Woodruff. The CNN reporter and host has interviewed Hagel often and said she thinks he sees himself first and foremost not as a Republican but as the senator from Nebraska. "My impression is he thinks one needs to get along with individuals in both parties to get things done," she said, noting this was not a course of action currently in fashion in Washington.

Senator Biden said he thinks Hagel is admired in both parties—and envied by some in his own—for his willingness to act on principle rather than pure partisanship. It's uncomfortable to take on your own party, Biden said. Most people's natural inclination is "to be part of the club."

Woodruff surmised that Hagel's outspoken independence meant that he was not exactly beloved at the White House. In fact a May 2004 column in the *San Diego Union Tribune* reported that, thanks to his outspoken candor, "Hagel [was] said to be tied for first place with McCain on the White House blacklist of Republican senators."

In December 2004 the Bush administration took a slap at Hagel for some of the discomfort the senator has regularly caused it when the president named Nebraska governor Mike Johanns to be secretary of agriculture during the second Bush term. Ordinarily the administration would give the senators from a nominee's home state a heads-up about the appointment, but no one told Hagel a thing, leaving him to hear it secondhand while he was traveling abroad. The syndicated columnist Robert Novak said the snub reflected the administration's anger over Hagel's criticism of its Iraq policy.

It also emphasized Hagel's place outside his party's core. In fact he's been called a congressional insider and outsider at the same time. "I assume that was a compliment," Hagel said, and then he pondered how the term applied to him: he said he thought he was an insider in that he tried to play a role as part of a team and tried to take on the responsibilities expected of him and because he gets along personally with his colleagues.

If Hagel is seen as an outsider, it's probably a result of his outspoken disagreements with his party's positions. "I think my responsibility is first to the people I represent and the nation I serve," he said. "I owe the people my best judgment." Anyone who allows his judgment to become hostage to insider relationships is not living up to his responsibility, Hagel said.

"Most of my colleagues respect that," Hagel said, although some may question his motives. "I'm not afraid to take on the insiders, the leaders—publicly or privately," he said. "That leads some in my party to ascribe motives to me that just aren't there: 'He's doing it for publicity' or 'He wants to run for president.'"

Sandy Berger, the national security adviser under Bill Clinton, said political maneuvering does not appear to be Hagel's primary motivation—at least not when it comes to international affairs. "Chuck is one of the most non-partisan senators—Democrat or

Republican—on foreign policy," Berger said. "This is deadly serious stuff for him and not the stuff of political jockeying."

Hagel was invited to speak in autumn 2003 at the founding conference of the Center for American Progress. Others on the program included Wesley Clark, who later ran for the Democratic presidential nomination; Joe Biden, the Democratic senator from Delaware; Mark Warner, the Democratic governor of Virginia; Democratic senator Hillary Rodham Clinton of New York; Richard Holbrooke, assistant secretary of state in the Clinton administration; and Jim Leach from Iowa, a Republican member of the House of Representatives.

"It was an all-star cast," said John Podesta, who runs the center. "We were looking for voices from the bipartisan tradition that had been the mainstream in this country for almost the entire period before World War II." Podesta said Hagel's conference speech reflected the fact that he wasn't afraid to differ with the Bush administration. Hagel's message wasn't harshly critical of the president, Podesta said, but it did challenge some assumptions. It was characteristic of Hagel's approach in the Senate and his "reputation as a guy who's kind of fearless, who will say what he thinks but also someone who does his homework and is thoughtful."

That description and others like it have led more than one observer to compare Hagel to his friend, Senator John McCain of Arizona—but with a few differences.

"He's McCain without the attitude," Podesta said. Both men say what they think, although McCain's voting record may put him slightly closer to the "moderate" label than Hagel's does. "But McCain is kind of unpredictable. He'll be a bomb thrower when you don't expect it," Podesta said. "He's a guy you like when he's with you, but he can just be way out there. Hagel's a more normal guy. . . . He's fearless but more mainstream."

Hagel and McCain got to know each other in the early 1980s when the two Vietnam veterans were involved with veterans' affairs and the development of the Vietnam Veterans Memorial. McCain campaigned for Hagel during the Nebraskan's 1996 Senate race. Since then they have been fast friends.

Hagel was national cochair of McCain's unsuccessful effort to win the Republican presidential nomination in 2000 and campaigned all over the nation for the Arizona senator. The two senators have offices across the hall from each other in the Russell Senate Office Building, and they periodically drop in on each other.

McCain said Hagel has earned his reputation as an outspoken maverick. His colleague places the country's needs first and foremost, McCain said. "Sometimes that will get you in trouble around here as the place is more dominated by special interests and partisan priorities." But he added that Hagel has been respectful when he has taken on the Bush administration and has offered constructive criticism.

From the middle of 2002 on, much of that criticism was directed toward the Bush administration's handling of the war in Iraq. The disagreements were deep and abundant.

### Questioning Iraq

As early as 1998 Hagel was concerned about the United States' attitude and actions toward Iraq. He disagreed with the senators from his own party when they and Republican leaders in the House called on President Clinton to remove Saddam Hussein from power because he wouldn't allow the United Nations weapons inspectors free access to potential weapons sites.

Removing Hussein would require a mammoth military operation, something the nation and its allies were not prepared for, Hagel said. And once Saddam had been removed from power, Hagel asked, who or what would take his place? Another despot? Civil war?

A year later Hagel urged Clinton not to attack Iraq and not to try to assassinate Hussein. If the United States' primary objective was to drive Hussein from power, the nation would do well to substitute real policy for sheer military force, Hagel said. He suggested the United States work with opposition groups in Iraq and in the Arab community and freeze Iraqi financial assets abroad.

When Bush came to power and began talking about the possibility of invading Iraq, Hagel spoke up again. "It's interesting to me that many of those who want to rush the country into war and think it would be so quick and easy don't know anything about war," Hagel said in August 2002. "They come at it from an intellectual perspective versus having sat in jungles or foxholes and watched their friends get their heads blown off. I try to speak for those ghosts of the past a little bit."[12]

Hagel had said it would be irresponsible to take America to war, to invade another nation unilaterally with no allies, no help, no support. Saddam Hussein, he said, was definitely a threat to the region and even to the United States but not the mortal threat the administration was making him out to be. Furthermore, Hagel believed that the political fallout could be devastating, with Central Asia and the Middle East being badly destabilized by a unilateral American invasion of Iraq. He had said, "We could potentially lose an entire generation of the Muslim world."[13]

Later that month Hagel was at it again, cautioning against unilateral action in Iraq. "Run for the diplomatic high ground first," he said. "Get the United Nations involved."[14] Commenting on two speeches by Vice President Dick Cheney in which Cheney had made a case for invading Iraq, unilaterally if necessary, Hagel said he couldn't imagine Cheney was doing that without the president's approval. "If that is the case, then we are probably in a lot more trouble than we know," he said.

Hagel said he didn't think Iraq had nuclear capabilities, although he assumed Saddam Hussein was trying to develop them. "But to scare the American public by saying this guy is a couple of months away from not only possessing nuclear weapons but a ballistic missile to deliver those, that's dangerous stuff here," Hagel said.[15]

When President Bush was preparing to explain his Iraqi position to the United Nations in September, Hagel approved of Bush's efforts to cast Iraq as an international, not simply bilateral, issue. But he said Bush had not yet explained to anyone who the United States' allies would be in a war against Iraq. Who would govern after Saddam? What was the administration's objective? Had the

RISKING THE ADMINISTRATION'S WRATH

United States calculated the consequences? What would war in Iraq mean for Afghanistan? For Israel and Palestine? For India and Pakistan? Hagel saw no easy, risk-free options.[16]

But when matters came to a vote that fall, Hagel joined 76 other senators and 296 members of the House in authorizing war in Iraq. Apparently, though, he still thought there was a good chance Bush would not actually take that final step. He told reporters he believed the president would and should exhaust all other avenues first and would not wage war rashly or unilaterally.[17]

In the emotional atmosphere surrounding the plans for war, Hagel's pleas for restraint drew fire from the far right. William Kristol of the *Weekly Standard* called Hagel an appeaser. The *National Review* labeled him "Senator Skeptic, R-France," alluding to France's unwillingness to support America's plans in Iraq and Hagel's insistence that America work with its traditional allies. The radio personality Rush Limbaugh said Hagel made his comments just to get media attention.

Hagel admitted that a politician takes some risks when he criticizes a president of his own party but added, "I just do what I believe is right."[18]

Hagel said in 2004 that Bush, Secretary of State Colin Powell, and National Security Adviser Condoleezza Rice had all assured him in fall 2002 that war would be the last option. They told him diplomatic efforts to avoid war would be played out to the end. Hagel applauded the United Nations' resolution in late October that demanded that Hussein allow weapons inspections to resume and that set a deadline for Iraq's compliance, although Hagel said he was afraid Hussein wouldn't comply. "The Iraqi issue is not just a United States issue. The Iraqi issue is a United Nations issue," he said.[19]

In December that year Hagel and Joe Biden, the ranking Democrat of the Senate Foreign Relations Committee, traveled to northern Iraq to meet with leaders of the Kurdish population. Hagel said the two decided to make the trip because they thought Kurdistan would be one of the most critical parts of a restructured Iraq and Middle East.

The Turkish government helped the two U.S. senators get into Iraq, providing bulletproof vehicles for their passage. About twenty armed escorts from the United States, Turkey, and Kurdistan accompanied the caravan that drove all night through rough terrain on narrow mountain roads.

When they arrived at the headquarters of the two largest Kurdish parties at 6 a.m. or so, the senators did some interviews with reporters at the scene, took quick showers, and changed clothes. Then they sat down to a meal and spent three hours talking to the Kurdish representatives who were their hosts. After that they visited schools and hospitals the Kurds had built since the end of the 1991 Gulf War.

The next morning the senators spoke to the Kurdish parliament then spent the rest of the day meeting with the families of men who had been rounded up and taken away by Saddam Hussein's forces in the previous decade. Hagel remembers, "There were hundreds of these black-shrouded women" who showed the U.S. visitors pictures of their children who had been massacred and pictures of the aftermath of a horrifying poison-gas attack.

The two-day visit helped the senators understand the nuances of the situation in Iraq and among the Kurds. So much of foreign policy depends on nuances, Hagel said, and "you never quite grasp an issue, a dynamic, a nuance the same way again after you see for yourself, after you're there." When they returned from their visit to Iraq—followed by a stop in Israel—Biden and Hagel wrote an opinion piece for the *Washington Post* in which they insisted that American should not go into Iraq without allies and had better be prepared for an enormous rebuilding effort once Saddam Hussein's regime had been toppled.

Furthermore the senators stressed that Iraq was only one piece in a Middle East region that was unstable. They said then—as Hagel had said before and has said since—that the United States must aggressively pursue peace between Israel and Palestine. The key to the long Israeli-Palestinian conflict, the senators wrote, was to empower Palestinian reformers and encourage Arab moderates. Trying to make peace between the Israelis and Palestinians should be done both for its own sake and because "doing so has ancillary benefits for the disarmament of Iraq."[20]

Their trip to the Middle East didn't make the senators experts on Kurdistan or Iraq, Hagel said. On the contrary, "It reflected how little we knew." But "a little insecurity is not all bad." Policymakers who represent the most powerful nation in the world need to pay more attention to what they don't know, Hagel said, to realize that even great powers have limits.

And that was the essence of the problem when the United States invaded Iraq in March 2003: the failure to understand those limits. "We didn't understand the culture, the history. This administration didn't take time to try to understand it," Hagel said. "We tried to apply Western standards and thinking and values to a part of the world we knew little about."

By early 2003, American sabers were rattling, and Hagel was having second thoughts about the reassurances Bush and others had given him back in September 2002. Hagel said he began to think, "I'm not sure this crowd ever was serious about getting a diplomatic resolution or even trying to." At that point, media attention was focused on what was likely to happen in Iraq. With the administration's battle drums beating ever louder, Hagel continued to insist that war should be the last option.[21]

He was pleased, a few weeks later, when his friend, Secretary of State Powell, spoke to the UN General Assembly, making a case that the world needed to stop Saddam Hussein before he used his weapons of mass destruction. Hagel thought Powell had laid out an effective and important presentation that would persuade other nations to back the American position. If the United States were really going to invade Iraq, he said, it was important to have the world on its side.[22]

As the invasion drew ever closer, Hagel continued to urge caution. He called for calm and for more time, saying America was wrecking coalitions and international relationships in its rush to war. "The idea of a quick, democratic replacement for Saddam Hussein is delusional," he said.[23] He suggested the UN convene a regional Middle East conference to try to prevent and resolve conflicts and to encourage political and social reform in the area.

In early March that year Hagel wrote an op-ed piece for the *Omaha World-Herald*, something of an open letter to the administration, warning about the pitfalls of heading into war alone. He made the case that the war on terrorism could not be won by simple military might. Victory, he wrote, would require international cooperation in a complex web of areas: intelligence, economics, diplomacy, law enforcement, humanitarian needs. America's success in Iraq would be measured by its ability to build lasting, flexible coalitions.

Hagel's pleas, like those of others who urged caution, fell on deaf ears, and the Bush administration ordered U.S. troops to invade Iraq on March 19, 2003. Hagel's criticism didn't stop, but his mantra switched to pleas for international help to rebuild Iraq after the United States ousted Hussein and warnings about highhanded U.S. tactics in the aftermath of the military attack.

Hagel made a brief visit to Baghdad in late June 2003, after President Bush had declared the official end of the military campaign in Iraq. And as hostilities continued and Iraqis and Americans continued to die, Hagel continued to push the administration toward cooperation with the United Nations and individual U.S. allies.

In September Hagel said it still was not clear whether the United States was better off having invaded Iraq, and he complained that the administration had done a miserable job of planning how to handle a post-Saddam nation. He said he would likely vote to support Bush's request for an additional eighty-seven billion dollars to help rebuild Iraq—and he did—but said "the Congress will damn well ask questions and get some answers" before forking over the money.[24] And he left no doubt how he felt about rebuilding Iraqi infrastructure and society: "We can't turn back. We own Iraq. The whole world knows it."[25]

## Blasting Administration Scandals

A mini-scandal tangential to the war developed during the summer and early fall of 2003 when the former ambassador Joseph Wilson went public with an assertion that one piece of evidence the administration had relied on in its case to invade Iraq—that Iraq had tried to purchase uranium from Niger for a nuclear-weapons program—was not true and that the administration knew it was not. A few weeks later the syndicated columnist Bob Novak, quoting "two senior administration officials," revealed that Wilson's wife, Valerie Plame, was an undercover CIA agent. Speculation arose that the White House, possibly via Vice President Dick Cheney, had leaked the information to punish Wilson and warn others who might speak out against its war rationale.

In October Hagel let loose on television, blasting whoever was responsible for feeding Novak the information and blowing Plame's cover. "If I was president," Hagel said, "the first thing I would have done is called my chief of staff and my national security adviser into my office and said, 'I want this figured out in forty-eight hours.' Not only would heads roll in my office—and they should once you find out what happened and who is responsible—but then criminal charges should be brought against those individuals."

The program's host asked Hagel how he could get by with criticism like that and his recent remarks about the administration's "miserable planning" for follow-up in Iraq. Did Hagel pay a political price for that kind of talk? "Well, I might not get invited to as many White House parties," Hagel said, "but the fact is, it's very simple: I take the same oath of office as the president does. And patriotism, in my job . . . is not about supporting my president or supporting my party."[26]

And so it went. In the following months, Hagel lamented that the reservoir of pro-American goodwill that had existed throughout most of the world since World War II had been drained. He opined that Congress had abrogated too much responsibility and allowed the president too much freedom in dealing with Iraq.

In 2004 Hagel told the incumbent president Bush and Senator John Kerry, who were facing off in the presidential election, that the United States must erase the global divide between rich and poor. The growing threat of terrorism worldwide, he said, was related to despair, endemic poverty, and hunger in many parts of the world.[27]

In 2004 Richard Clarke, a former Bush White House counterterrorism coordinator, accused the president of pressuring him to find evidence of Iraqi involvement in the September 11, 2001, attacks when none existed. While most in his party were trying to avoid the subject, Hagel recognized Clarke as a "serious professional" whose charges should be taken seriously.[28]

Hagel said that one year after President Bush declared an end to formal hostilities in Iraq the United States and its allies were on the edge of losing control of a dangerous and complicated situation.[29]

And then, in early May 2004, the difficult situation in Iraq turned grotesque as the public learned about American soldiers' abuse of Iraqi prisoners. The administration and Pentagon expressed their horror at the torture and mistreatment but also their certainty that the abuses were committed by only a few bad apples among the troops.

But Hagel wasn't willing to let it go at that. Speaking on NBC's *Today*, the senator said the situation required a harder look at the bigger issue: "Was there an environment, a culture that not only condoned but encouraged this kind of behavior? We need to look well beyond just the soldier. Who was in charge? Was there a breakdown in command here? . . . We need to understand all the dynamics of this."[30] In the following days he told reporters Congress needed to look at whether the Pentagon's culture facilitated the abuses. Depending on how high up the responsibility was found to go, he said, the administration would have to deal with the problem.[31]

In a personal interview Hagel said that besides being horrific in itself, "this is a dangerous, despicable episode in our nation's history," coming at the very moment when America should be reaching out to create a bond of trust with the Iraqis and the Arab world. The prisoner abuse undercuts America's credibility, he said, and "you can't lead without credibility and trust; it's the coin of the realm."

RISKING THE ADMINISTRATION'S WRATH

The incidents did damage at home, too, he said, by shaking the foundation of Americans' confidence in their military. The government needed to move swiftly to find out where things had broken down. "It's not good enough to end up punishing and disciplining the sergeants and the corporals. Someone must take responsibility," he said.

Asked whether the prisoner abuses in Iraq were just something that happens in war, similar to the My Lai massacre and other incidents in Vietnam where U.S. troops had mistreated or killed civilians, Hagel said the situations were very different.

It's true, he said, that war is a dirty business. "It's about suffering and passions and emotions that drive people to do things they would normally never even think about." The difference in this case, though, was that the prison guards and military police involved in the abuse weren't taking part in a battle, weren't reacting with an adrenalin rush prompted by the terror of an immediate threat. "This was a very controlled environment," he said. "The interrogators weren't under attack."

The easiest part of any war is the smart bombs and quick attacks, he said. The abuses that developed a year after the initial military victories were "a very clear example of how dramatically unprepared we were" to deal with the hard part of war: what to do in Iraq after Saddam Hussein had been deposed.

Soon after the scandal became public, Hagel said Defense Secretary Donald Rumsfeld and General Richard Myers, chairman of the Joint Chiefs of Staff, might lose their jobs as a result of the scandal. President Bush and some Republicans in Congress had defended Rumsfeld, but Hagel said, "Over the next couple of weeks, the president's going to have to make some hard choices."[32]

Furthermore, Hagel said, additional revelations of abuses were coming and should be made public and dealt with as quickly as possible. He also said he wasn't sure the United States could still win the war in Iraq, given the chaos in that nation in May.

Hagel's opinions were repeated in multiple media outlets in the following days and won him praise from some editorial writers. Salon.com, an online publication generally considered in the

liberal camp, said Hagel no longer looked like a romantic idealist but more like a prescient leader of his party and a good conscience in the Senate. Hagel and his friend John McCain, the piece
said, seemed to be setting the tone for the Senate's dealings with
Rumsfeld over the prisoner abuses.

A columnist in the Sarasota, Florida, *Herald-Tribune* credited
Republicans McCain and Hagel with making it clear that the outrage over the abuses was not simply something the Democrats in
Congress were trying to use to gain a partisan advantage. Hagel and
McCain, the column said, understood the seriousness of the abuse
and its ramifications for the larger battle against Islamic terrorism.

In congressional hearings Hagel began to push the administration to tell the Congress what would become of prisoners in U.S.
custody once governance was turned over to Iraqis on June 30.
Deputy Secretary of State Richard Armitage said he understood
that the prisoners would be put into the hands of Iraqis as rapidly
as possible after the turnover. Hagel asked him what "as rapidly
as possible" meant. Armitage said he didn't know. Hagel asked if
anybody did know. Paul Wolfowitz, deputy secretary of defense,
said no.

Considering the tension raised by the issue, Hagel said with
frustration, "I would have thought this government would put
some time into this, especially given what we have been through
the last few weeks." That comment, too, was quoted and reprinted
in multiple wire service stories and other media.

Then Hagel returned to his theme of UN involvement in stabilizing and rebuilding Iraq. He told reporters that the situation in
Iraq was too dangerous and complicated for the United States to
accomplish the goal of bringing freedom to the Iraqi people on
its own.[33]

He was unhappy that the administration wasn't being up front
with Congress about the handover and the rebuilding process. He
said administration representatives had given Congress all kinds of
answers—some inconsistent, some misleading, some incomplete,
and some downright wrong. The administration had not leveled
with the American people about the war's cost in lives or dollars,

he said. In fact, some officials had claimed taxpayers wouldn't have to foot any of the bill since income from Iraqi oil would cover it. That just was not true, Hagel said, adding, "and I think most of them knew it wasn't true."

He also harped on what looked to be an administration that shunned dissent in its ranks in favor of unquestioning support. In a May 2004 story about the Bush administration's leadership in Iraq, the *Los Angeles Times* quoted Hagel: "There is a general sense out there that the administration does not tolerate any points of view that are contrary to theirs. Good, sharp critical thinking is absolutely imperative to good policy."

Later that month Hagel said he was unhappy that the White House seemed to be pushing Congress away from the conduct of the war in Iraq. The U.S. Constitution intended Congress to serve with the president, not under him, he said. But the Bush administration was not including Congress in planning for the occupation and handover of Iraq or even keeping its members well informed.[34]

During that same week Hagel raised a national ruckus by suggesting during a Foreign Relations Committee hearing that the United States may have to reinstate the military draft to meet its commitments in Iraq and elsewhere in the world. It was partly a question of manpower, he said, but it also had a societal implication. "It's the middle class, lower-middle class that's always the rifleman in the field, that is always on the line, not the sons and daughters of the wealthy and the powerful," he said. If the war was, as Bush had recently asserted, a generational war, then shouldn't people from all walks of life be involved in it?[35]

In the following days Hagel's comments were the subject of wire-service stories, TV and cable news programs, and discussion in Internet chat rooms. Editorials and letters to the editor came down on both sides of the issue. His colleague on the Foreign Relations Committee, Senator Joe Biden, agreed with Hagel that the nation needed to consider the question. Hagel, sometimes with Biden, was a guest on multiple news shows and talk shows, elaborating on his original statement.

Hagel said repeatedly that he wasn't pushing to reinstate the draft, just asking Americans to consider whether it was needed. As things stood, the nation was engaged in a long-term war and making commitments to fight terrorism in the future that it could not fulfill with current resources, he said.[36]

The White House was having none of it. A draft was not under consideration or even on the back burner, the president's spokesman said. And Secretary of Defense Donald Rumsfeld said if the Pentagon needed more forces, it could find them in the Reserves and National Guard.

It is interesting that Democrats in both houses of Congress had introduced bills more than a year before to actually reinstate the draft, but it was Hagel's suggestion that the matter simply needed to be discussed that caused all the commotion. Perhaps the fact that Hagel is a Republican, a member of the dominant party, was what led people to give more credence to his suggestion than they had to similar ideas from Democrats. After the fact Hagel said he didn't expect the kind of response he got when he raised the possibility that a draft might be needed but thought it indicated "we've drilled into a bit of a nerve on this issue."

In June, Hagel and McCain stood out among their Republican brethren when they voted in favor of a measure to require the administration to provide specifics about the U.S. military commitment in Iraq after the planned handover at the end of that month. In an editorial, the *Lincoln Journal Star* praised Hagel's political courage.

"Not only did he break party ranks" the editorial said, but "Hagel also did something that makes partisan Republicans writhe in horror. He voted for an amendment suggested by Senator Ted Kennedy." Hagel had told the paper he thought Kennedy's proposal was an honest effort to provide for legitimate congressional oversight. "Unfortunately, an amendment by a stalwart liberal Democrat like Kennedy becomes radioactive to most Republicans," Hagel said.[37]

The Republican reaction to his vote was an example of just how partisan the Congress had become, Hagel said later. Too many

Republicans think if an idea comes from Kennedy it must be irresponsible—or even evil. In this case, he said, he thought Kennedy's measure was both responsible and important.

Hagel joined four other Republican senators in voting to support an amendment to the Pentagon budget bill that would have required the president to abide by the Geneva Conventions' rules about prisoners of war. The vote followed intense pressure from the administration and the Republican Policy Committee to kill the measure, and Hagel's refusal to be cowed by his party's minions earned him praise in a *New York Times* editorial.

Even what was meant to be a happy, hand-holding Republican National Convention in August gave Hagel reason to dissent. He said the Republican Party had forgotten its history as an internationalist party. Instead, Hagel said, many Republicans in 2004 questioned the value of working with institutions like the United Nations and NATO, institutions they once wholeheartedly embraced. Hagel added that he feared the protectionist instinct within the party and the ways in which it could threaten the Republican commitment to free trade.

Hagel got back on the administration's case in September for the situation in Iraq. State Department officials testified that they wanted to divert almost 20 percent of the $18.4 billion in reconstruction funds—provided in a bill Hagel had earlier sponsored—to security operations instead of public-works projects and economic development in Iraq. Hagel was appalled. He said the slow pace of reconstruction in Iraq was "beyond pitiful. It's beyond embarrassing; it's now in the zone of dangerous."

"You don't win the hearts and minds of the people at the end of a gun," Hagel said. "You do that through the process that we began in Congress by using the $18.4 billion for reconstruction in Iraq."[38]

That same month Hagel took issue with Bush and company's rosy assessment of the situation in Iraq. The administration's claims didn't add up to a picture that showed America winning, Hagel said. "We can't lose this," he said. "This is too important. There's no question about that. But to say, 'Well, we just must stay the course, and any of you who are questioning are just hand wringers' is not very responsible. The fact is, we're in deep trouble in Iraq, and I think we're going to have to look at some recalibration of policy." His remarks echoed and re-echoed as broadcast outlets and newspapers picked it up.[39]

After Bush was reelected in November 2004, Hagel continued to jab at the president's policies in Iraq. He said the United States had no good options in Iraq. "We are the guarantor of the security right now of Iraq. At the same time, we are the major force of instability in Iraq because of the oppressor anti-American sense that develops every day. Every time we blow down another house in Fallujah, there's more anti-American sentiment that goes throughout [the area]." But, Hagel continued, the United States did not have sufficient forces in Iraq to see the nation through its planned January 2005 elections and into some sort of stability: "I don't think we have enough troops. We didn't have enough going in. That's partly why we're in the mess we're in in Iraq."[40]

Hagel, Biden, and two other senators visited Iraq in late November 2004, assessing the situation for themselves. Hagel said he made it a point to talk privately with enlisted men in addition to attending official briefings and meetings. His assessment was that Iraq was becoming more dangerous, that security continued to erode, and that, as occupiers, U.S. troops were a destabilizing force. "I did not find one commander who said to me, 'We're winning,'" Hagel said. "They're doing everything they can. But we have constantly underestimated the insurgency force and the vitality of the insurgency."[41]

Soon after his return to the United States, Hagel made headlines with his harsh critique of Defense Secretary Donald Rumsfeld. Having admitted that he did not personally sign letters of sympathy to families of soldiers killed in Iraq, Rumsfeld made a trip to Iraq to try to mend fences with the military forces there. While the secretary was visiting with a group of troops, a soldier asked Rumsfeld why the United States had gone to war in Iraq with insufficient manpower and inadequate equipment. Rumsfeld responded that a nation goes to war with the army it has, not the one it might wish it had.

That televised response drew fire from pundits and Democratic critics—and from Hagel. "That soldier and those men and women there deserved a far better answer from their secretary of defense than a flippant comment," the senator said. "That might work in a newsroom where you can be cute with the television audience but not when you're putting these men and women in harm's way, who will be wounded. . . . Some will be killed." Hagel went on to criticize Rumsfeld and, by extension, the Bush administration for its handling of the situation in Iraq. One reason the troops were being forced to fight without enough weapons or body armor or armor for their vehicles, Hagel said, was that "we were unprepared for what we were going to face, what we are facing, in a post-Saddam Iraq. And this [Rumsfeld's response] is just one more manifestation of the problem."[42]

A few weeks later Hagel said deteriorating conditions in Iraq were the result of "the arrogance and incompetency of the civilian leadership at the Pentagon" and a series of bad judgments.[43]

Chris Matthews, host of *Hardball* on MSNBC, tried to put Hagel on the hot seat in early December. Hagel had asserted that the United States learned in Vietnam that it cannot win a war of attrition, and he had, generally, criticized the situation in Iraq.

Matthews told Hagel, "You're a Republican, you're loyal to the president. But was going to Iraq a blunder, or wasn't it? Was it a smart thing for our American interests, or was it a bad thing for our interests in the long run?" Hagel sidestepped, saying it was too early to tell, partly because what happened in Iraq would affect the entire Middle East—and, thus, the rest of the world.[44]

### Hitting Too Hard?

Some conservative observers think Hagel is too hard on his party and his president. In a 2000 profile of Hagel, *Business Week* said that while the business community loved Hagel for his advocacy of free trade and internationalism, critics saw him as too ambitious. His political foes called him an extremist, a tool of big business, the magazine reported. In another arena, Republican leaders said he was not a team player.

In a 2002 editorial the *National Review* reflected that, when Bill Clinton was being engulfed by the Monica Lewinsky scandal in 1998, Hagel had cautioned that Congress needed to be very careful how it dealt with the president. "We must be careful not to weaken or neuter the president in front of the world," he said. "America must speak to the world with some sense and some semblance of unity." Four years later the magazine charged that Hagel's behavior toward President Bush could be having exactly that same effect.

Hagel said criticism of Clinton-Lewinsky and criticism of Bush's foreign policy were two different issues. Clinton's case involved his personal conduct, Hagel said. He was concerned that if the world perceived Congress walking away from Clinton, other nations would cease to work with the president. "That would produce a very dangerous situation," he said, leaving a power vacuum in the international community.

His criticism of Bush is criticism of policy, he said, something that's acceptable and even expected in a democracy. When he receives letters berating him for his ongoing public differences with Bush, Hagel said he writes back, telling the letter writers that one reason the nation lost fifty-eight thousand soldiers in Vietnam is that Congress didn't do its job, didn't ask tough questions in the 1960s, and let the president implement whatever war policies he pleased. That must not happen again, Hagel said. "I owe the families of those dead, and those I served with, something better than that."

But it isn't just media pundits who think Hagel sometimes goes too far. Letters to the editor, for example, have sometimes chided Hagel for joining a "chorus of naysayers who are mostly Washington insiders" and who criticize without offering viable alternatives. People seem especially concerned that such criticism is not proper when the nation's troops are doing battle overseas.[45]

When Hagel spoke to the American Dental Association convention in March 2004, a member of the audience challenged him on that point, asking whether it was really appropriate to criticize the president in time of war. Hagel responded, "My oath is not to a party or a president. It's to the Constitution of the United States." The audience gave him lengthy applause.

Furthermore Hagel said he is concerned about Congress's constitutional role as a check on, and a balance to, the presidency and the judiciary. "Congress is the only thing that stands in the way between essentially a modern-day democratic dictator and a president who is accountable to the people," he said.[46]

Charlie Thone, a former Nebraska governor and Republican member of the U.S. House, said Hagel's attacks on administration policy were particularly hard for Republicans to swallow during the 2004 election campaign. "That's where it got a little 'ouchy' for some people," Thone said. "They thought he would be a better team player at that time." In fact Thone said he had talked to Hagel about toning down his criticisms—but to no avail. Thone said Hagel told him, "'A lot of good Nebraska Republicans think I should quiet down. But from my experience in Vietnam, I personally feel compelled to speak out, and I will continue to do so.' He just looked me right in the eye and let me know," Thone said.

Iraq was a long-term, highly visible target for Hagel, but it was not the only issue on which he disagreed with or voted against his party and his president. Hagel consistently criticized the Bush administration and Republican congressional leadership for running up a record deficit, and he took a stand against it in November 2004. The Senate was back in session after the election, forced to deal with a budget bill it had put off earlier in the fall. Hagel was one of six Senate Republicans who voted against the three-thousand-page, $388-billion omnibus spending bill, which later passed.

"It would be irresponsible for me to vote for this much federal spending when we do not even know what is in the bill," Hagel said of the measure, which was given to senators less than twenty-four hours before they were asked to vote on it.[47]

One definite sore spot in the bill was a provision that would have allowed congressional staff to review the tax returns of individuals and businesses without regard for privacy protections, a provision discovered after the House had already approved the package. Congressional leaders promised to repeal the provision, but Hagel said its inclusion highlighted a "badly broken" system. "Too many problems and too much unaccountable spending: that's partly why this country has been running record budget deficits the last few years," Hagel observed as he voted against the bill, even though such a move could make it more difficult for him to get Nebraska projects into the next year's budget bill.[48]

Hagel said in early 2005 that the Republican Party had to take responsibility for the unbalanced budgets and increased deficits accumulated under the Bush administration. It wasn't that the Democrats had "found the Holy Grail of fiscal responsibility," he said, "but the Republicans are in charge" with a majority in both houses of Congress and a Republican in the White House. "We have to reconnect with our principles."

Not that it would be easy. Bush had recently promised that his next proposed budget would cut the deficit in half by making substantial cuts in spending on programs for veterans, farmers, and housing. "Those are pretty explosive groups you're taking on," Hagel said.

When Bush announced that another of the cornerstones of his second term would be an effort to change Social Security, Hagel was underwhelmed. Yes, Social Security needed to be examined, he said, and sooner would be better than later—but the system was not in crisis in early 2005. The administration's focus on Social Security was simply an attempt to deflect attention from the real crisis facing social entitlements: health care costs. "Medicare drives health care," Hagel said. "You can't act like it's not a problem." The administration's credibility was riding on the way it dealt with these intertwined issues, he said.

Hagel's periodic defiance of Republican policy and leadership gains significance because it hasn't been made in private memos or one-on-one conversations. His criticisms have appeared in newspapers and magazines, in speeches and on television show after television show. He may vote with his party 93 percent of the time, but when he votes or speaks out against it, he frequently does so in high-profile cases like the president's three biggest domestic initiatives: the 2002 farm bill, the No Child Left Behind education bill, and the reform of Medicare, including creation of a drug benefit. Hagel's comments and criticisms create ripples that often extend well beyond the original media into which they are dropped.

## Media Mania

The mass media appear to love Senator Hagel. In fact it appears Hagel became a media darling within a few years of his arrival in the Senate.

Hagel's upset victory over Nebraska's governor in 1996 got him some initial attention from the national media, but Deb Fiddelke, the communications director for the 1996 campaign and for Hagel's first Senate office, said things didn't really pick up until 1998 when Hagel led the Senate drive to replenish funding for the International Monetary Fund. Soon thereafter he introduced his own first version of campaign-finance reform. Then he hit the trail for McCain's presidential bid in 2000 and introduced his friend at the Republican National Convention.

"Once you're on national media's radar," she said, "once they've met you and they like you and know you're going to have something interesting to say, they'll keep coming back to you." Fiddelke insists Hagel never asked her to court the media, to call the Sunday morning news shows to see if one of them wanted him as a guest. "They always came to him," she said.

The first of those appearances she recalls was on *Meet the Press* in 1997. Before long, Hagel was receiving more invitations from broadcast news shows than he could accept. The *Washington Post*'s 2004 profile of Hagel said Hagel's "interest in foreign affairs, eagerness to travel and learn and skills in front of a camera made him an instant star. . . . The television networks found him a cogent and attractive guest for the Sunday talk shows."

Those Sunday morning shows may not have the vast audience some other programs garner, but they do give their guests a chance to raise their profiles and influence other policy makers. The Sunday morning news shows give guests a megaphone to speak to the policy makers in Washington.

While he may not have asked for media exposure, Hagel certainly didn't run from it. The congressional scholar Ross Baker said some senators consider reporters nosy and impertinent adversaries. Not Hagel. He makes himself accessible to the media. Unlike some people in government, Baker said, Hagel does not immediately want to go off the record with journalists, and journalists tend to appreciate his candor.

Hagel's brother Tom said it's a quality he has long recognized in his older brother. "Whether you agree with him or not, you know where he stands. I think people find that refreshing, and people who understand that about him have a greater inclination to trust him," Tom Hagel said.

Janet Hook, who covers Congress for the *Los Angeles Times*, described Hagel as "kind of a reporter's senator," approachable and forthright. "He's not a publicity hound," she added, "but he likes talking to reporters." One observer after another remarked that Hagel makes a good media source because he answers the questions he's asked and because he says what he thinks. Furthermore, many said, the senator knows what he's talking about.

Particularly in matters related to foreign affairs, Hagel is approached as an expert. "He is someone who has done his homework," said CNN's Judy Woodruff. "He's one of those 'go-to' people on the Hill when it comes to national security and international affairs."

Senator Joe Biden, who frequently appears on TV news shows with Hagel, said the two of them, along with several other members of the Foreign Relations Committee, have built reputations for being knowledgeable about subjects that happened to be, in the early years of the twenty-first century, at the forefront of the national consciousness. "Chuck knows the subject matter," Biden said. "He's diligent, and people know it."

Of course, it doesn't hurt, either, that people find Hagel photogenic and good-looking. He dresses impeccably, like the successful businessman he was, in dark suits and cuff-linked shirts. *The Hill* named him one of Capitol Hill's fifty most beautiful people in 2004—one of only four senators who made the list—a fact that made Hagel laugh and drew a good deal of teasing from his Nebraska colleagues in Congress. But his looks alone wouldn't be enough to maintain his status with the press.

Being able to express his ideas clearly makes a big difference. Judy Woodruff said Hagel explains things in a way that viewers can understand and doesn't drift off into "convoluted speak." Hagel said the fact that he was a broadcast reporter himself back in his youth may make him more sympathetic to the media and better able to work with them. When he appears on TV, he said, he tries to remember the fundamentals: Speak in complete sentences. Try not to use slang. Don't fall into the unpardonable "you know" filler.

Hagel seems to relish the opportunity to speak his mind on the air, even when it means doing battle with one of television's more abrasive personalities. He doesn't appear frequently on shows like *Hardball with Chris Matthews*, but doing so occasionally seems to amuse him. During the first half of *Hardball*, guests actually get a chance to finish a thought before the host cuts them off, Hagel said. During the second half of the show, however, "you just strap yourself in," he said with a chuckle, adding that he found Matthews smart and engaging and the entire process more than just a shouting match.

Much of Hagel's success with the media may be due to his straight talk and his apparent comfort with taking on his own party as well as his penchant for the colorful phrase. For example, in May 2004 Hagel and many of his Senate colleagues complained that the administration was not being honest with them about the past or prospective costs of the Iraqi war. "Every ground squirrel in this country knows that it's going to be fifty [billion] to seventy-five billion dollars in additional money this year," Hagel said on NBC's *Today*. The ground squirrel reference was picked up and repeated in dozens of media. Asked about it later, Hagel said the metaphor just popped out. It wasn't anything he'd really thought about ahead of time, and he was amused that it got such widespread press.

As Hagel himself realizes, the media are drawn to someone who rebels against the party they assume he should be supporting. Former representative John Y. McCollister, Hagel's first boss, puts it bluntly. "[The media] are eager to find somebody who will throw stones at Bush." If the stone thrower is a Republican, that makes him all the more valuable as a source.

Senator Biden said Hagel wouldn't get the kind of media attention he gets if he were agreeing with the president. That's not as much of a story, he said, for journalists who judge newsworthiness in part on how much conflict it reflects.

Hagel himself recognizes the truth in McCollister's and Biden's comments. Reporters are looking for a Republican senator who will disagree with a Republican president, he said. "Some of it is a game." If it is a game, it's one in which the senator scores regularly. Observers unanimously agree that Hagel has become nationally prominent.

### Prominence versus Influence

Prominence and influence, of course, are not one and the same. Does Hagel's obvious prominence transfer into influence in the Senate? Has Hagel been able to make a difference within the institution? Observers are not unanimous on the answers to those questions, although many are willing to grant him influence in the foreign-policy arena.

If sponsoring successful legislation were the only measure of influence in Congress, Hagel might not rank high on the barometer. But debate—both within and outside the institution—is also an important part of the business of Congress. As former Nebraska senator Bob Kerrey said, "The most important thing in the Senate is your voice." Passing legislation is important, Kerrey said, but so are the debates in committees and on the floor. Hagel's independent voice influences policy debates pretty consistently, he observed.

Helen Dewar of the *Washington Post* said the fact that Hagel knows what he's talking about makes him influential in foreign-policy matters. But she also had another take on the question of influence. When the Senate is so closely divided between the two parties as it was in the early years of the twenty-first century, a maverick senator on one side or the other can become very influential when an issue's proponents or opponents have to build a majority. Hagel is not a moderate, she said, who would consistently hold the balance of power between the parties; but on some issues, his position and his vote do make the difference.

Generally, the Republican senators who have influence fall into one of two categories, said the longtime congressional reporter. Either they are moderates from swing states who have to cut deals to get things done and keep their constituents happy, or they are conservatives from safe states and have an independent streak. Dewar said Hagel falls into the latter category.

Mitch McConnell of Kentucky, the Senate's Republican whip in 2004 and Hagel's one-time opponent for a Senate leadership position, said emphatically that he thinks Hagel has been influential in foreign policy. Hagel is "a real big-league senator" who is more than simply prominent, McConnell said. "When he speaks on foreign policy, people in the Senate are interested in what he has to say."

Questioning the administration's positions but continuing to support what the president is trying to do has made Hagel influential in the Senate, McConnell said. Hagel doesn't hesitate to speak out, "but every time we've had a significant vote, he's been there," McConnell said. "I think he's a constructive critic."

Not that everyone appreciates the criticism.

CNN's Judy Woodruff said Hagel sometimes irritates his fellow Republicans. "We're increasingly living in a time when party loyalty is prized almost above all else," she said. But at the same time, she is certain both Republicans and Democrats listen to Hagel when it comes to international affairs.

John Podesta, who served in the Clinton White House, said much the same thing. During the Bush administration Democrats liked Hagel because he'd "take a poke at the president," Podesta said, but they liked him during the Clinton years, too. The

Democrats learned quickly to respect Hagel's knowledge of and positions on foreign policy and international affairs.

That's unusual, Podesta said. Very few real conservatives have any influence at all on their Democratic colleagues. "If [Trent] Lott says it's day, the Democrats say it's night," Podesta said. But if Hagel says something, the Democrats will stop and think about his point of view even if they don't agree. "That's what respect is all about," he said.

In a sense, that may also be what influence is about.

The fact that Hagel serves on some of the Senate's most influential committees has put him in a position to help shape the national conversation. Hagel's choice of Foreign Relations, which had become something of a political backwater, gave him the chance to contribute quickly to the international-affairs debate. And the turnover among committee members allowed Hagel a meteoric rise to seniority in the ranks. As foreign affairs have absorbed more and more of the nation's focus in recent years, Hagel finds himself informed on, passionate about, and in a position to speak out and to act on huge issues that really matter to the nation—and on a committee that has gone from political backwater to political lightning rod.

"I see him becoming a kind of Bill Fulbright," the political scientist Baker said, referring to the Arkansas Republican whose moderate foreign policy influenced the Senate for decades in the second half of the twentieth century. Since Fulbright left Washington in 1974, the Senate hadn't seen an internationalist from a state in the middle of the nation, Baker said—until Hagel appeared.

But not everyone is convinced that Hagel is influential in the Senate. Reporter Allison Stevens said someone who dissents from his party's positions will, indeed, get a lot of media exposure, but the increased likelihood that he might alienate his party's leaders will make it harder for him to push his issues along the Senate's procedural paths.

Janet Hook of the *Los Angeles Times* has mixed feelings about the question. Hagel isn't as influential as he would be if he chaired a committee, she said, but his colleagues do respect his opinions on foreign policy. On balance, though, she said, "I'd say he's more prominent than influential."

John Podesta joins the two traits, attributing both to Hagel. "Some people are just bloviators, out there on TV all the time," Podesta said. But Hagel's high profile results in some real clout, he said.

"Hagel clearly has the respect of the press corps, which is a different way of being influential," Podesta said. "It does feed back into the body.

"It will be interesting to watch this guy's career."

As Hagel's Senate term played out, many people were doing just that.

# 8

---

# Going for the Big One?

THOSE WHO THINK CHUCK HAGEL has been angling to run for president ever since he arrived in Washington may not believe it, but it looks as if Hagel is just as interested as anyone else to see how his career will turn out.

Having earned a reputation in the Senate for diligence and independence, he gets plenty of encouragement to do what his high school friends predicted he would do: make a run for the White House. That would be the ultimate step forward, the ultimate challenge in American politics. Hagel told the press in late 2004 that he was exploring his options, making sure he didn't accidentally close any doors against a run for president, but he said he was a long way from making up his mind.

Lilibet Hagel said her husband makes decisions carefully. "He's very, very planned out," she said. Not that he grew up knowing exactly what he wanted to be doing at a specific time in the future. "That would be kind of a program, and he doesn't do that," she said. But when he is considering an important step, he thinks it through thoroughly, trying to see all possible consequences down the road.

Conventional wisdom on Capitol Hill holds that each of the one hundred U.S. senators looks in the mirror every day and sees a potential president. It's safe to say Hagel sees the same image—on some days, at least. But apparently not all day, every day.

## Maybe; Maybe Not

During the years he's served in Congress, the senator has made conflicting statements about his political future. In January 2000 he told the *Lincoln Journal Star* that the thought of running for president sometimes crossed his mind. But in October 2002 he told the *Omaha World-Herald* he was not interested in the position.

In January 2003 he told the Associated Press he hadn't given serious thought to making a bid for president in 2008 but wouldn't rule out the possibility. "Do I want to be president? That's a question that you have to spend some time with, and I've never spent that time on it. You've got to want it deep down, and I've just never gotten close to making that determination," he said.

Speculation has continued. Web sites reported in March 2003 that Hagel had purchased the domain names "hagel2008.com" and "ChuckHagel2008.com," giving rise to rumors that the purchases were early steps down the presidential campaign trail. But Hagel said the names were probably purchased by cybersquatters who would want to sell them back to him if he decided to run for president. "It wasn't us," he said.

Speculation had taken a big leap forward when Hagel's chief of staff, Lou Ann Linehan, returned to his office after a stint at the State Department. Because of Linehan's reputation as a heck of a campaign manager and the fact that she had spent eighteen months learning from the inside how the executive branch of government works, some observers speculated that her homecoming meant Hagel must be preparing for a presidential bid.

Linehan's experience in the executive branch would indeed come in handy if Hagel decides to run for president, but she said that wasn't why she decided to go to work for the State Department. Instead, she said the new Bush administration had asked her several times to take the job as the State Department's deputy assistant secretary for legislative affairs with the Senate, she said, and she had finally said yes. A lot of her friends who had been chiefs of staff for Republican senators also took jobs in the administration. "It was not an easy decision to leave Senator Hagel . . . but I didn't know if anybody would ever knock on that door again," she said, adding that the opportunity to work for the executive branch was "huge."

At the State Department she was the person responsible for shepherding through the then-Democratic Senate all the confirmations for ambassadors, assistant secretaries, and under secretaries. She was also responsible for getting the State Department's priority legislation through the Senate, which involved working not only with the senators but also with groups like the Defense Department and Central Intelligence Agency.

But by January 2003 Linehan was ready to return to the Hill. She said she had missed Nebraska and had missed politics. As a State Department employee she was absolutely barred from any political activity. "I couldn't even put my name on an invitation to an event for Senator Hagel," she said.

Furthermore, with the Republicans back in the majority in the Senate, she knew her job at State was not going to be as much of a challenge. And Hagel had asked her to come back to run his office. She did not, she said, come back because Hagel asked her to begin planning for a presidential bid.

Regardless of Hagel's future plans, Linehan said, her experiences in the executive branch have made her a better chief of staff, a job that involves her deeply in procedure and strategy. In that regard, she said, she tends to be more cautious than Hagel, worrying about the fallout from the senator's attempts to block some of what he sees as bad ideas. "I frequently use the phrase, 'I don't know why we have to run in front of every bullet,'" she said. Hagel is more likely to take the risk, Linehan said, because he's good at seeing what's likely to be the end result of a course of action. "You get a gut instinct that he knows what he's doing."

One thing he's doing is building his reputation as someone with expertise and experience in international relations. Presidential candidates in recent decades have often been governors who have run on platforms that emphasize domestic issues: jobs, wages, health care, the overall economy. While he has not ignored those issues, Hagel has focused on foreign affairs.

In 1999 Hagel predicted that Americans in the twenty-first century would "demand national political leaders who understand the world."[1] He insisted he wasn't focusing on international affairs because he thought it would create an easy path to the White House. But he said his international credentials were the reason his name surfaced that year among potential Republican vice-presidential nominees.

But for all his leadership in foreign relations, his energy and work ethic and devotion to principle, Hagel may face a major logistical obstacle should he decide to run for president: he hails from a small state in the middle of the nation, a state with only five electoral college votes. Traditionally, scholars say, that's a big roadblock to a nomination. Parties generally turn to a candidate from a state that can be counted on to deliver a large block of electoral votes. Hagel can't do that. "He has no electoral base at all, even for the nomination, not to mention the general election," said Larry Sabato, a political scientist at the University of Virginia. "Being from a small state is a huge liability."

Other observers agreed. "A snowball's chance in hell" was the way Nebraska political scientist Brian Humes described the chances that someone from a small, midwestern state could win a presidential nomination. Hagel is on Nebraskans' radar because he is Nebraska's senator, but most of the rest of the nation doesn't even recognize his name, Humes said. He pointed out that Nebraska senator Bob Kerrey's 1992 run at the presidential nomination went nowhere.

But Ross Baker, a Rutgers political scientist, disagreed. "I think the small-state argument just doesn't make sense in the twenty-first century," he said. The twenty-first-century media are national in scope and can make a candidate from any state a familiar face in every state. And Hagel gets consistent attention from high-profile national media.

John Podesta, former Clinton chief of staff, also questions the conventional wisdom that the number of electoral votes a candidate brings to the race is paramount in selecting a good candidate. After all, Bill Clinton's home state of Arkansas has only six electoral votes. However, a small state may make a difference in terms of a candidate's financial base. For a candidate from a small state, the question is "Can you attract money?" Podesta said. If Hagel could do that successfully, it wouldn't matter where he's from.

Even Sabato concedes it's possible for a candidate from a small state to succeed, but he says the conditions would have to be exactly right: "Without a major electoral base, you really need lots of luck."

Sabato sees another roadblock to a Hagel presidential bid: his close relationship with John McCain and McCain's failed run for the Republican nomination in 2000. The two senators are often paired in news stories, referred to as GOP mavericks who give their administration plenty of grief.

"The McCain comparison limits what [Hagel] can do in the future," Sabato said. The McCain wing of the Republican Party is very small, he noted. "McCain was defeated overwhelmingly, and I think anyone identified with him would face the same fate." Hagel would have to develop his own identity, clearly separate from McCain's, he said.

The two senators are often considered a tandem, for better or worse. Stephen Hess, a senior fellow at the Brookings Institution, said Hagel looks like "a weak carbon copy of John McCain. And that's not an insult. McCain is pretty vivid and has a remarkable record." Hess said Hagel displays some of the same independence, pugnaciousness, and attractiveness that characterize McCain. But the maverick image they share may be insurmountable. "Since Republicans were not ready for McCain in 2000, will things have changed enough to make them more, or less, ready for Chuck Hagel in 2008?" Hess asked.[2]

But Senator Mitch McConnell of Kentucky, the Senate majority whip, said the "maverick" label doesn't apply to Hagel. "I'd apply that term to someone who frequently votes against what the Republicans are trying to do here, and that's not Chuck Hagel," McConnell said. Hagel is outspoken, particularly in foreign policy, about which he knows a lot and has strong opinions, McConnell said. But the Nebraskan votes consistently with his party. "That's why 'maverick' is not applicable to him."

Political scientist Baker said the experience Hagel had as a major figure in the McCain presidential campaign outweighs any negative effect his relationship with the Arizona senator might have. "Being identified with McCain is not the worst thing in the world," he said. But the tie with McCain could backfire in another way. In late 2004 and early 2005, as speculation about potential 2008 candidates really got rolling, both McCain and Hagel showed up on various lists. More than one prognosticator guessed that if McCain were to decide to try for the presidency one more time in 2008, his friend Hagel would bow out early.

### The Party Line

The McCain connection might have yet another impact. One reason the two senators are good friends and are often lumped in the same category is that both are willing to publicly disagree with their party's positions and leadership. That independent streak, observers say, could work against Hagel's presidential prospects, despite Podesta's analysis that Hagel has McCain's independent streak without McCain's sometimes pugnacious attitude.

But even tempered by a warm personality, that independence may not be enough to get Hagel a nomination. *Congressional Quarterly* reporter Allison Stevens said McCain's tendency to be outspoken catapulted him from long shot to second place in the race for the presidential nomination—but it was still only second place. "To go against the establishment has never seemed to be the way to win the establishment nomination," she said.

*Washington Post* reporter Helen Dewar said she wondered, too, if Hagel would be able to get the necessary support from the Republican power structure. "They tend to go for the more orthodox candidates," she said.

That's true, Hess said. "If he runs as a maverick, he's going to have an awfully tough time. True believers vote in Republican primaries and caucuses."[3]

And sometimes your political enemies can be your worst friends. For example, several times during the 2004 presidential race, Democratic candidate John Kerry approvingly cited Hagel's criticism of the Bush administration's handling of Iraq. Said Baker, "I think [Hagel] has got to worry about his Democratic friends speaking too highly of him," he said. "Those are not the strongest endorsements when you're trying to get a Republican nomination."

Ron Roskens, former head of USAID and a Hagel friend, said he didn't think Hagel had burned all his bridges with the Republican leadership, but he questioned the wisdom of opposing a president of one's own party "if you are thinking of trying to occupy that office down the road." A candidate will need the help of the incumbent president and his supporters, Roskens said. As Hagel has demonstrated repeatedly, currying presidential favor has not been high on his list of priorities. As a result the senator probably is not high on Bush's list of approved successors.

Democratic senator Joe Biden acknowledged the fine line Hagel has been walking. Biden said he sees no limits to Hagel's political future—other than Hagel's own party. "I'm not being a wise guy," Biden added with a smile. "I think he's out of step with the congressional Republican Party and in step with the national Republican Party." If the leadership continues to move hard right, Biden said, Hagel could have a hard time winning party leaders' support for a presidential run.

Biden isn't the only Democrat who's diagnosed that problem: Senator Christopher Dodd said Hagel is a bit of a pariah in the GOP because he refuses to go along with the party line on foreign policy. It would be hard for the people he has opposed to choose him to lead the party to the White House, he said.

Hagel has not chosen the conventional route to success in a vividly partisan setting. CNN's Judy Woodruff said the more likely route is to make oneself popular with the majority of the party in Congress and at the White House. The fact that Hagel has not done that made her wonder whether he really does have presidential ambitions.

So if he thinks he might like to make a run for the presidency some day, why does Hagel risk that future by flouting the conventions of politics? "I don't make my decisions based on what's risky or what isn't," he said. He knows disagreeing with the president or the party on major issues puts him outside the mainstream. But it doesn't bother him.

He said he tries to do his job in the Senate the same way he's done every other job in his life. "I try to do it straight up," he said. "I don't worry about my political future one way or the other. . . . I can't calibrate my votes and opinions and judgments on the political risk. That would be dishonest, and I won't do it."

While his stubborn independence may not make Hagel popular with the political powers that be, it could make him appealing to voters who think too many politicians calculate their every move on the basis of how much they have to gain or lose politically. "He's not one for a lot of games," the kinds of games that politicians often play to get attention on the national level, said the *Washington Post*'s Dewar. "He's pretty Midwest, pretty straightforward. . . . I don't see many demagogic genes," she said.

That Midwest demeanor and his Midwest roots could be a plus for Hagel, said his former Nebraska colleague Bob Kerrey. Kerrey said Bush's reelection in 2004 demonstrated the importance of being acceptable to voters beyond the East and West coasts. "I don't think Hagel's voting record is at odds with social and economic conservatives. I think he's a very attractive candidate, especially if McCain did not run," Kerrey said. "The most important thing he brings is that he's very likeable. Audiences will connect both to him and his story. They will like him, and that's a big deal."[4]

And Hagel's conservative voting record and Vietnam background can immunize him against charges that he's outside the mainstream. Were he to make it through the primaries and get the GOP nomination, his record of independence would be a "great token" to use in the general election, congressional scholar Ross Baker said—along with his expertise in foreign relations, his war record, and his success in business.

The combination of a conservative voting record and a predilection to disagree frequently with his party leads some to question whether Hagel is trying to have his cake and eat it too: keep his official record pristinely Republican but make his public profile indelibly independent. Is it a deliberate political strategy designed to set himself up for a run at the nation's highest office?

Probably not. "I'd be surprised if he were that Machiavellian," said Dewar. Hagel generally votes as a conservative or moderately conservative loyalist, she said. His independence seems to come from his commentary on foreign-policy and national-security issues "where he is not likely to dissent on votes," she said, pointing to the fact that Hagel voted to authorize the Iraq war even though he differed loudly with the administration over the conduct of and follow-up to hostilities.

Political scientist Brian Humes doesn't see a concerted strategy at work either. "I think he's just being who he is," he said. Hagel will criticize the Republicans' position, but sometimes when it comes down to a vote, he realizes his conservative roots leave him nowhere else to go. Most of the time voting with the Democrats would mean he wasn't being true his principles. "So he speaks his mind and chooses the best alternative available," said Humes.

So it's not a deliberate ploy. But would it work for or against him in an attempt to win the Republican nomination? Charlie Thone, Nebraska's governor from 1979 to 1983 and one of its U.S. representatives from 1971 to 1979, said Hagel's independence is a mixed blessing: some Nebraskans like it; others don't. The same might be true of voters at large if Hagel runs for president, Thone said. It does set him apart from the crowd, but it has also aggravated the current administration on numerous occasions. "I don't know how long those memories will continue," Thone said.

Hagel himself said voting Republican and speaking out against the administration at the same time is not a calculated strategy to enhance his chances to run for president. He was elected to represent the people of Nebraska, he said, and that means voting the way he thinks is best for the state and the nation. Generally, he added, his voting follows a strong Republican philosophical line. "But I also owe my constituents straight talk and my best judgment," he said. "My job is not to be an appendage of a party or a president's policy."

His response is pretty consistent. In late 2004 Hagel told reporters, "I ran for the Senate because I believed in things. I am not going to recalibrate my position on issues based on what I think might be more politically expedient. I've never been afraid of controversial issues. That's what leadership is about. The American people deserve to know the truth, whether it's a Republican or Democratic position, or a Republican or Democratic president. I can't do it any other way."[5]

In an interview, Hagel said, "People can criticize me on how I vote, what I say, my conclusions, my judgments, but this [suspicion of a calculated plan] is just not true."

## Questioning the Details

Of course his record in the Senate will be only part of what political opponents and the media will go over with a fine-toothed comb should Hagel choose to run for president. His status as a self-made millionaire is a matter of record, but two incidents along Hagel's road to wealth will be thoroughly examined: his role in the cell-phone-licensing process and his ownership of a voting-machine company.

To summarize the cell-phone brouhaha detailed in chapter 3: Hagel and his partners had assembled investors and teams of engineers and financial experts to put together applications for cell-phone licenses in the early 1980s. The FCC accepted several of their applications in a competitive process that awarded the first groups of licenses.

By the time preparations had begun for the next round of applications, the number of interested parties had increased exponentially, and the FCC changed the licensing process. Deciding they didn't have time to judge lengthy proposals, the board of governors told potential licensees to submit much-abbreviated applications. If the proposals met minimum requirements, they would be put in a pool, and winners would be selected by a lottery process.

Hagel and company decided to disband their investment groups and have individual investors submit applications, increasing the number of potential winners. The investors signed agreements that the winners would then share their licenses with each other—with Hagel's firm designated as the controlling partner.

During the 1996 Senate campaign the Democratic candidate Ben Nelson—then Nebraska's governor and later elected to the Senate—suggested that Hagel had improperly manipulated the licensing process to his own and his partners' advantage. Hagel vehemently responded that he had done nothing wrong and that the procedure his company followed was common at the time and had been okayed by the FCC ahead of time. He pointed out that, while complaints had been filed against his firm, they were dismissed with no finding of wrongdoing.

The implications were not enough to stop Hagel from beating Nelson in the election, but they are likely to come up again if Hagel decides to run for president. Political scientist Ross Baker said he doubted it would be much of a problem. "It's so esoteric," he said. "This isn't a woman problem," the kind of scandal that can titillate the public and grab its attention. "It's nothing other than the kind of thing that can rise up to bite anyone who's been in business and then gets into politics."

The voting-machine question, though, arose more recently and continues to be hashed over on various Web sites, if not in the mainstream media. If Hagel launched a formal presidential campaign, it would surely resurface everywhere.

It began a few weeks before the 2002 election in which Hagel defeated his Democratic opponent, Charlie Matulka, by 69 percentage points. Matulka held a press conference in which he denounced Hagel for owning an interest in the company that manufactures the machines Nebraska uses to tally its election results. Matulka said Hagel's holding shares in the McCarthy Group, which owned about 25 percent of the stock in Election Systems and Software—formerly American Information Systems—constituted a conflict of interest for the Republican senator.

Furthermore Matulka charged that it was improper for Mike McCarthy, head of the McCarthy Group, to serve as Hagel's campaign treasurer. And he complained that Hagel had at one time been the CEO of American Information Systems, which made the optical scanners Nebraska uses to count most of its ballots, and was still its president when he first won election to the Senate in 1996. In fact Hagel had ceased to be CEO in 1994 and had resigned from the board in 1995, before announcing his intent to run for the Senate.

After Hagel's landslide victory in which Matulka received just 14 percent of the vote to Hagel's 83 percent (3 percent went to other candidates), Matulka asked for a hand recount. The Nebraska secretary of state's office said the election results were not close enough to trigger an automatic recount. Therefore, if Matulka wanted one he would have to pay for it himself. That led Matulka to accuse Hagel and everyone associated with the election of creating a grand conspiracy to rig the outcome.

Neil Erickson, the Nebraska deputy secretary of state for elections, said the state would have paid for the recount Matulka wanted if the election results had been close. Since the automatic trigger point was not reached, Matulka could have contested the election in court, and the court could have ordered the state to pay for a recount, Erickson said, but Matulka chose not to do that.

Some observers asked why the state couldn't have recounted the votes only in areas where Matulka believed the results were suspect. Erickson said that became impossible when the state law changed after the 2000 presidential election with its disputed ballots: Through the 2004 election everyone in Nebraska used paper ballots except for absentee voters in Lancaster and Douglas counties who came to county offices before an election to cast their

GOING FOR THE BIG ONE?

votes by machine, Erickson said. About 85 percent of Nebraska's counties had counted their paper ballots with optical scanners.

In past elections, if a race were close and the vote count in a particular precinct showed only a small variation between the candidates, the ballots in the precinct would be recounted by hand, Erickson said. After the hair-splittingly close 2000 presidential election, with its recounts and its "hanging chads," however, it became unconstitutional to count some votes one way—by machine—and others another way—by hand. The courts had found that such a system violated the equal-protection guarantee of the U.S. Constitution, Erickson said.

So the Nebraska Legislature had to change the state's recount system: either recount all the ballots by hand or do all of them by machine. The counties with higher populations lobbied against hand recounts, Erickson said, and the legislature settled on a law that mandated machine recounts. So Matulka could have had a machine recount—at a cost of forty-two thousand dollars. He declined the offer.

Matulka's accusations of election fraud were covered by the Nebraska media during the campaign but didn't make it onto the national radar until the following January when a reporter for *The Hill*, a Capitol Hill publication, began looking not at a possible rigged election but at the alleged conflict of interest. The reporter asked the Senate Ethics Committee whether Hagel had declared, in 1996, his holdings in what was then AIS, the company that made the vote-counting scanners.

The publication found that Hagel had listed his holdings in the McCarthy Group but had not specifically reported the company's underlying assets, which included AIS—renamed ES&S after a merger with another company in 1997—and its entry into the voting-machine business. On the form Hagel had indicated the McCarthy Group was an "excepted investment fund," exempt from detailed disclosure rules.

A former Senate Ethics Committee staffer told the reporter the disclosure rule in question was originally designed to exempt only mutual funds that buy or sell thousands of different holdings over the course of a year. The McCarthy Group, the story said, owned fewer than twenty assets.

However, the instructions that accompany the disclosure report define a mutual fund as one that is widely held (with more than a hundred investors), publicly traded (or available), and held under circumstances in which the individual filing the disclosure has no control over the financial interests held by the fund. They say nothing about the volume of trading a company should have to be exempt.

Lou Ann Linehan, Hagel's chief of staff, told *The Hill* that the senator's financial forms had been reviewed and approved by the Ethics Committee. She said Hagel's staff had followed the instructions they had received from the committee staff. In a personal interview she said that after *The Hill* story appeared, the staff had gone through every disclosure filing Hagel had done and had double-checked with the Ethics Committee to be sure all was in order. "They assured us he'd filed appropriately," she said.

The story in *The Hill* said the McCarthy Group did not meet the definition of an excepted fund because it was not publicly available and so not easily traded on a market. The reporter said he had searched Moody's Financial Services Information, Standard & Poor's Register, and Barron's Dow Jones and Financial Weekly and found no reference to the McCarthy Group.

But the story quoted Mike McCarthy himself as saying his company is publicly available: "It's not SEC-registered, but it's available to the public by private exchange or private treaty." And the story quoted a Columbia University law professor's opinion that "publicly available" was a term created by the Senate Ethics Committee and that only the committee could define it. So Hagel asked the committee to define it for him. In a May 2003 letter to Hagel, the committee said the McCarthy Group met all the requirements of an excepted investment fund.

In a 2004 interview Linehan said the McCarthy Group was worth about $170 million. Hagel's investment in the company was worth between one million and five million dollars, or less than 2 percent of the Group's total. The McCarthy Group owns about

25 percent of the ES&S stock, which makes Hagel's share of ES&S minuscule, she said.

Alex Bolton, the reporter who wrote *The Hill*'s story, said he had been pressured by Hagel's staff to kill the piece, something that had seldom happened to him in the course of producing a story for his publication. Linehan said she did talk with Bolton before the story was published and told him it should not run because it was inaccurate. Hagel and his staff had followed the rules, she said, but the reporter decided the rules weren't tough enough. "That's a conversation we can have, but it doesn't change what happened," she added.

The story also faulted Hagel for failing to disclose, on the forms he filled out in 1996 to report on his 1995 financial dealings, that he had been the chairman of AIS during the first three months of 1995, until right before he announced he would run for Senate. However, copies of the 1996 form show Hagel listed his 1992–5 AIS chairmanship on the first line of "positions held outside the U.S. government."

Linehan said the discrepancy arose because the Ethics Committee keeps available to the public only documents from the previous five years. When Bolton asked to examine the records in 2003, the committee no longer had the 1996 form in its files. Hagel's office, though, keeps copies of every piece of information related to the required disclosures, she said.

The online fallout from Matulka's accusations and the stories in *The Hill* has ranged from implications that a conspiracy allowed Hagel to steal one or both of his senatorial elections to general declarations that the nation should not adopt electronic voting because the machines are unreliable and too easily rigged.

Even the *New York Times*, a far cry from a radical Web log, has opined that the nation should be careful about buying into electronic voting and cited Hagel's situation as part of its argument. The February 2004 editorial said no evidence existed to indicate Hagel did not win his elections honestly but added that a healthy democracy "must avoid even the appearance of corruption" and said the Nebraska election failed the test. People who were recently executives of companies that make voting machines and ballot scanners "should not be running for elections on those machines," it said.

If it's the case, Linehan said, that politicians must divest themselves of any interest that might influence their jobs, does that mean senators like Chuck Grassley of Iowa and Richard Lugar of Indiana have to sell their farms in order to serve on the Senate Agriculture Committee? Must members of Congress sell all their stock in order to deal with issues that affect businesses?

She acknowledged that some people think a senator's owning stock in a company that makes voting machines or vote scanners is different from owning a farm or stock in General Motors. But she said it's crazy to think the connection leads to fraudulent elections. "Even if he owned the company—which he doesn't—or had a significant interest in it—which he doesn't—there are so many people watching," she said. It would take a world-class conspiracy to rig the machines that record or count the votes. As it is, she said, the candidates and officeholders disclose all their investments and make their financial lives public. Voters can look at all that, she said, and "can trust them or not trust them."

Linehan concedes that concerns about the effects electronic voting might have on the system are legitimate and should be discussed. And Hagel responded in 2004 to e-mail questions about electronic voting asked by Ronnie Dugger, a founder of Alliance for Democracy, which bills itself as a new Populist movement "setting forth to end the domination of our economy, our government, our culture, our media and the environment by large corporations."[6]

One of Dugger's questions made the point that a senator's owning stock in a company that makes election equipment and that is operated by his close allies and friends is not a typical conflict of interest. Hagel answered that he has no direct investment in ES&S and no discretion over McCarthy Group investments. Furthermore, he said, the answer to what is a proper investment and what is not lies in disclosure: "That's why federal elected officials must file annual financial disclosure reports, which are made public. The people of America can determine if members have serious conflicts of interest."

He added that his involvement with AIS was over before he filed to run for the Senate and that, as interim CEO of the company, he had had no day-to-day involvement in hiring employees or running the company. His primary job had been to find a new CEO, he said. His work at AIS "is part of the record," he said. "I don't run from it." But he reasserted that he had laid it all out when he first ran for office.

When Dugger asked questions about the more general issue of electronic voting, Hagel didn't answer them directly. Dugger asked whether Hagel supported a Senate bill that would require a voter-verified paper audit trail to be attached to touch-screen voting machines to protect against fraud or manipulation. Hagel didn't really say whether he supported the bill. Instead he said election officials need to use "methods for voting that inspire the trust and confidence of voters." He thought those methods were best determined at the local level, implying he did not support the Senate bill.

Asked whether he thought elections could be stolen electronically if either the vendors or election-office insiders rigged the machines' software, Hagel again did not respond directly: "Elections have been stolen in the past, long before there were election machines," he said, and noted the sordid history of Cook County, Illinois, in that regard. "That's why bipartisan local and state election oversight, authority, and certification are so important."

But the questioning is unlikely to stop. Electronic elections could, theoretically, be rigged by someone who wants to be sure the election turns out his way—even without a candidate's knowledge. Yes, it would be a world-class conspiracy, but it's not impossible to imagine.

No matter how the nation decides to deal with electronic voting, Hagel and his staff's categorical denial of any wrongdoing involving election procedures or disclosure of his connections to AIS and the McCarthy Group seems plausible. And in fact Hagel was never formally accused of any legal or ethical violation. Also, the counsel to the Senate Ethics Committee sent a letter to the editor of *The Hill* on February 5, 2003, saying it seemed clear that Hagel had complied with the Senate's ethics rules in 1996 and "fully met his obligation . . . in publicly disclosing this particular investment." Hagel continues to hold stock in the McCarthy Group, which continues to hold stock in ES&S.

No matter what the explanations, the stories, questions, and online rumors will undoubtedly be reexamined if Hagel decides to run for president. For most voters it probably won't be a problem. "Ralph Nader's people won't vote for him [Hagel], but he won't get them anyway," Ross Baker said.

Nebraska political scientist Brian Humes said the 2002–3 commotion was much ado about not very much. In the 2002 election, he said, Hagel was an immensely popular incumbent running against an unknown. Matulka's accusations looked like the last gasp of a weak candidate trying to salvage some votes. Furthermore, Humes said, the connection between Hagel and the vote-counting scanners was pretty far-fetched: Hagel had an interest in a company that had an interest in a voting-machine company.

"If a conspiracy theory is going to capture the public, it has to seem plausible," Humes said. "You need a direct connection," and that connection didn't exist in this case. As one observer said of Matulka's 2002 accusations, if a politician were going to try to influence an election, why would he waste the effort on what was obviously going to be a lopsided race from day one?

Hagel's brother Tom, the law professor, said if the story had had a foundation in fact, the mainstream press would have smeared it all over the front pages. The fact that it petered out after a few stories and a couple of months "should tell you something," he said.

The senator himself said the whole thing was ridiculous: first of all he doesn't own the voting machines or the scanners. Second, he has always been open about his work with AIS in the early 1990s and resigned from the firm before announcing he would run for office. "I never had a thing to do with them after that," he said.

Unless something that has not yet come to light is unearthed regarding either the cell-phone licenses or the voting-machine connection, it's unlikely that either of those topics would seriously interfere with Hagel's run for the presidency should he choose to make it. He'd take some heat from opponents, as he has in his Senate campaigns, but the heat seems unlikely to be fatal.

But the cell-phone brouhaha and the voting-machine questions will not be the only parts of Hagel's life under the microscope if he makes a presidential bid. Over the course of the more than 215 years since the U.S. Constitution was written, the presidency has evolved into a position well beyond anything envisioned by the nation's founders. Instead of being an administrator, an executive whose primary job is to implement the wishes of the Congress, the president has become a focal point for the American people. The presidency has become personal, and voters expect to vote not just for someone whose policy views are similar to theirs but for someone they like, someone they can relate to.

Presidential candidates' relationships with their families, their staff members, and their colleagues are all fair game for the media and the American people, and Hagel's would be no exception.

### Getting Personal

Hagel's childhood appears to have been that of an all-American boy. He was energetic, on the go, a little rambunctious but never in any serious trouble. Even for small-town Nebraska, where families were expected to stick together, the Hagels were unusually close—and they still are. The senator and his brothers talk by phone regularly and see each other as often as possible. And all three of them speak of their late mother with near reverence.

Betty Hagel remarried in 1969, seven years after Charles Hagel died, and moved to Hastings with her new husband, E. J. Breeding. She worked there as an assistant librarian before she retired and moved to Lincoln. Her second husband died in 1990. The Hagel boys, including the senator from Washington, made it a point to see their mother—and each other—frequently. Tom Hagel said it wasn't until he was an adult that he realized that not every family is like the Hagels. He knows people who often don't spend Christmas with their parents or who don't see or talk with their siblings for six months or more. "I can't imagine that," Tom said.

Betty Hagel Breeding had emphysema. By December of 2002, when her sons and their families were with her for Christmas, it was obvious that the disease was wearing her down. She was at home, in hospice care. She died in January 2003 at age seventy-nine with her family at her bedside. A year and a half later, her sons were still missing her. Mike Hagel said she was not just their mother but also their best friend. "All three of us are having a hard time dealing with it." The brothers remain close to each other and to the traditional family model they grew up with.

Chuck Hagel has had no run-ins with the law, no arrests for drunken driving or drug abuse. He said he tried marijuana when he was in Vietnam but "got through about two drags of it, and that was it." He just didn't like smoking the stuff. He's tried tobacco and didn't like that, either, he said.

Hagel's personal life as an adult appears to be pretty straightforward. He dated a lot during his early years in Washington, and his brief first marriage ended in an amicable divorce. The senator is "nuts about" his current wife, Lilibet, Mike Hagel said, and about their children.

Hagel's relations with his staff seem to be good too. Current and former staff members are generally enthusiastic about Hagel as a person and as a boss. Hagel expects a lot of himself and of his staff, Lou Ann Linehan said. Everyone forgets to do something once in a while, she said, and something may fall through the cracks. But even if everyone else forgets, "he tends to remember."

"Our biggest struggle is keeping up with him," she said.

Charles Isom was deputy press secretary for Hagel in 1996 and 1997. He said Hagel expects his staff to get things right and is not happy when little things go wrong. "He takes responsibility if big things go wrong," Isom said, but he expects the staff to take care of the little things.

That's true, Tom Janssen confirmed. Hagel's former state director said he had enjoyed and learned from his job with Hagel, but it wasn't exactly a snap.

"It's not easy working for him," Janssen said. If a staff member makes a mistake, Hagel is not likely to let it slide. But Janssen doesn't see Hagel as a control freak or micromanager. "He's more like a coach, always pushing you to do more. The only way you'll get better is if you constantly challenge yourself." Pushing and challenging is something the senator does to himself as well as his staff, Janssen added.

"Demanding" was a word Richard Henry also used to describe Hagel. Henry, who went on to become an associate executive director for the American Association of Retired People, was Hagel's assistant at the USO in the late 1980s. As a boss, Henry said, Hagel expected a lot but also was very fair and thorough. "He was big on expectations and accountability," Henry said, but also adept at letting employees see and understand what his expectations were.

And Hagel made sure all the staff were included in the organization's business. Gladys Gordon, who worked for Hagel at the USO, said that before he arrived at the organization, only people at the executive level attended meetings and retreats. "He totally changed that," she said, when he started including the entire staff in board meetings and off-site retreats.

One result was that staff at all levels got to meet all kinds of prominent people. Gordon remembers when Henry Kissinger visited the USO headquarters. For some reason, she said, he came into the office where she worked—by that time she was a fund-raiser. When Hagel came from his office to greet Kissinger, he said, "Oh, Dr. Kissinger, have you met Gladys?" And the boss proceeded to introduce the former secretary of state to all the staff in the room. "It was incredible," Gordon remembers.

At the USO, too, Hagel expected a lot of his staff. "We worked until two or three in the morning for some events, but it was for a good cause, and you knew it was the right thing to do," Gordon said. And when the staff worked late, she added, so did the boss.

Gordon, who was Hagel's office manager during his first term in the Senate, said he demanded as much from his staff there as he had demanded from staff at the USO. In his Senate office, Gordon said, the staff referred to their boss as "always pleased but never satisfied."

Working for Hagel was tough, but it was a good kind of tough, Isom said, exhilarating and fast-paced—sort of like the senator himself.

Hagel seems to go through life in high gear, always moving on to the next duty, the next opportunity. His many and varied jobs have taken him all over the nation and the world, and he seems to know people everywhere, ranging from heads of state and international ambassadors to Vietnam buddies who never quite recovered.

Tom Hagel said his brother has an incredible sense of loyalty. As an example, he talks about a man the Hagel brothers served with in Vietnam, someone who was "really messed up when he got back." The man developed drinking problems, mental problems. "He was the kind of guy lots of people would write off as a loser," Tom said. "But Chuck stood by him," providing financial help and friendship. He's done the same thing with a friend from high school who ran into personal problems as an adult. "Lots of people disassociated themselves from the guy," Tom said, "but Chuck did not abandon him."

Many observers talk about Hagel's outgoing personality and friendly demeanor, his way of charming the people he's with. According to Senator Biden, it's a reflection of who Hagel really is: "He's a nice guy, a decent guy," he said. "I judge people by how they treat waitresses, taxi drivers, staff, elevator operators. Chuck treats everybody well."

Richard Henry said the same thing and remembered that one of the flower vendors on the street near the USO headquarters in Washington thought Hagel was "the cat's meow." Hagel bought flowers from her and treated her well, Henry said, made her feel special: "Chuck treated everybody, no matter who, with utmost respect."

Hagel would buy all the flowers the woman had left over at the end of the week, Gladys Gordon said. Sometimes he took them home; sometimes he left them at the office. When Gordon was married, during her time at the USO, she invited Linda, the flower vendor, to her wedding. It was then that the woman showed Gordon a surprise.

"Look at my teeth," Linda said. A recovering addict, Linda had lost a lot of teeth to the ravages of addiction and disease. But now they were perfect. "You know where my teeth came from?" Linda asked Gordon. "Chuck told me to go to the dentist and get them fixed, and he paid for it."

A South Vietnamese general was another beneficiary of Hagel's largesse, Gordon said. General Phan Tung had been a four-star general in the Vietnamese army. When the Americans pulled out, he initially refuse to leave his troops until the American military ordered him out at gunpoint. He, his wife, and their large family arrived in the United States knowing little English and looking for a way to survive.

The general's brother, also a Vietnamese military officer, got a job in Nebraska with Mutual of Omaha, and Hagel got to know him through Jim Barrett, a Mutual of Omaha executive who served on the USO board of governors when Hagel did. Barrett and Hagel found out one of the brothers was still unemployed and got him a job in the mailroom at the USO.

When Hagel took over at the bankrupt USO, he had to reorganize the operation, and that meant firing some staff. Before he decided who would go, Hagel interviewed each employee individually. He recalls that General Tung was trembling during the interview, sure he would be fired. Instead Hagel kept the general on. "I was predisposed to him because of his story," Hagel remembers. "He was a wonderful guy."

Once the USO was on its way to recovery, Hagel promoted General Tung, putting him in charge of the mailroom and adding responsibilities to his job description. In his new position of authority, the general occasionally hired Vietnamese young people to help out temporarily, and that's how Hagel got involved in the lives of a number of those young Vietnamese who wanted to go to college.

"I lent some money to some kids," Hagel said. "Actually, I just kind of gave them some." He told them he didn't want them to repay the money, just to get through college and be able to "do something [they] want to do." Like Linda the flower lady, all those young people needed, Hagel said, "was a little break, somebody to believe in them."

The opportunity to reach out like that is the most gratifying thing about being independently wealthy, Hagel said: "being able to help people along the way you could never help before."

All of General Tung's own children went to college on scholarships and graduated with professional degrees, Hagel said proudly. He continues to stay in touch with the family and has had them as his guests several times in the Senate dining room.

That kind of attention to people seems to be something Hagel ·learned in childhood. Lilibet Hagel said her proudest keepsake is a letter Hagel received from a woman in Columbus after he announced his candidacy for the Senate. "The letter said something like, 'Dear Chuck, you don't remember me, but I'm the girl from the wrong side of the tracks that you gave a ride home to such-and-such a night. You didn't have to do that, and I've never forgotten.' To this day, it makes me cry," Lilibet said of the letter. "This is what I want our children to know about their father."[7] Trying to define what makes her husband tick, Lilibet replied that he has a strong sense of who he is and what he believes. "And I think he is just a good soul," she said. "He's just a good soul."

Gordon describes the senator as incredibly thoughtful, sending hand-written notes to friends, family, and constituents; exchanging a series of letters with the troubled son of a friend who had died unexpectedly; sending engraved mugs to families with new babies, and gifts to college graduates. "He never forgets anything," she said. "He remembers your children's names and their birthdays."

Hagel attributes that to his lifelong interest in people: "I've always been fascinated with people. . . . I like to know about people, to get a sense of what makes them tick, where they come from, how many brothers and sisters they have, how they grew up. . . . I thrive on people."

Images of many of those people adorn the walls of Hagel's Senate office, which—like many of the walls in his home—are covered with pictures of the senator with family, friends, and prominent national and world figures. Hagel said he's always hung a lot of pictures on his walls. "I like being surrounded by things that mean something to me," he said.

When he moved into the Russell Office Building, he decided to hang photographs on the walls of the reception room, the conference room, and his own office. He thought it would be fun for people visiting from Nebraska to be able to look over the pictures while they waited to see him or a staff member. Some Nebraskans who have visited the office, though, roll their eyes as they ask, "Did you see all the pictures he has on his walls of himself with everybody?"

Hagel said the picture display wasn't intended to flaunt his connections. He just thought constituents would appreciate seeing some of the people their senator meets. "I think people are proud of their senators and their congressmen—if we don't make fools of ourselves. They're proud of who they send to Washington," he said. But some Nebraskans say the pictures are a bit over the top, an indication of a senator who thinks he's pretty important. And some add that they have a hard time getting on Hagel's schedule when they try to visit him in Washington.

Hagel admitted that was probably true: he can't see everyone he'd like to. "The fact is, I have only so many hours in the day," he said. He serves on four committees and spends time reading about and studying the issues the committees deal with as well as attending hearings and meetings. He develops legislation to introduce in the Senate and speaks to a variety of groups. "I don't know any senator who gives more speeches each week than I do," he said.

In addition he sees more foreign ministers, ambassadors, and trade delegations from foreign nations than many senators do. "I think it's very important to stay in touch with those people," he said, "not just because of the committees I serve on but in the interest of my country and state, too."

Bottom line: "No senator can meet with everybody who wants to meet with him," Hagel said, adding that if he can't see someone personally, he makes sure the person meets with a staff member. "That's why I have confidence in my staff. . . . All you can do is the best you can," he said.

Some critics see a kind of arrogance about Hagel, but Charlie Thone said those critics are few. "Yes, he is perceived by some to be arrogant," Thone said, "but it's sort of like a star basketball player. He could turn off his teammates and his fans if it's too much 'me, me, me,' but if he scores thirty-five points. . . . If he's successful, it's OK," Thone said. "Success leads to success, and he's kind of on a roll. I don't hear people in my circles calling him arrogant." As long as Hagel continues to do well in the Senate and in general, few are likely to worry about arrogance, Thone said.

### On the Run?

Combine the fact that Hagel has a Rolodex the size of a construction barrel—the Rolodex including both the famous and the unknown—with his experience and his rising profile and you have a man who looks as if he might be preparing to run for president.

Among those who touted Hagel as a good potential president was James Exon, Nebraska's retired Democratic senator whose seat Hagel filled in 1996.

"Of all the Republicans, the one the country could best turn to in these desperate times" is Hagel, Exon told the *Lincoln Journal Star* in 2004, a year before he died. Exon praised Hagel for being unafraid to speak his mind and said Republicans would do well to "treat Hagel as one of their honest power brokers to get something done for America."

Hagel's Foreign Relations Committee colleague Joe Biden said he hoped Hagel would run for president. "I think the American public—independents, Republicans, and some Democrats—would be very attracted to Chuck as a presidential nominee," Biden said. "I wouldn't want to run against him." But by early 2005 both Biden and Hagel were considered potential candidates.

Political scientist Ross Baker believes Hagel would be a wonderful president. "He'd be the kind of president even the French would like," Baker said with a chuckle.

Gladys Gordon said she wouldn't be surprised if Hagel took a shot at the presidential nomination. She recalls that after she'd known Hagel for six months or so, she asked him, "When are you going to run for president?" He laughed and asked her why she would say that. "Because you have the great American story," Gordon said.

Gordon's evocation of the great American story was echoed by the *Washington Post* in 1999 when columnist Mark Shields suggested that Hagel would be a good choice for the GOP vice-presidential nomination the following year. "Hagel's is a great American story," Shields wrote. After sketching the high points of Hagel's life, from his childhood in the Nebraska Sandhills to his high profile in the Senate, the columnist added, "Hagel embodies honor and duty. He is an independent and a reformer."

Experience doesn't hurt, either. A good president must have policy skills and judgment based on broad experience, said Mike McCarthy, Hagel's former business partner. "I can't imagine anyone better suited for the job." Although he thought in 2004 that Hagel was not likely to run, McCarthy believed that his friend has a strong vision for the nation based on the belief that each person must be able to exercise his or her freedom: "He understands better than anybody I know that individual freedom doesn't mean isolation," McCarthy said. "It means freedom in connection with all the other people in the world."

Hagel is an excellent campaigner, he added, although a national race would be different from a state election. "You can't make the personal connection across a cup of coffee with the entire nation," McCarthy said. But the skills Hagel has developed and his ability to communicate effectively through the media make him a viable national candidate who could run an effective campaign.

Being a senator—or even a president—does not appear to be the defining goal of Hagel's life. Former senator Bob Kerrey said that is what he likes about Hagel: "That's what makes him so much fun." "He's got lots of options and doesn't seem to worry endlessly about which he's going to pick. He's a happy guy."

Hagel's brothers said they would do everything in their power to support him if he were to run for president, but neither of them was thrilled with the prospect. "I'd rather he didn't do it," Tom Hagel said, adding he worries about a president's safety and hates to think of his brother in such a vulnerable position.

Mike Hagel said people ask him, "Wouldn't it be great to have a brother who was president?" He asks them, "Would you want your brother to be president?" All you need is one John Hinckley or Lee Harvey Oswald to bring it all to a horrible end, he said. But he added, "I'd do anything to help him. I'd bend over backwards to help him. I am his brother."

Tom Hagel said he thinks his brother will run if the opportunity seems right. And he would be a good president, he believes. "He's good at seeing past the obvious. He could be a person who has a vision on both domestic and foreign policy. . . . Plus, I trust him," said the good Democrat about his brother, the good Republican.

But despite his experience, his high profile in the media, and the cheering section urging him to run, it was not completely clear after the 2004 election that Hagel wanted to be a candidate for president in 2008. One thing that did seem clear was that he does not want a long career in the Senate.

When he ran in 1996, Hagel told voters he would serve two terms if they chose to give them to him. In 2004, one-third of the way through his second term, Hagel said he hadn't yet decided whether he'd like to try for a third. He does seem adamant that he will not settle in for a "lifetime" Senate seat even though many observers said he could probably have it if he wanted it. Barring a disaster, Nebraskans seem likely to keep returning Hagel to the Senate as long as he cares to be there.

Judy Woodruff at CNN said she could picture Hagel staying in the Senate and being a force for unity and bipartisanship, looking for solutions to difficult problems by bridging the gaps between the parties.

Former Hagel staffer Deb Fiddelke said she thought he might be willing to stay a little longer than two terms in the Senate because, eventually, he would likely be chair of the Foreign Relations Committee, a role she thinks he is ideally suited for.

But a long Senate career would break the pattern of Hagel's life. When he was elected to the Senate in 1996, his wife teased him, asking, "Are you sure you can stay in one job for six years?" Twelve years in the Senate would be the longest he had ever held the same job. Lilibet Hagel said her husband likes new experiences, new challenges, likes to keep moving ahead. "I remember him saying in the 1980s that the last thing in the world he wanted to do was run a phone company" long term, she recalled. That same desire to try the next thing will probably move him out of the Senate.

"I won't stay in the Senate indefinitely," Hagel commented in an interview. By summer 2004 he was thinking he might like to add six more years to the twelve years he originally said he'd sign on for. "But certainly not an indefinite Senate career," he said. Not that he didn't like being a senator. "It's the highest privilege I've ever had in my life," he said. "I like it; I enjoy it. . . . It just doesn't fit me to stay a long time."

He was thinking ahead, Hagel said, pondering, as he approached age sixty, how many years he'd have the energy and stamina required to do tough jobs. And he was thinking about other things he might still want to do. Being president was not at the top of the list. "I have no burning desire to be president," he said in 2004. But if he did decide to run, he wouldn't be doing it just for fun, just to see how far he could get.

Hagel did some background work during the 2004 Republican National Convention, meeting with the delegations from New Hampshire and Iowa, the states with the earliest primary election and presidential caucus, respectively. Although he insisted he had not decided whether his name would be on the list for those events in 2008, Hagel said he wanted to help influence his party's stand on the issues, especially international issues. "These conventions are about the future," he said. "We're going to be in a position over the next four years to develop and redefine our party. Right now, we have the least internationalist foreign policy since World

War II."[8] And he admitted that the decision to visit delegations from two such high-profile states was not entirely random.

During the convention, *USA Today* ran a story about the six presumed top prospects for the 2008 presidential race; Hagel led the story. The senator was interviewed on CNN's *American Morning* and met with editorial boards of various newspapers.

Hagel said during the convention, "In everything I've done in my life, I've tried to position myself on high ground to take advantage of opportunities as they come along. No leader can just stroll onto the national stage at his or her own time. However, there are a lot of uncontrollables ahead that I can't influence. I am very realistic."[9]

But once the election was over and Bush was returned to office, Hagel took another step toward throwing his hat in the ring. While continuing to insist that he hadn't made a firm decision, he was frank that he was trying to be sure he didn't accidentally cut off his options.

Days after the 2004 election, the *Washington Post* ran a long profile about Hagel and his political future. Following the senator during a visit to Nebraska, associate editor Robert Kaiser decided that Hagel was Nebraska's most popular politician. Hagel told the *Post* that if he decides to run for president, he will not dodge the hard issues: "I happen to believe that by 2008, this country is going to be ready for some people to talk very clearly, plainly—not frighten them, not demagogue them, but say it straight, say it honest."[10]

That may include being unfaithful to the Republican credo of "no new taxes," Hagel said. The nation will need more money to deal with Social Security and Medicare, if nothing else. Hagel said he would tell it as it is: "At some point somebody's going to ask you in a debate: 'Well, senator, will you pledge if you're elected president never to raise taxes?' I couldn't take that pledge. It would be irresponsible," he told Kaiser. "That may cost me the nomination."

In the meantime, though, Hagel said he wanted to be ready. "I've been around politics . . . long enough to know that no one

GOING FOR THE BIG ONE?

can accurately predict what the world will look like two years hence. . . . But I do know this: if one is serious about offering himself as a presidential candidate in four years, you are going to have to be suited up, and down on the field, and in the game."

Thinking about the decision to run for and serve as president, Hagel became thoughtful, almost agonizing over the answer. It would probably be the most difficult decision anyone would ever have to make, he said. "It changes everything—your family, your world, your life—forever. Forever!"[11]

The possible impact on his family seems to be one of Hagel's biggest concerns. His brothers and friends said they knew it bothered him. So did the political scientist Baker. He said he thought Hagel was worrying about giving up his cherished time with his family to "get into the meat grinder. I think that's the bottom line for Chuck Hagel." He may not want to sacrifice his home life for what has become one of America's most exhausting rituals, in which candidates and their reputations are routinely battered by their opponents and the media, and the winners are expected to enjoy living in a fishbowl.

Lilibet said having her husband in the White House "wouldn't be number one on [her] list of desirable occupations," adding, "I can think of a lot of other jobs that would be more fun." The presidency exacts a huge toll on the individual in the office, she said. Besides that, she thinks it's possible that a person could actually be more influential for good in some other position. "And, from a selfish standpoint, I'm not sure I'd want to give up as much as you'd have to give up."

A news story appeared in early 2005 about a group of students at Harvard's Kennedy School of Government who had done a study projecting who would be the two major-party presidential candidates for 2008. The study named Hagel as the Republican nominee—and as the winner of the general election. Asked what his wife thought about the story, Hagel said, "She acted like she never saw it."

Lilibet said she had done an interesting exercise with her English-as-a-second-language students, adults from around the world: "I had them write in their journals whether they would or would not want to be president." To a person, the students declined the honor.

The reasons were varied. One said she thought the responsibilities would be too great. Another said she thought it would be impossible to keep everyone happy and that she would be overwhelmed by criticism from every quarter. "The undertone was simply the idea that the job didn't hold out the chance for much joy," Lilibet said.

Lilibet's own opinion of life as a potential first lady could make or break her husband's decision to run. Hagel said he would not jump into the presidential race unless Lilibet were willing to commit to it without hesitation.

But even if the family agreed that this was a logical next move for Hagel to make, political circumstances would also be part of the equation. For example, Hagel's friend John McCain was also on the early list of potential 2008 GOP candidates. If McCain did decide to make a serious run for the nomination, Hagel would have to factor that into his own decision making, he said.

The outcome of the 2004 Bush-Kerry race also would be part of the calculation. If Bush had been returned to office with a big majority, the Republican Party might have decided it was doing just fine without an independent voice like Hagel's. But since Bush squeaked past John Kerry in a close race, it's possible the Republicans would consider Hagel a contrast, a way to draw more people into their camp.

And one more thing: an open seat in 2008 might be a break for the Democrats since the American people often demonstrate their desire for change after one party has held the White House for two terms, political scientists say. All those things will be part of Hagel's calculations as he decides what course of action to take.

One possibility he ruled out in spring 2004 was serving as Democrat John Kerry's vice-presidential running mate. Hagel's name was floated in the media for several weeks after Kerry clinched the presidential nomination, but the Nebraska senator consistently declined to be considered.

Hagel told CNN's Wolf Blitzer in May 2004, "A Democrat would surely not want to deal with me, Wolf. The Republicans have enough problems with me." Hagel told Blitzer he respected and liked Kerry but that he was not interested in crossing party lines to run with him. "I'm supporting George Bush for reelection," he said.

Hagel was officially the Nebraska chair for Bush's campaign and had supported Bush in 2000 after McCain dropped out of the race. But his comments about the 2004 race when Kerry announced he had chosen John Edwards as his running mate were hardly rabid partisan cheerleading for the Bush-Cheney ticket.

"The American people will have a very clear choice between Bush and Cheney, and Kerry and Edwards. The philosophical differences between the two tickets are stark," Hagel said. "For Nebraskans, I think the choice will be clear."[12]

It's safe to say Hagel never seriously considered pursuing a spot on the ticket with Kerry. But the suggestions that he might serve in a Kerry cabinet were a different matter. "I'd see that in a different light," Hagel said in May 2004. It would depend on what the world looked like at that point and what the American people seemed to expect from their administration. It would depend on the cabinet position in question and whether he thought he could really contribute, Hagel said.

Of course, he added, if he, a Republican, were to serve as a member of a Democratic president's cabinet, that would eliminate any possibility he could ever run for president himself. "I'd have to think about that," Hagel said. "Would it be worth it to give up that option" to serve as secretary of state or defense in a Kerry cabinet? Only if he were convinced the position would allow him to make a real difference, he said. As things turned out, the question was moot.

Hagel's future was far from settled in 2004 or early 2005, but it didn't seem to worry him. He said he's understood since he was young that a person can do lots of different things with his life if he's not afraid to fail and is willing to try different things until he finds his niche. When one door closes, another opens, he said.

"I had a great life before the Senate, and I'll have a great life when I leave to go do something else," whatever that may be, he said. Just as long as he can keep moving forward.

# Notes

*1. Who Is This Guy?*

1. *USA Today*, August 31, 2004.
2. PBS, *The NewsHour with Jim Lehrer*, September 1, 2004.
3. *Washington Post*, September 3, 2004.
4. *Time*, March 19, 2001.

*2. The Early Years*

1. *Washington Post*, November 15, 2004.
2. *Washington Post*, January 13, 1997.
3. *Washington Post*, January 13, 1997.
4. *Omaha World-Herald*, October 6, 1996.

*3. Vietnam*

1. *Omaha World-Herald*, August 16, 1999.
2. *Washington Post*, January 13, 1997.
3. Nebraska Educational Television, *Statewide*, October 1999.
4. *Washington Post*, January 13, 1997.
5. *Washington Post*, January 13, 1997.
6. *Washington Post*, January 13, 1997.
7. *Washington Post*, November 15, 2004.
8. *Washington Post*, November 15, 2004.
9. *Washington Post*, November 15, 2004.
10. *Washington Post*, December 8, 1996.

11. *Atlanta Journal-Constitution*, April 1, 2004.
12. *Atlanta Journal-Constitution*, April 1, 2004.
13. *Atlanta Journal-Constitution*, April 1, 2004.
14. *Atlanta Journal-Constitution*, April 1, 2004.

*4. Looking to Washington*

1. *Omaha World-Herald*, 1996.
2. *Omaha World-Herald*, 1996.
3. *Lincoln Journal Star*, 1996.
4. *Omaha World-Herald*, November 1996.
5. *Omaha World-Herald*, 1996.
6. *Omaha World-Herald*, 1996.
7. www.uso.org.
8. *Omaha World-Herald*, 1996.
9. www.privsect.org.

*5. Embracing a Political Future*

1. *Omaha World-Herald*, October 26, 1996.
2. *Omaha World-Herald*, October 26, 1996.
3. *Lincoln Journal Star*, October 26, 1996.
4. *Lincoln Journal Star*, October 25, 1996.
5. *Lincoln Journal Star*, October 31, 1996.
6. *Omaha World-Herald*, November 1, 1996.
7. *Omaha World-Herald*, November 1, 1996.
8. *Omaha World-Herald*, November 1, 1996.
9. *Omaha World-Herald*, October 27, 1996.
10. *Hastings (NE) Tribune*, November 6, 1996.
11. *Omaha World-Herald*, November 6, 1996.
12. *Lincoln Journal Star*, November 6, 1996.
13. *Lincoln Journal Star*, October 30, 1996.
14. *Lincoln Journal Star*, February 26, 2000.
15. *Omaha World-Herald*, November 3, 1996.
16. *Hastings (NE) Tribune*, November 6, 1996.
17. *Lincoln Journal Star*, November 6, 1996.
18. *Lincoln Journal Star*, November 17, 1996.

*6. Moving Forward in the Senate*

1. *Omaha World-Herald*, 1999.
2. *Times* (London), December 10, 2004.

3. *Lincoln Journal Star*, December 13, 2004.

4. *Lincoln Journal Star*, December 13, 2004.

5. Associated Press, December 14, 2004.

6. *Lincoln Journal Star*, May 5, 2003.

7. *Lincoln Journal Star*, March 9, 2004.

8. *Lincoln Journal Star*, September 30, 1999.

9. *Lincoln Journal Star*, February 13, 2004.

10. *Lincoln Journal Star*, November 25, 2003.

11. PoliticsOL.com, May 15, 2002.

12. PoliticsOL.com, May 15, 2002.

13. www.concordcoalition.org.

14. Nebraska Educational Television, *Statewide*, November 2002.

15. Associated Press, January 21, 2004.

16. Bloomberg News, January 22, 2004.

17. Associated Press, January 21, 2004.

18. *Lincoln Journal Star*, January 22, 2004.

19. *Phoenix Arizona Republic*, January 27, 2004.

20. *New York Times*, March 24, 2004.

21. *Lincoln Journal Star*, February 26, 1998.

22. *Wall Street Journal*, July 5, 2000.

23. *Time*, March 19, 2001.

24. CNN, March 27, 2001.

25. CNN, March 27, 2001.

26. *Time*, March 19, 2001.

27. Associated Press, September 3, 2004.

28. *Lincoln Journal Star*, February 25, 2004.

29. *Omaha World-Herald*, July 15, 2004.

30. *San Francisco Chronicle*, July 15, 2004.

31. *Omaha World-Herald*, July 15, 2004.

32. *Omaha World-Herald*, March 21, 2004.

33. *Omaha World-Herald*, March 21, 2004.

34. *Lincoln Journal Star*, March 12, 2004.

35. *Lincoln Journal Star*, March 12, 2004.

36. *Omaha World-Herald*, March 12, 2004.

37. *Omaha World-Herald*, March 14, 2004.

38. *Omaha World-Herald*, March 14, 2004.

39. *Omaha World-Herald*, March 18, 2004.

40. *Washington Post*, March 18, 2004.

## 7. Risking the Administration's Wrath

1. *Congressional Quarterly*, 2004 survey.
2. *San Francisco Chronicle*, June 30, 2004.
3. *Washington Post*, August 23, 1998.
4. *Washington Post*, November 25, 2998.
5. *Washington Post*, December 1, 1998.
6. *Lincoln Journal Star*, December 26, 1998.
7. *Lincoln Journal Star*, October 14, 1999.
8. *Lincoln Journal Star*, June 11, 2000.
9. *Lincoln Journal Star*, August 3, 2000.
10. *Lincoln Journal Star*, August 9, 2000.
11. *Washington Post*, December 22, 2003.
12. MSNBC, *Hardball with Chris Matthews*, August 26, 2002.
13. MSNBC, *Hardball with Chris Matthews*, August 26, 2002.
14. CNN, *Novak, Hunt and Shields*, August 31, 2002.
15. CNN, *Novak, Hunt and Shields*, August 31, 2002.
16. *Washington Post*, September 18, 2002.
17. *Lincoln Journal Star*, October 16, 2002.
18. *Lincoln Journal Star*, October 25, 2002.
19. Nebraska Educational Television, *Statewide*, November 2002.
20. *Washington Post*, December 20, 2002.
21. CNN, *Showdown: Iraq*, January 28, 2003.
22. CNN/FN, *Money and Markets*, February 5, 2003.
23. *Omaha World-Herald*, February 21, 2003.
24. *Lincoln Journal Star*, September 10, 2003.
25. *The Hill*, September 16, 2003.
26. CNBC, *Capital Report*, October 1, 2003.
27. *Lincoln Journal Star*, March 22, 2004.
28. *Guardian* (London), March 22, 2004.
29. *Washington Post*, April 6, 2004.
30. Associated Press, May 4, 2004.
31. *Pittsburgh Post-Gazette*, May 5, 2004.
32. *Atlanta Journal-Constitution*, May 10, 2004.
33. Associated Press, May 26, 2004.
34. CNN, *Lou Dobbs Tonight*, May 25, 2004.
35. CNN, *Lou Dobbs Tonight*, May 20, 2004.
36. *Washington Post*, April 22, 2004.
37. *Lincoln Journal Star*, July 7, 2004.

38. *San Mateo County (CA) Times,* September 21, 2004.

39. CBS, *Face the Nation,* September 19, 2004.

40. ABC, *George Stephanopoulos Hosts ABC's This Week,* November 21, 2004.

41. *New York Times,* December 4, 2004.

42. CNN, *Wolf Blitzer Reports,* December 12, 2004.

43. *Lincoln Journal Star,* December 21, 2004.

44. MSNBC, *Hardball,* December 7, 2004.

45. *Omaha World-Herald,* October 11, 2004.

46. *Washington Post,* March 14, 2004.

47. *Lincoln Journal Star,* November 22, 2004.

48. Associated Press, November 20, 2004.

*8. Going for the Big One?*

1. *Omaha World-Herald,* August 8, 1999.

2. *Lincoln Journal Star,* November 28, 2004.

3. *Lincoln Journal Star,* November 28, 2004.

4. *Lincoln Journal Star,* November 28, 2004.

5. *Lincoln Journal Star,* November 28, 2004.

6. www.thealliancefordemocracy.org.

7. *Omaha World-Herald,* October 6, 1996.

8. *Sacramento Bee,* September 5, 2004.

9. *Lincoln Journal Star,* September 6, 2004.

10. *Washington Post,* November 15, 2004.

11. Personal interview, June 2004.

12. Associated Press, July 7, 2004.